Cooper Rollow's

BEARS
Football Book

Jameson Books
Ottawa, Illinois

To Jake, Stacey, Charlie and Mia

Editorial assistance, Rich Lorenz.

CONTENTS

SECTION 1: THE BEARS STORY—1920-1985

SECTION 2: THE NEW BEARS

SECTION 3: BEARS PHOTOS 143
1985 Bears Team Roster By Number 152

SECTION 4: THE NFL: 1984 TEAM STATISTICS & 1985 TEAM SCHEDULES

SECTION 5: THE SUPER BOWLS

SECTION 6: BEAR/NFL BRIEFS

Section 1

The Bears Story 1920-1985

Chapter 1

A CHIP OFF THE OLD BLOCK

George Halas stunned the sports world in January, 1982, by plucking a diamond-in-the-rough, Mike Ditka, from Tom Landry's Dallas Cowboys coaching staff and naming him head coach of the Chicago Bears.

Dallas newsmen who had observed Ditka for years both as player and assistant coach were astounded. But they weren't tongue-tied.

"Ditka will never make it as a head coach," one Dallas sportswriter declared. "He's way too immature. He's not a leader. He throws clipboards when he gets mad. He acts like he thinks you're supposed to win all the time."

In Ditka's first year at the Bear helm, he hardly got his new playbook installed before the Bears went on strike along with the rest of the league. In his second year, Ditka angrily slammed his fist into an equipment cart and broke his hand. In his third year, he won the NFC Central title and took the Bears to within one game of the Super Bowl, their best finish in 21 years.

Suddenly, the diamond-in-the-rough had become a gem. Too bad George Halas, who died in 1983, couldn't have been around the following year to see the job Ditka did with the team Halas had founded in 1920 and taken to its last championship in 1963.

"I think he would have been pleased. Somewhere, he's smiling pretty good right now," Ditka said emotionally after the Bears clinched their first NFC Central Division title ever with a 34-3 rout of the Minnesota Vikings on Nov. 25, 1984.

Halas didn't smile often during the 19 years between the 1963 championship and the 1982 hiring of Ditka. Neill Armstrong's 1981 Bears won six games and lost 10. Armstrong's 1980 club finished 7-9. Armstrong's 1979 Bears and Jack Pardee's 1977 team both made the playoffs as wild cards, but both dropped their first playoff game.

Halas, who had nurtured and whiplashed the Bears to one championship after another in the early years and had personally coached the team to its last National Football League title in 1963, was 86 years old and his health was clearly failing when he astonished friends and foes by stamping Ditka as his personal choice to lead the Bears back from anonymity.

"For some time I have been working out a game plan designed to bring a winning football team back to Chicago," Halas said. "Now, with the signing of Mike Ditka as head coach, phase one of that plan is complete.''

The appointment of Ditka staggered former Bear players and veteran Chicago sportswriters who vividly remembered the shouting arguments Halas and Ditka used to have during Ditka's career as a two-fisted Bears tight end.

It was Ditka, the player, who uttered one of the great lines in sports history when he said, "George Halas tosses nickels around like manhole covers.''

But one of Halas' greatest attributes was his thick skin, and it was never more in evidence than when he hired Ditka. Halas perhaps even grudgingly admired the inspired "manhole cover" line just as he admired anything innovative and competitive. Ditka, with his love of combat and his unyielding, relentless urge to excel, was a chip off the old Halas block.

Ditka had left the Bears in a snit in April, 1967, when Halas traded him to the Philadelphia Eagles for quarterback Jack Concannon. The trade followed a lengthy contract dispute that centered on Ditka, once an All-American at Pittsburgh, signing to play with the Houston Oilers of the rival American Football League.

But now, all that was forgotten and Halas saw Ditka on the order of a son, a throwback to the Halas way, an eternal Bear.

"Halas hired me," Ditka now says, "because he thought I could win for him. It's as simple as that.''

"I think I was Halas' kind of player," Ditka declares, sitting behind his desk only a hop, skip and a punt from the practice field at Lake Forest College where Ditka orchestrated the Bears' 1984 divisional title and excited Bears fans like they hadn't been excited for two decades.

"That was the main reason Halas hired me," Ditka continues. "He was hoping some of those things would happen that happened when I was playing.

"Halas told me, 'You don't have to answer to anybody but me.' The main thing he said before we shook hands and signed a contract was that he wanted a football team that the fans could relate to. He didn't say it had to be like the old Bears, but he mentioned that they had always played with a lot of tenacity and toughness. He said he thought it was important that those qualities be instilled back into the ball club.''

"We talked quite a bit the first year [1982]," Ditka recalls. "I'm sure that at that point Halas got a lot of advice from a lot of people. He probably had a lot of people bending his ear.

"The only thing he ever disagreed with me on was when we failed on the goal line at Detroit my first year. [Quarterback] Bob Avellini got sacked. Halas thought you had to go with a quarterback sneak. It was a good point. We put the quarterback sneak in and we've scored many times with it.''

7

Ditka was awarded the Bears' head coaching job for the simple reason that he asked for it and convinced Papa Bear he could give him another championship. Ditka first made known his desire to return to his professional "alma mater" in an interview with this *Chicago Tribune* sportswriter while standing at the bar in Philadelphia the night before the Dallas Cowboys, whom Ditka served as an assistant coach, were to meet the Eagles for the NFC title in January, 1981.

At the time, Neill Armstrong was coach of the Bears and Ditka ventured that he was interested in the Bears' offensive coordinator post vacated by the recent resignation of Ken Meyer.

I expressed surprise that Ditka would be willing to return to Chicago considering his once-stormy relationship with George Halas.

"Listen," Ditka told me, "Mr. Halas and I get along just fine. All I ever wanted to do was go back to Chicago and be head coach of the Bears. You understand I have no designs on Neill Armstrong's job. But sooner or later . . . I'm 41 years old. I'm giving myself five more years to make a major move. I can't remain in Dallas forever as an assistant coach."

Ditka's remarks were printed the next week in *The Chicago Tribune,* along with the following comment from Halas: "It's certainly something to keep in mind for the future."

Ditka followed up on the interview by writing Halas a lengthy letter outlining his philosophy of coaching and spelling out, in detail, what he would do if named head coach of the Bears. The rest is history. Halas, fortified with dozens of memories of Ditka annihilating opposing defensive players who dared get in his way, went against the advice of many of his closest confidants, including general manager Jim Finks, and tabbed Ditka as the Bears' Moses.

Moses didn't take long to inspire the Bear exodus from the wilderness. Though his three-year contract was written on ordinary paper, not etched in granite, Ditka let it be known what he thought about the infighting that was traditional within the Bears' official family, often with Halas' blessing.

"They've been playing cutthroat in the Bear organization for 15 years," Ditka told Brian Hewitt of the *Chicago Sun-Times.* "I can work with anybody as long as they don't cut throats."

Ditka's implication was clear. The people who had been involved in the Bears' latest cutthroat political chess game were general manager Jim Finks and Halas himself, especially Halas. Ditka clearly was uncomfortable. Asked now what was wrong with the organization that had to be corrected, Ditka replies:

"You've got to create an atmosphere of trust, confidence and belief. I'm not only talking about our football team, I'm talking about the people in the organization. We're all working for the same goal. This applies to the secretaries in the organization as well as the coaches and players. You've got to have the right atmosphere, the kind of environment that is conducive to winning."

The new Chicago environment into which Ditka plunged himself after he and his wife, Diana, emigrated from Dallas in the winter of 1982 was not immediately conducive to winning. Ditka's first Bear team finished 3-6 in that strike-abbreviated year. The next season [1983], Ditka thumbed his nose at a 3-7 start and led his troops to a 5-1 finish and an 8-8 record. Then came 1984 when the Bears finally won a title, something akin to the breaking of the sound barrier. But let Ditka tell it.

"I don't think you can really consider the first year," he says. It is spring, and his eyes are already roaming the lush practice field at Lake Forest where soon his behemoths, old and new, will begin priming the pump for whatever glories await them in 1985.

"The first year was trial and error," Ditka reflects. "When we put our new [Dallas offensive] system in, I really don't think the players knew half the time what they were supposed to do. You'd call a play, and you'd wonder if they were thinking, 'What?' When the strike hit, it really hurt things. It took us a year to get involved offensively with what we wanted to do.

"The second year was a disappointment because I thought we had a better football team and had a chance to win our division. Last year, when we finally won the championship, the thing that was exciting was the adversity we had to overcome. Even though we had a good football team, that's a tribute to the players.

"We did what we had to do to win. We tried to look at the long-range picture. We couldn't win 'em all. Our objective was to get to the playoffs and that's what happened for us."

Did Ditka bring a magic wand from Landry's coaching arsenal in Dallas? What is the real secret to the Bears' resurgence?

"The attitude change," he replies instantly. "People started believing. We had the talent, although we still needed more people. We had to show our players that what we were doing was good, that what we were doing would work against everybody else.

"We had a good defense. We had to build a good offense. The Bears have always had the ability to play pretty good defense at times. The monumental change was at the quarterback position. What was here, you couldn't win with. I'm going to say that and I mean it. What's here now [Jim McMahon and Steve Fuller] you can win with.

"The thing I like about our club, and it came from the defense, is that we're a hard-nosed team. That's what people liked about this team when we were good [1963]. We might not have won them all, but we went out and knocked the crap out of people. These guys nowadays are the same kind of cats. They'll bite you, they'll hold you, they'll do anything. We have no pansies.

"One of the things that makes our offense so good is that it has to go up against that damned defense every day in practice. How would you like to be an offensive lineman and every day in practice you have to block Dan Hampton and Steve McMichael and Mike Hartenstine and Richard Dent?''

Ditka's critics may have faulted his methods while he was leading the Bears back from obscurity just as Halas had wanted him to do, but they couldn't argue with his philosophy.

"If we continue to play hard, good things will happen,'' Ditka said after the Bears lost an error-filled game to the Los Angeles Rams 21-14 on Nov. 6, 1982.

Ditka preached this gospel through his first three years as the Bears' new field boss. And suddenly he became a prophet.

"Put a chip on your shoulder in July and don't take it off until January,'' Ditka first told the players, and they loved it. The Bears had been existing on vanilla extract under the tutelage of nice Neill Armstrong and gentleman Jack Pardee. Now they were told to gargle with vinegar and smile, damn it.

"It's nice to know we're not going to be playing for a 0-0 tie most of the time,'' veteran defensive tackle Jim Osborne said when Ditka had made it clear he expected the offense to produce points to go along with the Bear defense's kick-em-in-the-butt philosophy.

Most of the Bears initially reserved judgment on their new boss. Except for garrulous Gary Fencik, the outspoken safetyman from Yale and the Ivy League, who said he sensed an ''urgency'' in Ditka right from the beginning that he never saw under Ditka's predecessors.

"Now we've got a head coach who gets sick when he loses, even in the preseason,'' Fencik said. "We might have some second thoughts about some of the things he does, but we never question that the guy is absolutely committed to winning right now.''

Chapter 2

1984: TO THE SHADOWS OF THE SUPER BOWL

The Bears' first championship season in 21 years began some 180 miles from Chicago. Coach Mike Ditka, searching desperately for some sort of emotional thread to tie together the disparate elements of his football team, took the Bears away from their traditional Lake Forest College camp and into the southwest corner of Wisconsin for the initial phase of their summer exercising.

In the small farming community of Platteville, the Bears set up bivouac at a remote branch of the University of Wisconsin. The facilities turned out to be wonderful, and the Bears had nothing to do for 3½ weeks but eat, sleep, talk and practice football.

And at night, as Ditka had hoped, they got to know one another.

"Maybe if you go to a bar with a guy you thought was a noodle, you'll find out he's a pretty good guy," said Ditka, who had gone to a few bars with the championship 1963 Bears.

But bar-hopping wasn't the reason Ditka took the Bears to Platteville. His first Bear team in 1982 had finished 3-6 in a strike-shortened season and his 1983 club was forced to put on a tremendous late drive to finish 8-8.

After a horrific 3-7 start in the first 10 games of 1983 in which Ditka's detractors were salivating all the way from Chicago to Dallas, Ditka somehow motivated his troops to a 5-1 finish and a near-playoff berth in the Super Bowl tourney. The Bears weren't mathematically eliminated until the second to last weekend of the regular season. And Jim McMahon, who set three Bear career passing records, was blossoming in his second year at quarterback.

Ditka knew what he had and what he needed to win with the 1984 Bears. He also knew that a banner season was essential in this third year of his three-year contract.

"Why shouldn't the Bears win? Why shouldn't we be as good as anybody else? These were the points we had to keep hammering home, beginning in Platteville, and then in Lake Forest and on into the season," Ditka says.

"The second key factor, other than attitude, was that we put good people in there. The Bears have drafted pretty well, not only the last three years but the three before that. You're talking about Keith Van Horne, Mike Singletary, Todd Bell, Otis Wilson, Matt Suhey, Dan Hampton and Al Harris. Those were very good drafts [1979 through 1981]. I felt we had the right people playing the right positions last year."

The Bears started eight first-round draft choices in 1984. They also started four second-rounders, a tribute to the astuteness of personnel director Bill Tobin and his longtime sidekick, scout Jim Parmer.

"I felt that if we could get off to a quick start, which we did, we could become a good football team," Ditka reflects. "The most important thing is we controlled our own division. We were 7-1 in our division and easily could have been 8-0. Anytime you can control your division, you shouldn't have problems."

Ditka's office in Lake Forest overlooks the practice field where he accomplished what many old-time Bears would regard as a modern miracle.

"We finally got the defense and the offense talking to each other," Ditka says with a mirthless chuckle. "I think that was our biggest accomplishment, our biggest challenge."

Ditka, like any of George Halas' former players, remembered how Papa Bear used to pit one coach against another, one player against another, the offense against the defense.

The rivalry between the Bear offense and defense was so intense that when guard Stan Jones, now a Denver Bronco assistant coach, was switched to defensive tackle before the 1963 season, the defensive players wouldn't allow him in their team meetings until they were convinced the move was permanent.

"We didn't want him spying on us," drawled defensive tackle Fred Williams.

Ditka finds it difficult to laugh about such memories.

"I don't think it's good," he says. "Halas did those things for a lot of reasons. It's not my place to go into that. I just know I couldn't run a team like that.

"When I first came here, cripes, our receivers were getting killed out there. Sure, that looks good and it's fun to hit, but we're on the same team. I had to keep telling the players, 'Hey, we don't play the BEARS this year. We've got to help each other, not kill each other.'

"That was one of the reasons we went to Platteville. The players came together. Lived together. What's the end result? What are we looking for? We're trying to win and get into the Super Bowl and win the Super Bowl. If you achieve that because your defense is No. 1, that's fine. If you achieve it because your offense is No. 1, that's fine also. It's still the Chicago Bears achieving it."

Three separate and extremely critical components keyed the Bears' impressive rush last season to their first championship since 1963—quarterbacking, defense, and the irrepressible Walter Payton.

First, there was the quarterback situation, which started out as positive as a Christmas stocking and became an increasing worry because of injuries. The greatest testimony to Ditka's coaching job is the fact that the third-year coach was able to hold the Bears together through such adversity and put together a winner.

Ever since the retirement of Sid Luckman many light years ago, the Bears traditionally have had problems at quarterback. Supposedly, the arrival of Jim McMahon and his new backup, Steve Fuller, had finally put the situation to rest. But injuries struck, as first McMahon, then Fuller, became casualties.

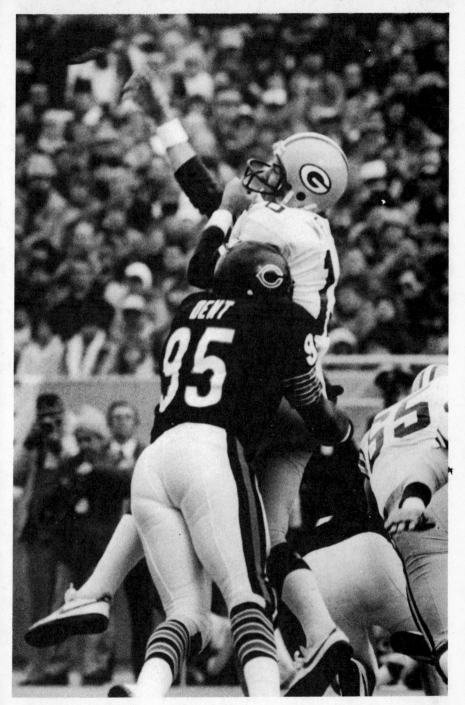

Richard Dent makes one of the 17½ sacks that led the league in 1984. The victim is Green Bay quarterback Randy Wright. (Chicago Tribune Photo)

Ditka, fighting a season-long battle to bring the offense up to the level of the Bears' super defense, used six different quarterbacks, including five different starters.

McMahon, who played in just nine games, performed with a fractured right hand and a bruised back early in the season and then suffered a lacerated kidney against the Raiders Nov. 4 that sidelined him for the year. Fuller, who played in only five games, bailed out the offense in November when he was the top-rated passer in the NFL, sandwiching four starts between a pair of shoulder separations. The Bears never were able to develop a consistent passing attack and finished the season ranked 26th in the league in that phase.

But, oh, that Bear defense. If they didn't know it before, Chicago fans found out last year why George Halas rehired defensive coordinator Buddy Ryan before he had even named Ditka as head coach to succeed Neill Armstrong. Ryan's defenses can be criticized for being too complicated, too flambuoyant and too reckless. But their track record is there for the world to see. In an era when defense supposedly was dead in the NFL, Ryan's Renegades dominated opponents week after week. The Bear defense, designed to "put pressure on everybody," in Ryan's words, uses 60 different coverages, including the exotic so-called "46" named after Doug Plank and featuring a five-man line.

Ryan's defense was simply the best unit in the NFL in 1984 and certainly one of the best ever put on the field anywhere. The Bears just missed ranking first in all three key categories of defensive stax—total, rush and pass. They were No. 1 in total defense, No. 1 in rushing defense, and their 72 sacks broke the NFL record by five.

And then there was Walter Payton, who sends sportswriters scurrying for superlatives every time he touches the ball.

"When it's all said and done," Ditka says, "Walter may be remembered as the greatest runner in history. And talk about toughness—who's any tougher than Payton?"

Who, indeed? The spotlight beamed on Payton as never before throughout the early part of the 1984 season as the Bear phenom chased and finally destroyed Jim Brown's all-time NFL rushing record.

Payton felt a lot of heat and so did his teammates as he gradually chopped away at Brown's career record of 12,312 yards set 19 years earlier with the Cleveland Browns. Payton started the 1984 season, his 10th as a pro, with 11,625 rushing yards. He needed to gain 687 to catch Brown, but Walter said his sights were considerably higher.

"I want to get the record so high that the next person who tries for it, it's going to bust his heart," Payton told Robert Markus of *The Chicago Tribune.* "Instead of 12,000 yards, how about making it 15,500 or 16,000?

That's what I'm shooting for before I retire. Jim Brown's record means something, because it means I'm gaining on my goal.''

Payton had little difficulty breaking Brown's record. He had six straight 100-yard games en route to the dramatic moment. But he was admittedly nervous and anxious to get the whole thing over with.

"Records are like dreams," Payton told Kevin Lamb of *The Chicago Sun-Times*. "Good while you're having them, but when you wake up, you can't remember what you were dreaming about.''

The historic day came on Sunday, Oct. 7, when Payton and the Bears met the New Orleans Saints in Soldier Field. Payton needed 66 yards. Before the pregame calisthenics, Walter told his teammates to "forget the record. We're going to win.''

At halftime, Payton needed just two more yards to equal Brown's record. On the second play of the second half, Payton's 2,795th career rushing attempt, quarterback Jim McMahon called Toss 28 Weak. Payton took a pitchout around left end as he had been doing all of his life, paused briefly, and darted upfield. Three yards were open for the taking but Payton, of course, gained six before the Saints brought him down.

Walter had just become, in the minds of all who were witness, the greatest running back in the history of pro football.

Payton was mobbed on the sideline. He let the celebration go on for a couple of minutes, then yelled to photographers, "Get off the field.'' And the game went on, with the Bears winning 20-7.

"When I finally got the record, I felt relieved," said Payton, who gained 154 yards rushing on that momentous day. "For the last three weeks—and I've tried to conceal this—it's been hard on me and my family and friends. If you had to do this all the time, I can see how you might go astray.''

Ditka was feeling pressure during the 1984 preseason, he now admits, and the tension extended throughout the season.

"I was under a lot of pressure to win and I put a lot of pressure on myself. My biggest problem in coaching is myself. I think I take things way too seriously. It's pride. What's happened in our whole league is that everybody worries about each individual week too much. It's the big picture that counts. You have to look at what the 16-game season is going to bring to you.''

Ditka lost his well-known temper after the Bears had bowed to the Green Bay Packers 17-14 in a Milwaukee exhibition, accusing his players, among other things, of not trying, feeling sorry for themselves and lacking leadership. Ditka threatened an immediate shakeup.

"That's ridiculous," snapped safety Gary Fencik, flashing his Ivy League pedigree. "The guys are trying hard. This was a preseason game. Mike is on a learning curve. A lot of the things he says are true and honest, but sometimes they're mistimed.''

15

After a good night's sleep and a look at the same films, Ditka backtracked and did everything but apologize to the squad.

"I told you a long time ago coaches should never talk after a game," Ditka said to reporters. "It was just frustration. We wanted to win. I was just ticked off. I saw a lot of good things in the game films."

But Ditka wasn't through fuming for the season. He saved an even stormier caper for the last day of September after the Bears, who had won their first three regular season games in a magnificent burst out of the state, sank to 3-2 with a 23-14 loss to Ditka's old Dallas Cowboys team in Soldier Field.

Dallas quarterback Gary Hogeboom had a sparkling day, hitting 18 of 29 passes for 265 yards including a 68-yard screen pass for a touchdown to Tony Dorsett. Rafael Septien kicked three field goals and the Bears' Bob Thomas missed two. But the amazing twist in the day's scenario was Ditka's refusal to give the ball to Walter Payton in the second half. Payton gained 130 of his 155 yards on 20 carries in the first half, including a 20-yard touchdown scamper. Inexplicably, Ditka decided the Bears needed to try to pass in the second half, even though quarterback Jim McMahon had a broken hand. McMahon completed only 6 of 14 passes for 79 yards. Ditka called Payton's number only four times in 22 plays in the third quarter.

"We were outcoached today. That's all. Period," Ditka snarled in front of sportswriters from all over the nation, including several old media adversaries from Dallas.

"I have no statement outside of the questions asked," Ditka began his press conference.

Was the end of the first half the turning point?

"No," snapped Ditka. "Next question."

Did you want a time out called?

"Yes. Next question."

Did you want the ball thrown out of bounds on third down?

"Yes. Next question."

Why did you run two running plays right before that?

"Because we thought we wanted to."

Why did Walter Payton run only four times in the third quarter?

"No kidding? I don't know."

Did you want the pass at the end of the half thrown into the end zone?

"No."

Why not?

"Why would I?"

The clock ran out.

"So what?"

Now that he has had time to look back on the above dialogue, Ditka has a ready explanation for his testy behavior which added to his image of belligerence.

"I thought the questions were asinine," Ditka says. "A guy was trying to bait me. I felt bad because I wanted to win the game, but not because I had been with the Cowboys. I wanted to win it because the Cowboys were the first team that were on the plateau we had to reach. You have to beat a team on that level before you get the confidence and the recognition you need. It finally came five weeks later with the Raiders."

The Bears devastated the hated Los Angeles Raiders 17-6 on Nov. 4 in Soldier Field in a game that moved Ditka to declare: "That was a real heavyweight football game. I don't know that there was a harder football game played in the last five years."

Don Pierson of *The Chicago Tribune* called the Bears' win "their most meaningful victory since their 1963 championship. For the moment, it proved to much of the rest of the National Football League, to Bear fans and to the Bears themselves that cigars were in order, if not champagne."

The bone-jarring triumph brought the Bears' record to 7-3, their best start since 1963. It put them 3½ games up in the NFC Central Division with six to play. But it cost them the services of McMahon, who was lost for the season with a lacerated kidney.

The contest was waged on such an intensely physical level that practically every fan in the stadium could feel the zing and zap of every blow. The Bears were brutal, if not murderous. Linebacker Otis Wilson knocked out Raider starting quarterback Marc Wilson and replacement David Humm, both in the first half, forcing Marc Wilson to finish the game with a bandaged right thumb. Steve Fuller took over for McMahon after a shoulder separation and began an inspired month at the Bears' helm.

When the world champion Raiders lined up against the Bears, defensive end Howie Long decided to intimidate Bears guard Kurt Becker.

"I'm going to spit in your face," Long told Becker.

"Howie, he likes that," warned Bears tackle Keith Van Horne.

Long tried again.

"I'd like to get you in a closet and beat the hell out of you," Long said.

"Can we leave the light on?" asked Becker.

"Howie, he likes that, too," warned Van Horne.

It was my privilege to cover the Raiders' dressing room on that day. I've been in the sportswriting business for over three decades, and have never seen a dressing room like this one. The angry Raiders fumed, fussed and fretted through bloody lips.

"I haven't had my butt kicked like that since the eighth grade," Long said. "And that kid moved out of the neighborhood before I got a chance to get even."

"This is the Bears' back yard," yelped offensive tackle Shelby Jordan. "When you're world champs, it's like the Old West. You'd better keep your six-guns handy and your rifle on the side. The history of the Raiders is to take what we want. But we didn't do much taking today."

Long fired a verbal blast at Bear tight end Jay Saldi, reclaimed by Ditka from Ditka's old Cowboy team. "I was wrenching his head off and he's saying, 'Look at the scoreboard, look at the scoreboard,' " Long said in a mocking tone. "It reminded me of when I was a kid and my sister was always finking on me."

Through no fault of Fuller, the ex-Kansas City Chief who was acquired from the Los Angeles Rams for backup insurance, the Bears lost Fuller's first start—at the Rams 29-13. But they clinched their division by winning the next two games, at Detroit 16-14 and at Minnesota 34-3.

"This team isn't looking for ways to lose," Payton told Terry Bannon of the *Arlington Herald* after the victory in Viking country. "We fell behind 3-0 today, and that's all they got. In the past, we'd fall behind and everybody would throw in the towel."

With a huge lead, the Bears had plenty of time to plan a dressing room celebration at the Metrodome. The only hitch was that the NFL doesn't allow champagne in locker rooms. So tackle Dan Hampton filled a jug with ice water. When tackle Steve McMichael and safety Todd Bell grabbed Ditka, Hampton doused him.

"You poured it on his back," McMichael said.

"Close enough," Hampton said.

The Bears' NFC Central victory sent them into the postseason playoffs as divisional champions. That meant they didn't have to play in a wild card game as they had in 1977 when they were wiped out by Dallas and in 1979 when they lost a controversial decision to Philadelphia.

The Bears went into the nation's capital as champions for a change, and they gave the Washington Redskins, their first playoff foe, a lesson in pro football, Chicago style.

One Redskin had an ankle broken, another had his collarbone fractured, and another was introduced to the edge of night by Bell, one of the many current Bears who employ the tricks of such old-time Bear mayhem artists as Ed Sprinkle, Ed "Country" Meadows and Dick Butkus.

"It's time for Chicago to take a bow," Ditka said after the Bears had stuck the Redskins with their first playoff loss in history in RFK Stadium 23-19 in a bruising battle that lasted 3½ hours.

With Bell playing cornerback for the first time in his life late in the game, the Bears frantically protected leads of 13, then 6, then 4 points. Time after time, quarterback Joe Thiesmann went after Bell, looking for a crack in the Bears' defensive armor. Time after time, Thiesmann and the famed "Hogs" of the Redskin offensive line were slaughtered by the Bear defenders.

Bell was moved to cornerback in the fourth quarter after big John Riggins' 1-yard touchdown run, his second of the game, had whittled the Bears' lead to six points at 23-17. Ditka handed the Redskins their last two points on a safety with 8:08 remaining to give coach Buddy Ryan's defense better field position.

"Todd Bell is the best athlete I've ever played with," exclaimed safety Gary Fencik after Bell had separated Joe Washington from his senses and the ball following a second quarter pass from Theismann when the Redskins had moved to the Chicago 34 and were threatening to go up 10-0.

The Bears' often-dormant offense, ignited by a fine performance by the offensive line, exploded with Payton's second quarter 19-yard touchdown pass to tight end Pat Dunsmore. Fuller hit wide receiver Willie Gault with a short pass on the second play of the second half and Gault used his sprinter's speed to turn the play into a 75-yard touchdown. After Fuller's 16-yard TD strike to wide receiver Dennis McKinnon made it 23-10 with 4:05 left in the third quarter, the Bear defense took over.

The Redskins seemed punch drunk as they stumbled up the ramp to their dressing quarters.

"It was like two heavyweights out there—a lot of knockdowns going on," said Riggins, who was held to 50 yards in 21 strenuous rushes and virtually ignored by coach Joe Gibbs in the second half.

The Bears' season ended that December day under the shadow of the Washington Monument. For the record, they played one more game—against the soon-to-be-again Super Bowl champion San Francisco 49ers a week later in Candlestick Park.

For the very first time, the Bears were within two weeks and one game of their first Super Bowl. But when the artistic, athletic 49ers finished with them, Ditka and his troops knew they had gone as far as they should have expected to go in one season. The final score of the National Football Conference title game was 23-0, and it wasn't even especially embarrassing.

1984 BEARS DEPTH CHART

OFFENSE

Wide receiver—Willie Gault, Jack Cameron, Brad Anderson.
Left tackle—Jim Covert, Andy Frederick.
Left guard—Mark Bortz, Rob Fada.
Center—Jay Hilgenberg, Tom Andrews.
Right guard—Kurt Becker, Rob Fada.
Right tackle—Keith Van Horne, Andy Frederick.
Tight end—Emery Moorehead, Pat Dunsmore, Jay Saldi, Mitch Krenk.

Wide receiver—Dennis McKinnon, Brian Baschnagel, Brad Anderson.
Quarterback—Jim McMahon, Steve Fuller, Greg Landry, Rusty Lisch.
Fullback—Matt Suhey, Calvin Thomas.
Tailback—Walter Payton, Dennis Gentry, Anthony Hutchison.

DEFENSE

Left end—Mike Hartenstine, Tyrone Keys, Henry Waechter.
Left tackle—Steve McMichael, Jim Osborne, Henry Waechter.
Right tackle—Dan Hampton, Richard Dent, Henry Waechter.
Right end—Richard Dent, Tyrone Keys, Henry Waechter.
Left linebacker—Otis Wilson, Ron Rivera, Dan Rains.
Middle linebacker—Mike Singletary, Brian Cabral.
Right linebacker—Al Harris, Wilber Marshall.
Left cornerback—Mike Richardson, Terry Schmidt.
Right cornerback—Leslie Frazier, Jeff Fisher.
Strong safety—Todd Bell, Kevin Potter, Jeff Fisher.
Free safety—Gary Fencik, Dave Duerson, Kevin Potter.

SPECIALISTS

Punter—Dave Finzer.
Place kicks, kickoffs—Bob Thomas, Dave Finzer.
Holder—Brian Baschnagel, Dave Finzer.
Kick center—Jay Hilgenberg, Ron Rivera.
Punt center—Dan Rains, Jay Hilgenberg.
Punt returns—Jeff Fisher, Dave Duerson, Jack Cameron.
Kickoff returns—Jack Cameron, Dennis Gentry, Anthony Hutchison, Willie Gault.

COACHING STAFF

Mike Ditka, head coach; Jim Dooley, Dale Haupt, Ed Hughes, Steve Kazor, Jim LaRue, Ted Plumb, Johnny Roland, Buddy Ryan, Dick Stanfel.

Chapter 3

HOW IT ALL STARTED

There is a simplistic irony in the fact that George Halas and pro football were born the same year, 1895. No other single figure in the history of

America's favorite game of violence played as significant a role in the development of the sport as the Papa Bear.

The first professional football game was played on August 31, 1895, in Latrobe, Pennsylvania, as a Latrobe team sponsored by the local YMCA defeated a pickup club from Jeannette, Pa., 12-0. Twenty-five years later, sitting around on the running boards in an auto showroom in Canton, Ohio, George Halas and a few other visionaries peeked into the future and formed what was to become the National Football League.

In later years, Halas often laughed when he looked back at the modest economics of those hard-pressed days. He paid more for a month's supply of shoe laces than it cost a team to get into the American Professional Football Association.

"Membership, we decided, would cost $100 per team. We awarded franchises to eleven teams, then sat back and crossed our fingers. I guarantee you there wasn't a hundred bucks among all of us in the room that day. But we wanted the new league to have credibility so we established what we regarded as a stiff entry fee."

One of the franchises went to Halas' Decatur Staleys, the forerunners of the Chicago Bears. Only one of the other ten teams anointed on that historic day in Canton still exists—the St. Louis Cardinals, then the Racine-Chicago Cardinals.

Though Halas was only twenty-five, he already possessed many of the qualities which were to be his trademarks during a lifetime as the impresario of pro football. A native Chicagoan whose parents had emigrated from Bohemia, Halas acquired a boyhood toughness and shrewdness which was to be his stock in trade as he clawed and cajoled his way to the top.

"I always hated to go into that man's office," big Doug Atkins, an all-pro defensive end who had his own particular brand of toughness, said many years later. "No matter how fired up I was when I went in to talk contract, no matter how many fine points I made about my ability, I always walked out of Halas' office and realized I had lost."

Halas was the youngest of three sons. His father, Frank, operated a tailor shop in the heart of Chicago's Bohemian neighborhood on the west side. George was fifteen when his father died. His mother kept the family together by operating a grocery store and managing the apartment building in which the family resided.

Halas played sports of all sorts during his boyhood. Encouraged by his brothers, Frank Jr., and Walter, young George acquired easy skills in football, baseball, and basketball. At Crane Technical High School, he weighed only 140 pounds while playing tackle during his senior year in 1913.

When Halas matriculated at the University of Illinois, the venerable Illini football coach, Bob Zuppke, took one look at the slender, reckless kid who had gone out for halfback and bellowed to an assistant: "Get that kid out of the backfield! Try him out at end. At least he may live through the day."

Halas not only lived through the day; he became a regular end on the Illini. It was at the annual Illinois football banquet in 1917 when Zuppke made an off-the-cuff remark which, Halas later said, planted the seed from which sprouted the National Football League.

"Illinois had won the Big Ten championship," Halas recalled. "Zup looked around the room sadly at his graduating seniors. Then he said, 'It's too bad. Just when all of you begin to know something about football, I lose you. Football is the only sport in which a player's career ends just when it should be beginning.' "

Zuppke's words struck home to young Halas, who carried them in his heart until that fateful day in Canton.

Halas had earned a degree in civil engineering at Illinois. But his professional future, whatever it was to be, had to wait. The United States was engaged in World War I. Halas joined the Navy and became an ensign at Great Lakes Naval Training Station near Chicago which, happily, had a fine football team. Halas was the star of the 1919 Rose Bowl game, catching two passes from Paddy Driscoll as Great Lakes shut out the Mare Island Marines, 17-0.

As much as he enjoyed football, Halas had long dreamed of a major league baseball career. When the New York Yankees opened their spring training camp in Jacksonville, Fla., Halas was there waiting. His glove dangling from his left hand, he picked up a pen with his right hand and signed a contract.

Yankee Manager Miller Huggins liked Halas from the start. But Halas simply couldn't hit a curve ball. Additionally, he hurt his right hip sliding into third base in a spring game. Halas was in the lineup for the Yankees against the Washington Senators in New York's Polo Grounds in 1919. The pitcher was Walter Johnson, famous for his blazing fast ball. Johnson threw Halas curve balls. Halas scorched a pair of line drives into the right-field stands, but both went foul by a foot. Halas went hitless.

Eleven games later, after compiling a lofty batting average of .091, the pride of the Yankees was cut. He played out the remainder of the season in St. Paul, Minn., in the minors.

After his short-lived baseball career, Halas got a job in the bridge department of the Chicago, Burlington and Quincy Railroad. At the age of twenty-four, he was making $55 a week. But Zuppke's words kept coming back to him, creating an irresistible craving for pro football.

Halas didn't take long to find a game. He joined up with the Hammond team and made his professional debut against the Canton Bulldogs at right end. The game thrilled Halas on two counts. First, he was paid the unbelievable sum of $100. Second, he had the frightening privilege of playing against the legendary Jim Thorpe.

"Our big fullback, Gil Falcon, tackled Thorpe by the ankles on one play and sent the famous Indian crashing into our bench with blood trickling from a cut over his right eye," Halas recalled. "On the next play, Thorpe smashed through our line, drove under Falcon, and knocked him three feet into the air. The trainer had to pump the air back into him. That Indian was in a class by himself."

Not far from Chicago, in Decatur, a sports fanatic named A. E. Staley owned and operated the Staley Starch Works. Staley already had a top-flight semi-pro baseball team managed by the great Joe McGinnity.

"Why not a football team, too?" Halas asked Staley.

Sold. The 1920 Decatur Staleys—recruited, managed, and coached by Halas and starring Halas at end—lost only one of thirteen games.

Halas talked Staley into letting the players practice for two hours on company time each afternoon—the first time in pro football's short history when a team had engaged in organized daily drills. Add to this "job benefit" the chance to share in the profits of the gate receipts, which Staley permitted Halas to offer his recruits, and it is easy to see why Halas was able to lure a veritable all-star team to live and die for the greater glory of the Decatur Staleys.

The Staleys' roster included such future sports luminaries as Jimmy Conzelman, Charley Dressen, Dutch Sternaman, Bob Koehler, George Trafton, Burt Ingwerson, Guy Chamberlain, Hugh Blacklock, and many others.

Halas enjoyed the coaching and playing far more than he did the paperwork involved in setting up the playing schedule, picking sites, finding suitable dates, and so forth.

"I wrote to Ralph Hay of the Canton Bulldogs," Halas later remembered, "and suggested it would be easier for all of us if we formed a league and played a set schedule."

Then came the famous meeting in the Canton auto showroom. The groundwork for a professional league had been laid the previous year by Hay and others. Now, prodded by Halas, the grand design took shape.

Thorpe, the Carlisle Indian, was named president of the American Professional Football Association. Franchises were granted to the Canton Bulldogs, Cleveland Panthers, Dayton Triangles, Akron Professionals, Buffalo All Americans, Chicago Tigers, Columbus Panhandles, Detroit Heralds, Rochester (N.Y.), Rock Island (Ill.), Muncie (Ind.), Racine-Chicago Cardinals, Hammond (Ind.), and the Decatur Staleys.

A. E. Staley enjoyed watching his football team perform and win. But he didn't enjoy picking up the tab. He sent for Halas after the season.

"George," he said, "we simply can't underwrite the football project any longer. Why don't you move the boys up to Chicago? I think you can make a go of pro football there.''

Then Staley said the magic words: "I'll give you $5,000 to get started. All I ask is that you continue to call the team 'The Staleys' for one season.''

Thus, incredibly, a football franchise which was to become a gold mine was not only given away free, but a bonus was attached. Halas took the money and ran. He took Ed (Dutch) Sternaman, his star halfback, with him as co-owner, thus saving Sternaman's $100 weekly salary. This move caused Halas a goodly amount of cash in later years before the two split.

In 1922, Halas changed the name of the team to the Chicago Bears. That same year, the American Professional Football Association officially became the National Football League. Modern pro football had arrived. But it was still a long way from respectability.

Chapter 4

GRANGE, NAGURSKI, AND A POT OF GOLD

George Halas gambled everything he owned that Harold (Red) Grange, the greatest college player of his day, could pull in the fans as a pro as Grange had done at Illinois.

The Bears and the National Football League were doing reasonably well. In 1924, the Bears showed a net profit of $20,000. But this was the beginning of the era dubbed romantically by historians as The Golden Age of Sports. Names such as Babe Ruth and Jack Dempsey had promoters talking in terms of millions, rather than thousands, of dollars.

"Why not us?" Halas wondered. So Halas went after the biggest prize he knew of. Grange, the Wheaton ice man, had become a legend as the Galloping Ghost of the Fighting Illini. He was a picture of grace, balance, and speed, and yet he was as tough as the cleats on a football shoe. Halas didn't have to be clairvoyant to know that Red Grange, who had scored thirty-one touchdowns in three seasons at Champaign, was the key to the future of pro football.

Unto his death, Halas refused to concede that anybody—Walter Payton, Gale Sayers or O. J. Simpson, Jimmy Brown or Hugh McElhenny or Ollie Matson—could carry the football with any more finesse, cleverness, or daring than Grange.

"I wouldn't say Grange was the greatest back I've ever known," wrote Grantland Rice, the sportswriter who canonized the Four Horsemen of Notre

Dame, "but he had more influence on both the college and pro game than any other player."

Halas went out to get Grange with every weapon at his disposal, including cunning, skulduggery, and blatant disregard for the rules.

"I had to have Red on the Bears," Halas told me many times. "I don't imagine any football player will ever again be as universally popular with the fans as was Red. They simply exploded every time he ran out on the field. And so did Grange."

Reports that Grange had signed a Bear contract in violation of the rules were widely circulated before Illinois met Ohio State in the 1925 season finale. Grange hotly denied the rumors. He was quoted by the *Chicago Tribune* as saying, "You can be sure I haven't signed a scrap of paper with anyone, and I haven't told anybody what I'm going to do."

Cash and Carry Pyle knew what the fabulous redhead was going to do. Pyle, a Champaign movie house impresario, was pro football's first big-time agent, an early day Bob Woolf with a bit of Mike Jacobs and Ben Bentley thrown in. He was a born promoter. Until then, his world had been confined to the city limits of Champaign. But with Grange as a client, he was ready to make his move.

Halas and Dutch Sternaman wrote Grange several times in the summer of 1925 as the Galloping Ghost was preparing for his senior year at Illinois. The redhead didn't respond. Then Pyle dropped in on the Bears, offering Grange's services as a pro. Halas, suddenly forgetting his allegiance to his alma mater, began to wheel and deal.

The day after Grange had helped Illinois beat Ohio State, 14-9, Grange was in a Chicago hotel to sign with the Bears, having eluded the press down a Columbus fire escape the night before. The famed redhead became pro football's first $100,000-a-year player with a contract which stipulated a gate percentage and other benefits.

Grange sat on the Bear bench the day he signed, as Halas' team zipped the Green Bay Packers, 21-0. Finally, the following Thursday, Thanksgiving Day, Grange made his long-awaited professional debut against the Chicago Cardinals. The intracity game drew 36,000 instead of the usual Turkey Day crowd of less than 14,000.

Unfortunately, Grange totaled only thirty-six yards as Paddy Driscoll, the Cardinals' kicker, punted away from the Galloping Ghost continuously. But despite the scoreless tie, Halas declared later, "I knew then and there that pro football was destined to be a big-time sport."

So, probably, did Grange. The redhead made $12,000 during his scoreless pro debut.

Then came the barnstorming tour which Halas and historians agree "made" pro football. Grange and the Bears went on a nineteen-game coast-to-coast junket interrupted only by one two-week rest. Highlight of the tour was a battle against the Giants in New York's Polo Grounds, where 73,561 fans became the biggest pro football throng ever assembled up to that date.

The Giants kicked the stuffings out of Grange, the "up-start" All-American pro from Illinois. But Red intercepted a pass and ran thirty yards for a touchdown as the Bears won, 19-7. The game impressed the staid *New York Times* enough so that *Times* editors ran the story of Grange's appearance on page one.

Fifty years later, the *Times* recognized Gale Sayers in much the same belated fashion when the Kansas Comet dazzled a Yankee Stadium crowd with two touchdowns and passed for a third in a 35-14 Bear victory over the Giants during Sayers' rookie campaign.

The arrival of Grange made an instant success of Halas, the Bears, and the National Football League. Yet the struggle for big-time recognition continued. Halas needed more magic for his Bears. Grange, with recurring knee problems, was not the sole answer.

Halas fired himself as head coach in 1930 and brought in Ralph Jones, a schoolboy coach from Lake Forest Academy. Halas, of course, would return later to the Bear sideline.

The Bears' T formation was sick. It had impressive power over the middle but little strength to the outside. Jones eliminated the tight formation which Halas, the traditionalist, had favored, by splitting one end out some five yards. Jones widened the backfield spacing. And he introduced the man-in-motion.

But above all, he shook hands with Bronko Nagurski, a one-man football team. Nagurski was so huge, strong, fast, and versatile that he played both tackle and fullback at Minnesota. When the big fellow graduated in 1930, Halas offered him $5,000 for one season. Bronko demanded a two-year pact, got it, and became the ultimate Bear—until Dick Butkus the only Bear who really qualified for the title, "Monster of the Midway."

Nagurski, born of Ukranian immigrants in Canada, spent his boyhood in International Falls, Minn. "We don't have summer," he told his Bear teammates. "We just have a season in the middle of the year when the sledding is tough."

The sledding seldom was tough for Bronko as a Bear. Just for opponents who tried to bring down the Paul Bunyan of football. One time Johnny Dell Isola, New York Giants linebacker, tackled Nagurski on first down. "It was the hardest tackle I ever made," Dell Isola said later. "I thought Nagurski might have a yard at the most. Then I heard the ref saying, 'Second down and two.' "

Nagurski's two-yard pass to Grange gave the Bears a 9-0 victory over Portsmouth for the 1932 NFL title. The game was played indoors in Chicago

Stadium on an 80-yard gridiron.

Halas, having tired of administrative duty, reclaimed the coaching reins "temporarily" in 1933, the first of three times he was to make a comeback. Jones had left behind him a modernized T formation, later to be polished to a rich luster by the wise Clark Shaughnessy.

It turned out to be an exhilarating year for the Bears, who finished 10-2-1 and played at home before an average of 20,000 fans a game. The Bears beat the Giants, 23-21, in the first championship game ever played after the league was split into two divisions.

Thanks to Nagurski and Beattie Feathers, Halas' 1934 Bears were undefeated in their thirteen league games. With Nagurski clearing the way, Feathers, running much of the time off his old Tennessee single wing, averaged 9.9 yards per carry and became the NFL's first 1,000-yarder even though he missed the last two games of the season with a dislocated shoulder.

Feathers always credited his success to The Bronk. "I had the greatest blocker in history," cackled the old Vol. "Whichever way Nagurski knocked them, I cut into the opening."

Feathers' 1,004 yards were history before the Bears got into the 1934 championship game against the Giants in the Polo Grounds. But even with Feathers nursing his injury, Halas had faith in the ability of the undefeated Bears.

Halas, however, hadn't reckoned with the resourcefulness of the Giants' coach, Stout Steve Owen. The Polo Grounds turf was frozen solid on that December day. So Owen had his trainer raid the Manhattan College locker room. The trainer came back with a supply of rubber-soled shoes which gave the Giants the traction they needed. New York won, 31-13, to end the Bears' unbeaten skein at thirty-three games.

"It was humiliating," Halas groaned. "We encouraged our players to step on the Giants' tennis shoes, but it didn't work. I don't mind getting beat by a good team, but when the equipment man beats me. . . !"

The Bears never again were caught short of footwear for all occasions.

A few weeks later, in an exhibition game in Los Angeles, the Bears gained revenge over the Giants with a 21-0 shutout. The game was significant only because it marked the end of the Red Grange era. Near the end of the contest, the old redhead broke loose on the Chicago 20-yard line. But his thirty-nine-year-old legs failed him and he was dragged down from behind.

Grange was through. Nagurski remained until 1937 when he retired to join the pro wrestling circuit and go fishing with his sons. He returned briefly later for a last hurrah, but was never the same.

Chapter 5

SID LUCKMAN AND THE GREATEST VICTORY OF ALL

"That game was the greatest thrill of my lifetime. And George Halas was such a great coach. To this day I thank the Good Lord that I was a part of the team that played one of the greatest games in the history of football. It's something you can never forget."

Sid Luckman was sitting on an airplane on the way to the Kentucky Derby when he made the above comment to me. Time obscures the year, but his words come back vividly. They are the same words Luckman always uses, whether on the banquet circuit or in private conversations, when he talks about George Halas and "that" great football game.

Halas always claimed that Luckman never called a wrong play in his twelve years behind the center. Luckman was, indeed, the perfect quarterback in the most perfect football game ever played by one team.

After the Bears had shocked the Washington Redskins, 73-0, in the 1940 championship game, Luckman summed up the rout as modestly as he could:

"That was the greatest football game ever played," said Sidney. "Everything we did was right. Everything they did was wrong."

How true. Ten Bear players scored touchdowns in the most memorable game in Bear history, the game which marked the beginning of a Bear dynasty. In the fourth quarter, officials told Halas not to kick any more extra points because the supply of footballs was running low. So Halas ordered his team to run or pass for extra points. And the Bears missed only one of *them*.

Sammy Baugh, the Redskins' superlative quarterback, was helpless. Early in the game, Baugh threw what appeared to be a certain touchdown pass to end Charlie Malone. But Malone dropped the ball in the sun. Afterwards, Malone was asked if the game would have wound up differently had he made the catch.

"Yeh," he said dryly, "the score would have been 73 to 7."

The 1940 Bears, certainly the finest pro football club assembled up to that point, were the culmination of a rebuilding program by Halas which began after he bought out Sternaman's half-interest for $38,000.

Halas borrowed money and pledged to make the final payment to Sternaman in 1933. Only the friendship of Charlie Bidwill, who later bought the Chicago Cardinals, enabled Halas to keep the Bears. Bidwill bought $5,000 in Bears stock and arranged a $5,000 bank loan for Halas, who got all the money up for Sternaman just thirty minutes before the final deadline for payment.

Halas' rebuilding plan took advantage of the new college draft. Such mainstays as Joe Stydahar and Danny Fortmann helped lead the Bears to the Western Division crown in 1937. But it was becoming increasingly obvious that the Bears needed a top-flight quarterback to run the T formation which Clark Shaughnessy had helped Halas install. Halas was amazed by the brilliance of Shaughnessy's facile mind, though somewhat frightened by the 400 plays which the former Stanford coach had written into the Bear playbook off the T.

On October 28, 1938, Sid Luckman's picture appeared on the cover of *Life* magazine. Luckman had had no experience with the T formation. He was strictly a single wing tailback at Columbia University. But Luckman's college coach, the respected Lou Little, pronounced Sid to be the best passer he had ever seen.

"I went to see Luckman in his last college game at Bakers Field, which was played in a downpour," Halas once recalled. "I saw him do tricks with the ball as a halfback and in the rain, and I said, 'We've got to have that young man.' " Halas was to make almost the identical remark about Gale Sayers nearly thirty years later.

Halas shrewdly made certain he'd get Luckman by offering the Pittsburgh Steelers a gang of good players if they'd draft the Columbia ace and pass him on to the Bears in 1939. The Steelers kept their word and Halas had Luckman. He made a similar deal with the Philadelphia Eagles a year later in acquiring the rights to the great runner from Duke, George McAfee.

Fullback Bill Osmanski also joined the fold in 1939, and the dynasty was complete in 1940 when Halas recruited a sensational array of rookies. Along with McAfee, in came center Clyde (Bulldog) Turner, end Ken Kavanaugh, halfbacks Harry Clark and Scooter McLean, and tackles Lee Artoe and Ed Kolman.

McAfee, who had been a track star at Duke, had a unique ability to shift direction without warning, luring tacklers with a deceptive kick of the leg. Halas always refused to compare McAfee with his legendary predecessor, Red Grange, or with the great runners who followed him, Gale Sayers and Walter Payton.

"When you talk about George McAfee and Red Grange," Halas told many a banquet audience, "you are talking about immortals. Both were in the same cast. The same goes for Gale Sayers. The highest compliment you can pay a ball carrier such as Sayers is to liken him to McAfee."

Grange himself called McAfee "the most dangerous man with a football in the game."

When Luckman joined the Bears in 1939, it was with some reluctance. Luckman knew nothing about the T formation and was apprehensive about his projected conversion from halfback to T formation quarterback.

Halas didn't rush him. "I didn't dare start him at quarterback," Papa Bear recalls. "So the first four games I played him at left halfback so he could see what the quarterback was doing up there. I had Carl Brumbaugh, who had retired in 1937, coach him. All Sid did after that was win championships for us."

With the sensational Luckman at the helm, the Bears roared to National Football League championships in 1940, 1941, 1943, and 1946.

The mutual admiration between Halas and Luckman was unending.

"Luckman was like a coach on the field because he studied constantly," Halas said admiringly. "We coaches would work all day on the plays for the following Sunday's game. After we were through about eleven o'clock at night, I would call Sid at home and give him the list of plays. The next morning I would have Sid repeat the plays to me. He repeated them so fast, I usually had to say, 'Wait a minute. Go a little slower!' "

Halas delighted in talking about the championship rout of the Redskins in 1940.

"Three weeks before that game, they beat us, 7 to 3. George Preston Marshall [Redskin owner] called us a lot of cry babies. He said we were a first-half team only and had no real great ability. Of course, I made certain all those newspaper quotes appeared on the clubhouse wall."

On the eve of the game, Halas began to have misgivings. "I've overplayed my hand," he confided to Assistant Coach Luke Johnsos. "These guys are so mad they'll be busy trying to kill the Redskins instead of beating them at football."

The Bears' game plan was very simple. Halas described it to Luckman thusly: "I'm gambling that the Redskins are going to use the same defense they've been using. There's one way to find out. On the first play I want you to send George McAfee inside right tackle. Then, if the defenses are the same, turn Bill Osmanski loose."

Luckman sent McAfee bursting inside tackle on the first play after the kickoff for an eight-yard gain. Luckman was smiling when he returned to the huddle.

"Same defense, fellows," he said. Halas' guess had proved correct. Coaches do not change winning defenses.

Luckman then called for an off-tackle slant by Osmanski. George Vass, the veteran pro football writer for the *Chicago Daily News*, described what happened:

"McAfee, the right halfback, went in motion to the right, taking out Redskins linebacker Jimmy Johnston," Vass wrote. "Bear right guard George Musso pulled out and went to the left. Luckman, on a reverse pivot, faked to halfback Ray Nolting, then pitched to Osmanski. The fullback went to the left—counter to the direction of McAfee, the man in motion to the right.

"Osmanski noted that someone had missed the block on the Washington right end. So instead of cutting off tackle, he swerved wide and, turning the corner, sprinted down the sidelines. Halfway home, at the 35, he was about to be cornered by a pair of Redskins, but Bears right end George Wilson cut all the way across the field, hurtled into them, and took them both out with one tremendous block to spring Osmanski the rest of the way to a sixty-eight-yard touchdown run. Automatic Jack Manders kicked the extra point, and the Bears had a 7 to 0 lead after a minute of play."

Arthur Daley, sports editor of the *New York Times*, wrote that Wilson's dynamic block was "like a double-barreled shotgun." Halas exclaimed, "I've never seen one like it."

Almost immediately thereafter came the crucial point of the game as Charlie Malone, free in the end zone but blinded by the sun, dropped Sammy Baugh's perfect pass. From that point, the Bears marched eighty yards for a touchdown.

It was 38-0 at halftime, 54-0 after the third quarter, and by the time the Bears headed for their joyous dressing room celebration, Luckman was already making dinner plans to pay off the guys in the offensive line.

Chapter 6

THE MIDDLE YEARS

The lopsidedness of the Bears' 73-0 victory over the Redskins focused attention on the T formation. And after Clark Shaughnessy's Stanford Indians, starring Frankie Albert and using the T, routed Nebraska in the Rose Bowl on New Year's Day, 1941, it seemed as if every university and college in the nation from Notre Dame to the Chanute Black Panthers switched over to the "new" formation.

Halas was privately amused, although hugely pleased, by the adulation and mimicry of a football system which was at least as old as the single wing.

World War II depleted the ranks of the Bears, just as it decimated all professional teams. The exodus, in the case of the Bears, started at the top. Halas again entered the Navy after the Bears, led by Norm Standlee, George McAfee, and Ken Kavanaugh, routed the Giants, 37-9, in the 1941 championship game. Halas became a lieutenant commander in this second naval tour of duty.

During Papa Bear's absence, Luke Johnsos and Hunk Anderson served as dual coaches of the Bears. One of their prime pleasures, and also acute agonies, was to watch the return of Bronko Nagurski. Now thirty-five years old, the former fullback came back as a tackle for his reincarnation.

Against the Detroit Lions, Nagurski waited patiently for Frank Sinkwich to try to find a pass receiver. Nagurski didn't bother to chase Sinkwich. He merely felled him with a mighty blast of the forearm as Sinkwich tried to run by.

"Sonny, I'm too old to go chasing you," Nagurski said. "You'll have to come to me."

By the start of the 1944 season, Nagurski again had retired after returning to his old fullback position long enough to score his last Bear touchdown in a 41-21 triumph over Washington for the 1943 NFL crown. Luckman hurled five scoring passes in the rout.

The manpower shortage caused by the war produced several "discoveries," the most important of which was Ed Sprinkle, who came from Bulldog Turner's alma mater, Hardin-Simmons. Bulldog brought Sprinkle to Johnsos for a tryout and the ferocious, blond young man made the team as a walk-on at guard. Over the next twelve years, Sprinkle, who became an end, gained a reputation as the meanest man in football, fitting well into the mold of the physical Bears, who always have sought to intimidate.

"I was proud to let Sprinkle wear my old jersey No. 7," Halas said recently, "because he was one of the toughest, roughest ends the Bears ever had." No argument.

Halas returned from the Navy late in 1945, but the Bears already were hopelessly out of the running and finished 3-7. The old coach used the final two games (both victories) to test his returning servicemen against the Pittsburgh Steelers and Chicago Cardinals.

Halas especially wanted to see McAfee in action again, but told the star halfback he didn't expect him to play more than a few minutes. McAfee played only twelve minutes in one game, scoring three touchdowns.

The following year, with Papa Bear around full time, the Bears spurted to a record of 8-2-1, then beat the Giants for the NFL title, 24-14.

Sports historians are generally agreed that the Bears' arch enemies, the Cardinals, were responsible for the beginning of the deterioration of the Bears which extended until their next conference championship in 1956, and never really ended then.

The destruction of the 1947 Bears didn't take place until the final game of the season, but when it happened, it was devastating. The Cardinals, with their "dream" backfield of Paul Christman, Charlie Trippi, Pat Harder, and Marshall Goldberg, went into the finale that year tied for first place with the Bears in the Western Division, both with 8-4 records.

Coach Jimmy Conzelman's craftily planned opening play from scrimmage was adroitly executed. The Cards' best receiver, Mal Kutner, raced deep into the secondary, drawing two Bear defenders with him. Meanwhile, Boris (Babe) Dimancheff swung to the outside, turned to take Christman's perfect pass, and sprinted to the goal line on an eighty-yard touchdown play. The Cards went on to win, 30-21, for the divisional title, and the next week beat Philadelphia, 28-21, for the NFL crown.

The loss in a crucial, climactic game seemed to symbolize the plight of the Bears, who were gradually losing their great players of the previous decade and finding them difficult to replace.

Halas, like all other NFL owners, got into a bidding war with the fledgling All-America Football Conference. Papa Bear signed three of college football's biggest names—quarterbacks Johnny Lujack of Notre Dame and Bobby Layne of Texas, and George Connor, the magnificent tackle from Notre Dame.

Nowhere was the Bears' personnel situation more critical than at quarterback, the department which appeared superficially to be one of the strongest. When Halas brought in Lujack and Layne as potential replacements for the aging Luckman, he bought himself nothing but trouble.

"Halas broke me in by having me start the game while Sid sized up the defense," Lujack recalls. "Then Sid would take over while I played defense myself." Lujack tied a Bear record by intercepting nine passes in his 1948 rookie season. Meanwhile, Layne, the fun-loving Texan, was fidgeting on the bench, planning his evenings.

Lujack's finest day came in 1949 when he threw six touchdown passes against the Cardinals in a 52-21 victory. But the ex-Irish quarterback permanently injured his passing arm in 1950. Luckman retired the same year (along with George McAfee, and Ken Kavanaugh). And Layne was no longer around, having been sold by Halas to the New York Bulldogs the previous year in a deal which may have been the biggest mistake in the history of pro football.

Layne quickly wound up in Detroit, leading Coach Buddy Parker's Lions to three NFL crowns and a divisional title in the early fifties. Lujack retired after the 1951 season. It seemed incredible, but the Bears, who only three years earlier were loaded with quarterbacks, now had none.

The Luckman-Lujack-Layne fiasco set in motion a musical chairs chain of unhappy quarterbacking competitions that persists with the Bears to this

33

day. After the three "L's," there were the three "B's"—Ed Brown, Zeke Bratkowski, and George Blanda—competing testily for the QB job. Then there were Bill Wade, Rudy Bukich, and Larry Rakestraw; then Rakestraw, Jack Concannon, and Virgil Carter; Concannon, Carter, and Bobby Douglass; Douglass, Carter, and Gary Huff; Bob Avellini, Huff, and Carter; Avellini, Mike Phipps, and Vince Evans; and now, in 1985, Jim McMahon and Steve Fuller.

Wow!

George Connor, the last of the two-way players, became a perennial all-pro and a Chicago favorite. The ex-Notre Damer started out playing offensive tackle and wound up doubling on defense as a linebacker. One of big George's greatest regrets was that the Bears never won a title during his illustrious pro career. They almost made it in 1950, but lost a conference playoff to the Los Angeles Rams, 24-14. That year marked the Bear baptism of defensive end Bill Wightkin, another Notre Dame great.

Halas always came up with one or two special "finds" each decade. His big discovery of the 1950s was Harlon Hill, a lanky speedster from obscure Florence (Alabama) State. Hill was spotted by Clark Shaughnessy on a scouting mission. Halas drafted the youngster on the fifteenth round in 1954 and was immediately impressed. Hill had no "moves" and never developed any. But he could fly.

At the end of his first three years as a Bear, Harlon was ahead of the Packers' legendary Don Hutson in every statistical department of pass catching. The Bears' rebuilding program had suddenly started to pay dividends. In 1952, Halas had drafted ends Bill McColl and Jim Dooley, plus middle guard Bill George and tackle Bill Bishop.

McColl, with his 6-foot-4, 230-pound size, helped Halas "invent" the slot halfback, forerunner to today's flanker. Dooley, an agile split end with loyalty to match his keen football mind, was to receive his reward in later years when he was named head coach.

Fred Williams added talent at defensive tackle and Ozarkian humor to the Bears in 1953. The 1954 crop included quarterbacks Ed Brown and Zeke Bratkowski, center Larry Strickland, tackle Stan Jones, and defensive end Ed (Country) Meadows. The latter was to achieve notoriety in 1956 as the man who broke Bobby Layne's jaw with a blindside tackle.

In 1955, Halas gambled and drafted an injured fullback from Florida to make the slot attack work. When Rick Casares came out of the Army, the Bears selected him on the tenth round to go along with a hard-running halfback, Bobby Watkins of Ohio State. In his rookie year, Casares led the league with a 5.4-yard rushing average. The next season, 1956, he gained 1,126 yards and scored fourteen touchdowns. He was a demon throughout his career who drew tremendous respect from his teammates.

Halas stepped down as Bear coach for the third time in 1956. To nobody's surprise he nominated his old pal, John L. (Paddy) Driscoll, to succeed him. Paddy was the only one of the long-time Halas colleagues with the exception of Phil Handler who had not yet held the coaching reins, and Papa Bear felt he was handing over a championship team.

Driscoll's Bears, with Halas making no pretense of staying in the background, forged to a 9-3-1 record and a conference title in 1956. But the championship game was a disaster. "We kicked hell out of them," boasted a vengeful Frank Gifford after the New York Giants had ripped the Bears apart, 47-7.

A casual visit to a Florida race track led one of Halas' valued lieutenants to Willie Galimore. Phil Handler heard from a jockey at Hialeah about the sensational youngster from Florida A. & M., and telephoned Halas in Chicago. Galimore's college coach, Jake Gaither, confirmed that Willie was, indeed, something special. The Bears drafted him as a "future" for 1957.

Galimore's sensational running was about the only bright spot during Driscoll's second and final campaign as head coach in 1957. After Willie scored four touchdowns against the Los Angeles Rams, Sid Luckman pronounced the rookie "the nearest approach to George McAfee the league has seen."

The 1957 Bears finished 5-7 and Halas, having given his old pal a two-year taste of coaching, bumped Driscoll and once again returned to the sidelines.

"When I quit coaching," Halas explained, "I couldn't think of any reason I would ever come back. But looking over the situation, I felt coaching methods in pro football were changing. I developed some new ideas; now I wanted to try them out."

Halas, of course, wanted one more championship. But he found the road ahead far more difficult than he had anticipated. His 1958 and 1959 clubs both finished a respectable second in their conference (to John Unitas and the potent Baltimore Colts), with 8-4 records. But in 1960 the Bears skidded to 5-6-1.

Fans and sportswriters began calling upon Papa Bear to fire himself once again—this time for good. "After all, he wouldn't be out of a job," pointed out columnist Bill Gleason.

There was at least one bright spot in 1961. One of the Bears' eight victories came at the expense of the San Francisco 49ers and it shattered Coach Red Hickey's publicized "shotgun" offense, which had overwhelmed opponents and charmed naive sportswriters for three weeks.

The "shotgun" was simply a variation of the short punt formation, with the quarterback taking a direct snap from center. When the 49ers came to Wrigley Field, Defensive Coach Clark Shaughnessy, the genius who once had helped Halas refine the T formation, muzzled the new offensive weapon with casual simplicity.

Shaughnessy moved linebacker Bill George back into the line where he once had toiled as a middle guard, overshifting slightly to the right or left of center. The Bears' defensive ends moved out to prevent the 49er wingbacks from slanting over the middle for short passes. The outside linebackers helped George intimidate the three San Francisco tailbacks—John Brodie, Bill Kilmer, and Charlie Waters—and the Bears coasted to a 31-0 victory.

The Bears finished 8-6 in 1961, fourth in their division, and moved up to third in 1962 after a whirlwind windup brought them home 9-5. But the fans wanted more. And so did Papa Bear!

Halas was having trouble keeping his assistants from open warfare as he moved toward a 1963 season which he sensed might be his greatest year of personal triumph. Shaughnessy and George Allen were running the defense. Luke Johnsos and Jim Dooley were running the offense. Shaughnessy and Allen were feuding, often publicly, as the ambitious Allen moved closer and closer toward command level.

Finally, the situation became too much for the embittered Shaughnessy to take. Late in the 1962 season, he quietly packed his bags and went home to California.

Flanker Johnny Morris, now a Chicago television sportscaster, blames Halas himself for the friction among his underlings.

"Halas had a philosophy that competition within his ranks was healthy and good," Morris explains. "There was great competition between the offensive and defensive coaches, which was translated into competition between the offensive and defensive players.

"For years there was a duel between Luke Johnsos and Clark Shaughnessy. Halas liked this. He did the same thing between the offensive and defensive platoons. He would go to an offensive meeting and tell them the offense wasn't doing the job. Then he would go to a defensive meeting and tell them they were letting the offense down."

Chapter 7

1963: THAT LAST CHAMPIONSHIP SEASON

It was a long time coming. Seventeen years had gone by since the Bears had won their last world championship. Now, going into the 1963 campaign, George Halas knew he had the ingredients to silence his critics forever.

Throughout the season, Divine Providence seemed to smile upon the Bears. No matter how they flipped the coin, it always came up heads.

In a crucial November game against the Pittsburgh Steelers, the Bears were fighting desperately late in the game to protect a 17-17 tie which was essential to their title hopes. Bear quarterback Bill Wade, on his own 3-yard line, inexplicably tried to throw a screen pass to fullback Joe Marconi. The pass sailed into the hands of John Reger, a Steeler linebacker. Reger was so startled he dropped the ball. He could have cakewalked into the end zone.

Big Doug Atkins, the Bears' all-pro defensive end not known for looking upon his fellow man with kindness, turned his eyes heavenward and intoned in his Tennessee drawl, "Somebody up there likes us."

Halas had the Bears fighting mad before the season even began. The old coach, then sixty-eight, had himself fighting mad, too. Near the end of the first half of a preseason game against the Giants, Halas, inflamed by a scuffle on the field, picked up a helmet and tried to fashion a new skull for one of the Giants.

New York Coach Allie Sherman tried to restrain Halas. "George, cut it out," Sherman implored. "This is just an exhibition."

"It's a game, isn't it?" Halas snorted.

When they started playing for real, the Bears went swinging through the former Titletown, U.S.A., and chopped it to ribbons. Packer fans had dubbed the little Fox River city of Green Bay "Titletown" when Vince Lombardi won his first NFL championship there in 1961. The name had been held in reverence through the following season, when Lombardi and the Pack won again.

With Bill Wade concentrating on percentage ball control and a revitalized defense shackling the Packers' power, the Bears came back to Chicago with a thrilling 10-3 victory.

"When we won that opener," linebacker Bill George recalled once, "all of the old timers—Doug Atkins, Fred Williams, Larry Morris, and myself—knew we had a shot at the title. Yet we always had a strange feeling after every game that year. A feeling that the bubble had to bust sooner or later. It never did."

As the Bears poured into their dressing room in Green Bay, they were as happy as a troop of Boy Scouts suddenly unleashed in a candy store.

"We did it," screamed tackle Earl Leggett. "I didn't think we could do it, but we did."

"I knew damned well we'd do it," shouted George, the greatest middle linebacker in history up to that point and the captain of the Bears' aroused defense.

Blood was gushing from Bill Wade's eye.

"We got a lot we can do, Baby," end Mike Ditka yelled into Wade's ear. "We didn't hit one-fifth of our potential today."

For the first time in perhaps a decade, there was rapport between the Bear offensive and defensive units. That's what a victory over the mighty Green Bay Packers could do in those days.

"You saw what our defense did," hollered flanker Johnny Morris. "They played a whale of a ball game. They won it for us."

"No, we didn't," countered defensive halfback Dave Whitsell. "The offense won it. You guys got that ball and stuffed it down their throats."

Halas tried to make it clear that the triumph over Lombardi's hallowed team was no miracle. "This effort today culminates months of planning," the Papa Bear declared. "The coaches have worked hundreds of hours toward this one game. But the victory belongs to the players. They were ready physically and they were ready mentally."

The happy triumph over Lombardi and Company set the tone for the rest of the season, both tactically and spiritually. The 1963 Bears were to be a defense-oriented team. Offensively, they were to play ball control, emphasizing execution and taking as few chances as possible. And they were to be tough and resolute.

"It was a one-shot year, the one year where it all molded together," Johnny Morris reflected as he prepared for his ten o'clock sportscast on Chicago's CBS affiliate, WBBM-TV. "There's no question that the offense was motivated by the defense. It was the greatest overall defensive performance I had ever seen by a football team.

"Offensively, we didn't score a lot of points. But we scored enough to get the job done. We were able to move the ball four or five yards at a time, consistently, all season. This meant the defense didn't have to be on the field all the time as they had had to do in previous years."

Wade, the sharpshooter from Vanderbilt with a football brain as keen as his throwing arm, had been impressive in the last six games during 1962. During that span, Bullet Bill tossed eleven touchdown passes. His backup man was Rudy Bukich, who could throw a football farther with accuracy than any man in history. Bukich was to lead the league in passing in 1965, but in this championship season, he played a low-key second fiddle to Wade.

Wade's pet aerial targets were right end Mike Ditka, the strong man from Pittsburgh and spiritual leader of the offense, and Morris, who the following year was to lead the NFL in *his* specialty with a record ninety-three receptions.

When he wasn't looking for Ditka or Morris, Wade threw to halfback Ronnie Bull, the 1962 top draft choice and rookie of the year from Baylor. Or he tossed short swings to fullback Joe Marconi, who increasingly had replaced heavy duty Rick Casares. The split ends were John Farrington,

Angelo Coia, and Bob Jenks.

Ditka is worthy of special mention. The Bears haven't had a tight end with a fragment of big Mike's ability or aggressiveness since Ditka left.

"The minute he walked out on the field for the first practice in 1961," Bill George once said, "I knew Ditka was an instant pro. I can only say that about one other player. When Dick Butkus made his first tackle in 1965, I knew my playing days were numbered."

"Ditka was an offensive player in the mold of a defensive man," Morris declares. "He was our enforcer. If there were any problems on the offensive team, it was Ditka who took over. One time a fan ran out onto the field in the Los Angeles Coliseum. Ditka decked him with one punch. Mike just figured the guy had no business being out there."

The Bears' 1963 running game was built around Bull and Willie Galimore at halfback, and Marconi and Casares at fullback. The offensive line, anchored by the veteran center, Mike Pyle, featured Bob Wetoska and Jim Cadile on the "strong" side, and Herman Lee and Ted Karras on the other.

But defense was the key to the vindication of George Halas' decision to hang on as coach until his beloved Bears won one more championship. There may never have been a finer trio of linebackers than the Bears' Bill George, Joe Fortunato, and Larry Morris. Doug Atkins and Bob Kilcullen, backed by Ed O'Bradovich, were the most feared defensive ends in the league. Tackles included Fred Williams, Stan Jones, and Earl Leggett. The defensive secondary of Richie Petitbon, Rosey Taylor, Dave Whitsell, and Bennie McRae (with J. C. Caroline sparking the special teams) was peerless.

There was no mutual admiration society between Halas and Atkins. The big defensive end had his own training rules. These included going over to the side of the field and spending entire practice sessions reclining on a rolled-up tarpaulin while his teammates toiled. Strangely, nobody seemed to mind.

"My big old body hurts 'most all the time," explained the 6-foot-8, 260-pound Tennessean, who at thirty-three was in his eleventh pro year. "I still ache on Saturdays from the Sunday before. When it gets so I hurt on Sunday mornings from the previous week, I'll know it's time to quit."

Halas admits he "had a little trouble with Atkins now and then. But I thought I handled him pretty well. He was undoubtedly the greatest defensive end in football. You're not going to throw a championship out the window trying to discipline a guy like that."

The Bears' offensive performances in that championship year made dull viewing for fans who savored the memory of long bombs going back to the days of Sid Luckman. No longer was there an Ed Brown throwing to Harlon Hill. Even Wade's dramatic instincts had to be curbed.

The fans occasionally booed Wade for failing to unload to his deep receivers. But the veteran quarterback was merely following the game plan, which limited the aerial game to short flare passes to the backs, slant-ins to Ditka, and hooks to Morris.

The offensive modernization, in which Halas was assisted by Jim Dooley, Luke Johnsos, and Chuck Mather, was accomplished smoothly. But to this day there is confusion as to the genesis of the Bears' 1963 championship defense. George Allen, who had won out in a bitter duel with Clark Shaughnessy for Halas' favor, has repeatedly claimed credit for junking the Bears' old man-to-man defense and installing a modern zone. Shaughnessy loyalists insist Allen was merely walking through an intricate routine carefully choreographed by Shaughnessy.

When the conflict between Allen and Shaughnessy obviously had become irreconcilable in 1962, Halas began taking more and more control of the defense. The Bears had been the object of some ridicule for their constant "jitterbugging" (stunting by linebackers).

A casual boast by end Max McGee of the Packers convinced Halas that the Bears must put in a zone. "As long as the Bears keep playing me man-to-man," McGee bragged, "I'll stay in this league forever."

Halas, Shaughnessy, and Allen installed what Halas termed the "buz and rub" defense in 1962. In the "buz," the linebackers zoomed back to help out the deep backs on pass defense. In the "rub," they stayed up on the line to protect against the run.

"Shaughnessy lacked enthusiasm for the buz," Halas declared. "But he agreed to go 75 percent buz and 25 percent red-dogging (the Bears' term for blitzing). We wound up as the number one team on pass defense and Shaughnessy quit without waiting for the season to end."

Bill George had a totally different and somewhat bitter version. The big middle linebacker's forte was blitzing, and George remained loyal to the departed Shaughnessy throughout the 1963 title campaign in which Allen was widely acclaimed as the Bears' defensive wizard.

"We already had the buz and rub long before Allen knew what it was all about," bristled George, who was killed in a car wreck in 1982. "We just used different names. Clark taught me a lot. He taught everybody a hell of a lot. They [Halas and Allen] claimed in 1963 they'd changed the defense. They hadn't changed a damned thing. All they did was change from colors to numbers.

"Practically everything we did that championship year had already been put in by Shaughnessy," George asserted. "Sure, I favored the red dog. I liked to red dog. But that was only because we didn't have the personnel to zone a lot. In 1963, Bennie McRae [cornerback] more than any other person enabled us to use a lot of zone. He was the first guy we had who was able to handle the zone on the vital left side of the defense.

"Hell, Allen didn't even know the zone very well. His main contribution was getting us ready for the games. The only reason he took me along with him to the Los Angeles Rams when he went out there to coach was to cover up for him. I got along with Allen fine. But I don't like to see Shaughnessy cheated out of the credit he deserved."

From their opening victory over Green Bay on, the Bears were never out of first place in 1963. They rolled past Minnesota and Detroit, then escaped in a squeaker against Baltimore in which Bukich came off the bench to bail out Wade. They were 4-0 and then 5-0 after a 52-14 rout of the Rams.

"We are not yet the greatest in history," chuckled Halas after Ditka had caught four touchdown passes and the Bear defense had pilfered six L.A. aerials.

But then the Bears ran into trouble, losing 20-14 at San Francisco. The Bears and Packers were neck-and-neck the next three weeks. The decisive game of the season was the return match with Green Bay at Wrigley Field on November 17. It had been commonly assumed that the Packers, playing without suspended Paul Hornung, would come into Chicago and gain a bloody revenge for their earlier defeat by the Bears.

But J. C. Caroline made clear the Bears' eagerness on the opening kickoff when he drove through two blocks and cut Herb Adderley down inside the Packer 20 on Adderley's opening kickoff return.

The Bears took a 6-0 lead on the first two of Roger Leclerc's four field goals. To all intents and purposes, they won the game before the first quarter ended when Willie Galimore cut off left tackle behind Herman Lee's block, squirmed away from Bill Forester and Jesse Whittenton, and sprinted twenty-seven yards for a touchdown. With the 26-7 triumph, the Bears had a 9-1 record.

Disaster struck the nation the following week with the assassination of President John Kennedy. Commissioner Pete Rozelle, in an unpopular and unwise decision, decided to let the National Football League play its Sunday games as usual. Commissioner Joe Foss of the upstart American Football League called off his conference's Sunday schedule.

Sunday, November 24, thus was a day already charged with hysteria. It became more so with the news of the killing of Lee Harvey Oswald, President Kennedy's accused assassin, by Jack Ruby. The news of this second killing reached Forbes Field in Pittsburgh only two hours before the Bears and Steelers kicked off.

It was in this setting that the two teams played a game supercharged with emotion in which tempers frequently erupted. The contest ended in a 17-17 tie, but the final score seemed insignificant.

Three individual episodes enter my mind as I recall that traumatic day in Pittsburgh.

First, there was Mike Ditka's 65-yard run on a pass from Wade in which the great Bear tight end dragged nearly half the Steeler team with him before finally collapsing on the Pittsburgh 20. Johnny Morris still calls it "the greatest individual effort by a football player I have ever seen."

The second incident has already been briefly described—Wade's inexcusable screen pass while deep in his own territory which narrowly missed being intercepted by a linebacker.

After remarking that "somebody up there likes us," Atkins charged over to Halas, shook his fist, and said: "Let's get out of here. We'll take the tie and go home."

The third nervous episode that day occurred after the game. Pat Livingston, sports editor of the *Pittsburgh Press* and usually an admirer of Halas, charged up to Papa Bear in the dressing room, accused him of stealing the game with "your usual bleeping deplorable dirty tricks," and began slapping Halas on the cheeks, first gently, then gradually with more force.

Joe Stydahar, one of the assistant coaches, and Atkins, of all people, gave Livingston a free ride out of the dressing room. In more ways than one, the Bears were happy to escape with a tie as they boarded their plane for the return flight home.

When the Bears came into their regular season finale at Wrigley Field against the Detroit Lions, they had to win it. Vince Lombardi's Packers, though beaten twice by Halas' team that year, had brought the Western Division race down to the wire by winning the previous day at Los Angeles.

The Bears, unable to get their offense untracked, trailed the Lions, 7-3, at halftime.

"You guys are simply too tight, too tense," Halas told his players during the intermission. "Forget the score. Just go out and play your regular game in the second half."

The Bears took their coach's advice. Relaxing discernibly, they suddenly started moving the ball, scoring three times in a frenzied second half spree.

Johnny Morris, the frisky little flanker, ignited the parade, running a down-and-in pattern past young Tom Hall to take Bill Wade's pass for a fifty-one yard touchdown.

Wade didn't see Morris' spectacular run after the catch because "I was unconscious. I got hit hard and saw stars. When I woke up, Johnny was already running into the end zone."

The nifty catch was one of eight totaling 171 yards by Morris, who made a mockery out of the Detroit secondary as the Lions doubled up on Mike Ditka. Three minutes and twenty-one seconds after Morris' touchdown, however, Ditka was open and Wade hit the husky tight end for twenty-two yards and a TD.

The last Bear touchdown of the day was the most spectacular of all. Little

Davey Whitsell, the gutsy right cornerback, stepped in front of Gail Cogdill near the sideline, stole a pass from quarterback Earl Morrall, and returned thirty-nine yards to the end zone.

"It was a gamble," Whitsell beamed later. "I'd been playing Cogdill tight all day. I decided we needed the ball. Morrall fired it out there and I just cut in front of Cogdill and grabbed it."

Richie Petitbon, a compatriot of Whitsell's in the great Bear secondary, said Whitsell pulled a Babe Ruth in making the game-clinching interception. "Dave called his shot," explained Richie. "He told me earlier in the week he was going to get one of those 'out' passes Morrall likes to throw and go all the way."

Whitsell's grand larceny, which came with only twenty-five seconds to play, sealed the Bears' 24-14 victory, gave them the championship of the Western Division for the tenth time, and set them up for the NFL title game.

The big one was played on December 29, 1963, in Wrigley Field. The grass was all but frozen and the famous Lake Michigan wind was whipping in to chill the capacity crowd.

A few hours before the opening kickoff, Bill George and Fred Williams were observing a weekly ritual. They were having coffee in a small restaurant near the ball park, and Williams made the same observation he voiced every Sunday morning during the football season, rain or shine.

Peering out the window at the frigid winter scene, the hefty tackle said, "It sure is a great day."

Another customer stared at him and asked, "A great day for what?" Williams had been waiting for this question for twelve years.

"A great day to freeze your bleepin' ass, that's what!"

Williams turned out to be a prophet. Despite the weather, it was a great day for the Bears and their avid fans. Writing in *The Chicago Tribune*, George Strickler summed up the game as follows:

"Greatness came to the Chicago Bears yesterday in the frigidity of Wrigley Field where the team of destiny gave the New York Giants all the best of the breaks and a thorough whipping to win the championship of the National Football League. The score was 14 to 10.

"Before 45,801 mittened, blanketed, and shivering spectators, the Bears brought the title back to Chicago for the first time in seventeen years by rallying twice, then throttling New York's desperate last challenge.

"Both Bear touchdowns were set up by interceptions and came on quarterback sneaks by Bill Wade, a gallant and steady performer this day. The Bears intercepted five passes, including two long ones into the end zones.

"By their triumph, the Bears climaxed the career of one of football's greatest coaches, sixty-eight-year-old George Halas, the venerable pro pioneer who is virtually everybody's candidate for coach of the century."

Halas knew that the Bears' task was to stop Giant quarterback Y. A. Tittle, the thirty-seven-year-old Bald Eagle. With fullback Alex Webster and halfback Hugh McElhenny aging, Tittle would, Halas was certain, be trying to pass to flanker Frank Gifford and split end Del Shofner.

The game was in its infancy when Halas' analysis proved correct. After the Giants recovered a fumble by Wade, Tittle lobbed a soft pass to Gifford, who ran a flag pattern on cornerback Bennie McRae and took the ball into the end zone for a fourteen-yard touchdown. Don Chandler's extra point kick gave the Giants a 7-0 lead with 7:22 played.

Near the end of the first quarter, Tittle had Shofner all alone in the end zone, but Shofner's numbed fingers couldn't hold the pass. Now Tittle tried a screen, this time to Phil King. But Larry Morris, the Bears' right linebacker, was waiting.

"Fred Williams and Doug Atkins gave Tittle a big rush," Morris said later, "and Tittle had to throw fast. I was lucky. I caught the ball and started to run. Why did I zigzag a lot? Because I'm no gazelle halfback. I wanted to score."

Morris didn't quite make it. After sixty-one yards, he "just ran out of steam." But his interception, which won him a new car as player-of-the-game, got the Bears down to the New York 5-yard line. After Ronnie Bull gained three yards on the first play, Wade sneaked for a touchdown and Bob Jencks' conversion knotted the count at 7-7.

The Giants took a 10-7 lead on Chandler's thirteen-yard field goal at 5:11 of the second period. But the Bear defense continued to pound Tittle. With six minutes remaining until halftime, a blitzing Larry Morris drove his helmet into Tittle's left knee as the Giant quarterback faded to pass. Tittle left the game, not to return until the next half, and New York carried its 10-7 edge into the intermission.

Bear fans gasped in horror when McElhenny, who had been one of pro football's super runners during an illustrious career with the San Francisco 49ers, took the opening second half kickoff and moved past midfield. At the Bear 46-yard line, Rosey Taylor tackled Big Mac to save a touchdown.

"It was my biggest satisfaction of the day," exulted Taylor, whose nine pass interceptions had led the league during the regular season.

It was ironic that Ed O'Bradovich, who started at defensive end only because the incumbent, Bob Kilcullen, was injured after starting every previous game that season, should wind up the hero in the break that turned the game.

With three minutes remaining in the third quarter and the ball on his 24, Tittle called a play. Bears linebacker Joe Fortunato, his eyes sparkling, warned his defensive colleagues, "Watch out for the screen."

"We put a regular four-man rush on Tittle," O'Bradovich said later.

"When my man, tackle Jack Stroud, dropped back in a hurry and Tittle also dropped back, I knew Fortunato was right. I was playing kind of wide, and Tittle threw the ball, I think toward Joe Morrison. It was chest-high. I caught it and started to run."

O. B. bulled his way ten yards to the Giants' 14 with the interception. Four plays, including Wade's key "lookie" toss to Ditka, carried to within two inches of the goal line. Wade sneaked the rest of the way, and Jencks' extra point gave the Bears the lead at 14-10. But the entire fourth quarter still remained.

The Bears spent a large part of the final period waiting in dread for the bomb they knew Tittle would try to detonate. Finally, with ten seconds left and a first down on the Chicago 39, Tittle let Shofner go down, then in, from the right side. Tittle fired. But when the ball left his hand, it went into orbit. As one sportswriter noted, "Shofner could not have gotten there in a taxi."

Richie Petitbon, one of the Bears' old pros, could and did get there. He intercepted in the end zone and pandemonium broke loose.

It was a half minute before Tittle, kneeling on the frozen turf in dejection, jerked his helmet off his bald head and flung it to the ground. Three times he picked it up and smashed it into the turf. Then he walked to the sidelines, weeping unashamedly.

After the field was cleared of premature celebrators, the Bears used up the remaining two seconds with a quarterback sneak by Wade. Then they broke for the dressing room. There was no immediate uproar. Finally, George Halas walked in. Papa Bear set the pace for the postgame festivities, just as he had called the shots all year.

"Go!" screamed Halas.

Then, and only then, did the Bears start yelling. They hollered magnificently, but not so magnificently that the microphones failed to pick up the Bears' victory chant for national television.

It was a song bequeathed to the Bears many years ago by the villainous Ed Sprinkle. This time it was for George Allen. As Fortunato tossed Allen the game ball, the squad rose up and rendered its traditional victory anthem:

"Hooray for George, hooray at last; hooray for George, for he's a horse's ass."

1963 NFL CHAMPIONSHIP GAME
BEARS DEPTH CHART

OFFENSE

Split end — John Farrington, Angelo Coia, Bob Jencks.

Left tackle — Herman Lee, Roger Davis.
Left guard — Ted Karras, Roger Davis.
Center — Mike Pyle, Bob Wetoska.
Right guard — Jim Cadile, Bob Wetoska.
Right tackle — Bob Wetoska, Steve Barnett.
Tight end — Mike Ditka, Bob Jencks.
Quarterback — Bill Wade, Rudy Bukich.
Flanker — John Morris, Angelo Coia, Bobby Joe Green.
Running back — Willie Galimore, Ronnie Bull, Billy Martin.
Fullback — Joe Marconi, Charlie Bivins.

DEFENSE

Left end — Ed O'Bradovich, Bob Kilcullen, John Johnson.
Left tackle — Stan Jones, John Johnson.
Right tackle — Fred Williams, John Johnson.
Right end — Doug Atkins, Ed O'Bradovich, Roger Leclerc.
Left linebacker — Joe Fortunato, Tom Bettis.
Middle linebacker — Bill George, Tom Bettis.
Right linebacker — Larry Morris, Roger Leclerc.
Left cornerback — Bennie McRae, J. C. Caroline.
Right cornerback — Dave Whitsell, Bennie McRae.
Left safety — Richie Petitbon, Larry Glueck.
Right safety — Rosey Taylor, Larry Glueck.

SPECIALISTS

Place kickers — Bob Jencks, Roger Leclerc.
Holder — Dave Whitsell.
Kickoffs — Roger Leclerc.
Punter — Bobby Joe Green.
Punt returns — Johnny Morris, Rosey Taylor, Charlie Bivins.
Kickoff returns — Ronnie Bull, Johnny Morris, Rosey Taylor, Charlie Bivins.

COACHING STAFF

George S. Halas, head coach; John L. (Paddy) Driscoll, Luke Johnsos, Phil Handler, Jim Dooley, George Allen, Joe Stydahar, Sid Luckman, Chuck Mather.

Chapter 8

DOUG ATKINS: REBEL WITH A CAUSE

Doug Atkins deserves a special chapter in any Bear history. Perhaps more than any other player in the swashbuckling Bears saga, Atkins personifies the brawling, don't-give-a-damn character that George Halas liked his players and his teams to have.

Halas and Atkins didn't always get along. But they shared a commitment to excellence. The owner-coach and the huge, strapping, 6-foot-8 defensive end from Tennessee often argued openly in front of the rest of the squad. Nobody thought anything about it in those days.

"Once in awhile I would call Doug a dirty bleep-bleep and he would call me a no-good blankety-blank," Halas once said. "But we agreed on one thing. We both knew we could win with him in the lineup."

"Doug was incredible," says Ed O'Bradovich, who played with Atkins on the Bears' 1963 championship team. "He and the old man used to fight all the time. Doug could get away with calling him any name in the book. It was the old love-hate thing. We used to just love to sit back and watch those two go at it."

O'Bradovich, also a defensive end, recalls a 1962 game in San Francisco's Kezar Stadium, where the previous year a fan had jumped out of the stands and taken a couple of swings at Halas.

"We all figured the old man would use this as a psychological weapon to juice us up," O'Bradovich said. "But, instead, he told us just before the game, 'The first man that gets in a fight here today, it's going to cost him a thousand bucks.'

"As usual, we lost the flip of the coin, so the defense was on the field right from the start. On the very first play of the game, Doug got in a fight with the 49ers' second-string center. He just stretched this guy and got kicked out of the game. So Halas comes running out on the field and says to Doug, 'What did you do that for, you big dummy?'

"Doug turns around and says, 'Anybody that whoops me, I'm gonna whoop him back.' And the old man says, 'You're goddamned right, Doug. But the fine sticks.' "

Halas, well aware of Atkins' nocturnal habits and amazing tolerance for alcohol, used to assign defensive tackle Fred Williams to "chaperone" Atkins at night. The problem, Halas recalled years later, was that Atkins

47

could drink 12 martinis without becoming noticeably intoxicated, whereas Williams often was out after two drinks.

On one particular evening, Williams was able to match Atkins in staying power after Atkins challenged him to a martini-drinking contest. Even though they tied at 21, Williams claimed to be the winner because he had to drive Atkins home. But there were mitigating factors which appeared to turn the final count in Atkins' favor. Williams took a bath upon arriving home and couldn't get out of the bathtub. Williams' wife called Atkins for help. After launching his buddy from the tub, Atkins proclaimed himself the winner.

Atkins once assaulted a man with a $20 bill. Again on this occasion, Atkins' accomplice was his patient "chaperone," Williams. The two were in a bar one Sunday night when another customer began complaining because the Bears hadn't beaten the point spread in the game that afternoon. The man said he had lost a $20 bet.

Atkins listened for a while, then pulled a $20 bill out of his pocket and rubbed it in the man's face until his nose began bleeding.

Atkins says he couldn't figure out for many years how Halas knew so much about his personal life.

"One time I was drinking beer with [offensive end] Harlon Hill," Atkins recalled, "and the old man told me the next day exactly how many beers we had had.

"Halas said, 'A true Chicago Bear fan called and told me you were drinking beer last night at the Somerset Hotel. You had 12 beers, and Harlon Hill had 10.' Halas then told me everything Harlon and I had talked about at the bar. Finally, I found out that the 'true Chicago Bear fan' sitting at the bar was actually a Burns detective hired by Halas. The guy was reporting everything we said to the old man."

One day during Bears practice at Wrigley Field, which was the Bears' home until they moved to Soldier Field 15 years ago, all the Bears were accounted for except Atkins.

"Where's Atkins?" Halas bellowed.

Finally, somebody spotted Atkins in the upper deck behind home plate.

"Atkins," Halas yelled, "What in the hell are you going up there?"

"Talking to the pigeons," Atkins said.

There were two sets of training rules during the 12 years that the gifted giant, Atkins, toiled for the Bears. One set of rules applied to Atkins and the second to the other 39 members of the active roster.

On many a Wednesday or Thursday, his huge back, legs and shoulders aching from wounds incurred the previous Sunday, Atkins would sit on a rolled-up tarpaulin in Wrigley Field wearing an appropriately pained look while his teammates exercised. Halas paid no attention to the languishing

Atkins. He knew the big guy would be there when it counted the following Sunday.

Sometimes Atkins could be found on the sidelines, playing with his dog, a Rottweiler named Rebel. Atkins' idea of playing with the 100-pound dog was to twirl him around at the end of a rope, like in the hammer throw.

Atkins brought his dog to training camp in Rensselaer, Ind., where Halas annually took his team for summer concentration far from the enticements of the Windy City. Atkins used to invite other players to his room to listen to him tell stories. Just to make certain everybody stuck around for the dozens of punch lines, Atkins would station Rebel at the door.

"Rebel," Atkins would say when a rude guest inched toward the door, and the dog would growl and expose his bicuspids. When a listener tried to excuse himself to go to the bathroom after hours of beer drinking, Atkins would chuckle, "open the window."

Halas always kept an eagle-eye on the weight charts, looking for signs of excess.

"When you first got to training camp," Atkins recalls, "Halas always asked what's your best training weight. We used to tell the rookies to add a few pounds. If you weigh 250, tell him your best playing weight is 255 or 258. That way you had a little leeway.

"Halas would assess fines for excessive poundage over a player's assigned weight. If my assigned weight was 270 and I weighed in at 273, that was 25 dollars a pound. All over three pounds was fifty dollars a pound. And you didn't get that money back.

"We used to take silver dollars and wrap them in tape and tape them on the bottom weight to bring our reading down a little. We spent more time trying to doctor the scales. We messed up lots of scales. But we usually got caught sooner or later.

"The weekly weigh-in was Thursday morning. Lots of times I'd weigh 280 on a Wednesday and my assigned weight was 270. A bunch of us would go to steam baths. We'd quit eating, take steam, dry out hot, take laxatives and water pills—anything to make the weight. Then after we made the weight, we'd have a big meal and be right back the next day where we started."

Atkins always had plenty to say about the Bears' coaching, most of it distinctly uncomplimentary. He fumed about the team's "pansy offense." He didn't like the political games constantly waged by Clark Shaughnessy and George Allen, the coaching bosses of the defense, which finally ended when Allen convinced Halas his simple zone defense was better than Shaughnessy's ultra-sophisticated man-to-man, and Shaughnessy stalked out.

"Shaughnessy had a lot of crazy things he wanted us to do," recalls Atkins. "Lots of times Bill George [middle linebacker and defensive captain] didn't call them in the games, just in practice. We played too many Mickey Mouse defenses. After Shaughnessy left, Bill handled most of the things for George Allen. Allen was just smart enough to get the job done with Bill calling the signals. And Allen was easy to work with.

"Bill George was the smartest linebacker in the business, maybe the smartest player. I used to get mad because they lined me up so far out on the flank. Bill used to say they put me out there where I could get the quarterback without anybody on me. I used to tell them, 'Put me in a standard 4-3 defense so I can work like Gino Marchetti of Baltimore. Don't line me up outside of the ballpark.' I felt like I wasn't in the game sometimes."

But Atkins was always in the game. When big Doug was finally named to the Pro Football Hall of Fame in 1982, one of his ex-Bear teammates, Stan Jones, now on the Denver Broncos' coaching staff, exclaimed, "It wasn't a legitimate Hall of Fame until Doug got in. He was so tall that when we used to play volleyball in the end zone, he would spike the ball over the crossbar. He had the highest tolerance for pain I have ever seen."

Atkins, who played 17 years with the Bears, Cleveland Browns and New Orleans Saints, compiled a personal roster of injuries that included two damaged knees, a torn bicep, numerous cracked ribs, a broken collarbone, two hands broken twice, both ankles sprained, a ripped groin muscle, and a broken leg.

"Doug came out of a game in New Orleans with a compound fracture of the leg and actually walked off the field," Jones said in awe.

But even playing in pain, Atkins was a model of improvisation.

"One of his favorite tricks," Baltimore quarterback Johnny Unitas said, "was to throw a blocker at the quarterback."

"After my first meeting with Atkins," said Colt offensive tackle Jim Parker, "I wanted to quit football."

"I used to hurt most of the time," recalls Atkins, who was a perennial all-pro. "I learned over the years that it's what you do on Sundays that counts. Practice don't mean a darn. Heck, there's nothing more fun than to get out and run in practice, but you can only do that if you're feeling good.

"One time Halas asked me to play a game against Green Bay even though I had two bad ankles after a hard week of practice. I couldn't even walk on them. I had to shoot both ankles up. Well, somebody blocked me once, and I heard an assistant coach saying, 'Atkins, all-pro? Bull!' I decided then and there that practice isn't important. I decided to save my strength for the games. That's what everybody is going to judge you on."

Atkins got the job done magnificently with an almost total lack of the finesse found in today's breed of defensive ends.

"Doug was totally unsophisticated," Williams said. "George Allen would tell Doug to go one way if the back did this, or go another way if the tackle did that, or do this or that depending on what the wide receiver did.

"Doug would tell him, 'George, cut the crap. Just tell me if you want me to get the runner or the passer. Whichever one you want, I'll get.'"

Encouraged by Atkins, other Bear players of the sixties generation also occasionally summoned up the courage to challenge Halas. Harlon Hill once asked Halas why the Bears had to practice on Sundays during training camp when the Baltimore Colts had Sundays off.

"Because we're not as good as the Colts," Halas said.

"What does that have to do with it?" Hill asked Papa Bear. "I could work my mule for 24 hours, and he still wouldn't win the Kentucky Derby."

Williams once asked Halas for a $5,000 raise. Halas responded with a counter-offer of $500. "I guess you'll just have to trade me," Williams said. "I've been trying," Halas said, "but nobody wants you."

Atkins used to enjoy his annual bouts with Halas about money.

"I got along with Halas just fine," Atkins now insists in his high-pitched Tennessee drawl. "When I left the Bears [in 1967 for the New Orleans Saints], I had a $25,000 salary and a $5,000 bonus.

"Halas used to hold that bonus over our heads. Say you were making $12,000 on your contract, and he'd give you a $1,000 bonus for having a good year. But if you didn't have such a good year, he'd tell you he was raising you to $13,000 and then he'd conveniently forget about the bonus, so you were playing next year for the same amount."

"The old man and I had a few little cuss-fights," Atkins says with a chuckle. "He could hold his own with those words. We kind of put a show on for everybody once in awhile. He was from the old school. He demanded the best from everybody. After you get out of football, you can understand what he was driving at.

"We never had any trouble off the field. People kept trying to get me to knock him after I got out, like a lot of them did. I always told them, 'You should have knocked him while you were playing, not now.' I said what I wanted to say when it was time to say it."

Chapter 9

SAYERS, BUTKUS, AND A DC-3

Two of the greatest stars in Bear history—Gale Sayers and Dick Butkus—burst upon the scene in 1965. The two followed parallel courses, from instant success as rookies to national recognition as super stars, and then to premature retirement because of knee injuries.

Ironically and sadly, there were no Bear championships during the time of Sayers and Butkus, one of the most exciting and agonizing of all Bear eras.

The ten-year period from 1964 to 1974 ran the gamut of human experience. It was a time of tribulation and trauma, a time of wonder. There were moments of joy, and of tragedy.

Willie Galimore and John Farrington were killed in a training camp auto accident in 1964 near Rensselaer, Ind. Another beloved member of the Bear family, Brian Piccolo, died of cancer in 1970. George Halas hung up his coaching hat for good in 1968, to be replaced by Jim Dooley. Dooley was fired in 1972 and succeeded by Abe Gibron, who lasted through 1974.

All of these were ingredients in the continuing saga of pro football's oldest and most storied franchise, the final chapters before the Jim Finks housecleaning.

George Halas' friends had hoped he would retire after winning the 1963 championship, still savoring the thrill of accomplishment and never again to know the anguish of defeat. But they couldn't talk the stubborn old pioneer into quitting.

"I'd better keep on going," Halas would say with a laugh. "Where's a sixty-eight-year-old going to find another job, anyway?"

Injuries felled many of the key Bears in 1964. Bill George, Joe Fortunato, Larry Morris, and Doug Atkins all were hurt, leaving the proud 1963 championship defense in shreds. The offense also was hurting. With Rick Casares and Joe Marconi fading, Ronnie Bull had to carry much of the rushing load along with Jon Arnett, newly acquired from the Los Angeles Rams. Johnny Morris led the league in pass catching with a record ninety-three receptions. But the Bears' magic touch of the previous year clearly had been lost.

"It seems like we have a black cloud over our head," lamented safety Richie Petitbon on the airplane ride home after the Bears had lost to the Washington Redskins, 27-20, enroute to a dismal 5-9 record.

Halas once again started hearing boos. The fans also resumed the vocal harassment of quarterback Bill Wade and demanding Rudy Bukich. Halas acquiesced and began alternating his quarterbacks. This, too, drew criticism, even from other Bear players.

"I think they should decide on one quarterback and stick with him for four or five games," said Morris. Mike Ditka said nice things about both quarterbacks, but made it clear he preferred Bukich.

The quarterback situation, always a Bear worry, was not the only thing on Halas' mind. The 1965 draft loomed hugely important to Papa Bear, who saw the chance to give his faltering football team a twin injection.

The tonics, Halas vowed going into the draft, were to be Gale Sayers, an All-American halfback at Kansas, and Dick Butkus, a Chicago-born linebacker known for his violence while performing for Halas' alma mater, the University of Illinois.

Halas had been sold on Sayers since the Bear mentor saw a "totally unique" move by the dazzling youngster in a Kansas game film. "I knew right then and there we had to get that boy, no matter what the cost," Halas said later.

The Bears used their two first-round picks to select Butkus and Sayers in that order. Then Halas went out to nail down his two potential superstars. He knew they would be expensive, but this was no time to pull a Jack Benny. Or a George Halas.

It took a $150,000, four-year contract plus some cunning cloak-and-dagger maneuvers to protect Sayers from the Kansas City Chiefs of the rival American Football League, who also had drafted the Kansas Comet. But Halas won out, with the help of the onetime Illinois and Baltimore Colt star, Buddy Young.

Young "babysat" Sayers in a New York hotel at the request of the National Football League until Sayers' contract could be worked out. Young delivered his valuable guest at a press conference in Chicago's LaSalle hotel amidst the popping of flash bulbs and the whirring of TV cameras.

"Gentlemen," said Halas with a dramatic flair, "I would like to present the newest member of the Chicago Bears, Mr. Gale Sayers. And I would like to thank Buddy Young. Buddy gave us many headaches in the NFL. It just goes to show that if you live long enough, you get compensated."

"I'm happy to be a Bear," Sayers said with a grin. "I just got back from New York, where Mr. Lamar Hunt [owner of the Chiefs] invited me over to his hotel. When millionaires start opening the door for me, I get suspicious."

Young said he made his first approach to Sayers by telephone after being asked to protect the young draft choice from the evil AFL. "I simply called him up and told him who I was. If he hadn't recognized the name, I'd probably have told him I was Jackie Robinson."

The negotiations with Butkus were nowhere nearly as intriguing, but just as tough. The Illinois linebacker was represented by Arthur Morse, to this date probably the shrewdest and most competent of the player agents. Halas paid another $150,000 for the rights to four years of Butkus' services. Butkus was coveted by the New York Jets, who acquired bidding rights to him from the Denver Broncos.

"The decision was up to Dick," said Morse. "I told him that a lawyer can only go so far, that it was his body and his family."

"I didn't like Denver's approach," said Butkus. "There's more to it than just money and that's all Denver wanted to talk about. I saw a Jets official just once in New York, and that was my last contact with the AFL."

Sayers and Butkus, the two new rookie prizes, were the subject of much speculation and awe as the Bears went through the 1965 exhibition season. Sayers, like every college runner graduating into the pro ranks, was unproven. Could he mesmerize professional defenses as he had those in the Big Eight Conference? Butkus, though tough and belligerent, had been wrongfully tagged by *Sports Illustrated* with a "not-so-smart" rep at Illinois. Would he be bewildered by the intricate defenses of the pros?

Sayers was held largely under wraps until the third preseason game. Then the Bears made an appearance in Bill Wade's home town. Here is the way the *Chicago Tribune* described the event, under a Nashville, Tenn., dateline:

"A new star burst upon the professional scene today when Gale Sayers, 195 pounds of dynamite in a football suit, touched off a 28-14 Chicago Bear explosion at the expense of the Los Angeles Rams.

"Breakaway threat? Kick returner? Passer? The Bears have them all in Sayers, the young gazelle from Kansas. All Sayers did on this day was:

"1. Run a punt back seventy-seven yards for a touchdown.

"2. Return a kickoff ninety-three yards for a touchdown.

"3. Throw a pass twenty-five yards for still another touchdown.

"The scintillating performance by Sayers overshadowed a dramatic debut by Bill Wade, who returned to Vanderbilt University, where he starred fifteen years ago."

It didn't take Butkus, aided by the scholarly Bill George, long to pick up the eccentricities of the Bear defense. As Sayers thrilled the fans during his rookie season with twenty-two dazzling touchdown runs for an NFL record, Butkus was spectacularly restoring the Chicago defense to its oldtime respectability.

Sayers scored four touchdowns in a 45-37 victory over the Minnesota Vikings. "How about that, Gale?" chortled George Connor, the former Bear, waving a television microphone in front of Sayers. "Wasn't that ninety-nine-yard run about your greatest thrill ever?" "No," replied Sayers matter-of-factly. "I've had a lot of them."

After Butkus and the Bear defense had walloped the Detroit Lions, 38-10 in Wrigley Field, Mike Ditka, a towel draped around his midsection, stood holding a football in the center of the dressing room. Calling for quiet, the all-pro tight end said, "Listen, fellows. The defense did a hell of a job today and I wish we had eleven footballs to pass out. The game ball goes to Dick Butkus."

A week later, with Butkus playing a starring role, Halas' team destroyed Green Bay, 31-10. Packer Coach Vince Lombardi muttered admiringly,

"This is a better Bear club than the one that won the championship in 1963. Far better."

And so it went all season. By the end of 1965, Sayers had won rookie-of-the-year honors and achieved all-pro. He scored six touchdowns in a remarkable performance in the slop against the San Francisco 49ers, and would have scored a seventh if Halas hadn't taken him out with the Bears on the 49er 3-yard line late in the game.

"I had a sudden premonition that Gale would get hurt on the next play and I took him out," Halas told announcer Hugh Hill of WLS-TV, Chicago's ABC affiliate. "I've been kicking myself ever since for not letting him score that touchdown. It would have been an NFL record."

Meanwhile, Butkus was being described as one of the greatest, and the meanest, linebackers of all time.

"I'm not so mean," Butkus disclaimed. "I wouldn't ever go out to hurt anybody deliberately. Unless it was, you know, important—like a league game or something."

The older Bears were immediately awed by the 6-foot-3, 245-pound Butkus.

"He never has to open his mouth, except to call defensive signals," declared end Ed O'Bradovich with awe. "You can see the intensity in his eyes. He has complete and total desire. Even if we're down forty points with a minute to go, Dick just has to get in there and hit."

Butkus didn't much mind who, or what, he hit. One time when business manager Rudy Custer scheduled the Bears on an old-fashioned DC-3 for a short hop from Green Bay, Butkus punched out a rear window to get some air.

Due in large part to the contributions of Butkus and Sayers, the Bears reversed their 5-9 record of 1964 and finished 9-5 in 1965. Many others, of course, contributed. Rudy Bukich forced Wade to the sideline and won the NFL passing title, leading the Bears to victory in nine of their last eleven games.

Andy Livingston, who had been drafted the previous year, appeared destined for greatness. Against Green Bay, teaming with Sayers in a tandem which excited the fans, the Phoenix Junior College product ran seven times for seventy yards and caught two passes. But Livingston, who sometimes paused like a startled chicken thief in the middle of a run, was hampered by injuries and never made it big.

One of the largest controversies of Halas' career erupted when he tried to prevent George Allen, the forty-three-year-old architect of the Bears' defense, from jumping to the Los Angeles Rams, owned by Halas' old friend, Dan Reeves. Halas, refusing to promise Allen the eventual head coaching job, took him to court.

Whether Halas succeeded in "upholding the validity of this contract and the integrity of the National Football League," as he sought to do, is a matter of interpretation. Fearing possible antitrust involvement if the case dragged on too long, Halas, hot-dogging like a character in a Perry Mason novel, leaped upon the witness stand, introduced himself to the judge, and dropped the lawsuit.

Turning to Allen, Halas said, "George, a few of those statements you made on the stand I do not like. They weren't true, George. And please don't forget to return your Bear playbook."

The cries for Halas' scalp resumed in 1966 when the Bears slipped to a 5-7-2 mark. Tired of abusing the thirty-six-year-old Wade, the fans turned on Bukich, their hero of the previous year. Now the crowd wanted Larry Rakestraw, a seldom-used four-year "pro" from Georgia. So Halas gave the fans Rakestraw, throwing him in against the San Francisco 49ers. At last report Rakestraw was alive and well and prospering back in Georgia.

"There is no way I could quit on the downbeat," Halas said after the 1966 campaign. "I know the mistakes I made. I think I am the only one who can turn it around. It will involve some changes of personnel."

The changes Halas had in mind were the slicing of malcontents Mike Ditka and Doug Atkins, two of the stars of the 1963 championship team. Halas unloaded Ditka to Philadelphia for quarterback Jack Concannon and sent Atkins and tackle Herman Lee to New Orleans for guard Don Croftcheck.

Concannon—a witty, cocksure Irishman—delighted Chicago sportswriters. He had a strong arm, fair aim, and a fair share of irreverence. He liked to run with the football. Concannon frankly said he expected to take the quarterback job away from Bukich. In later years he exhibited the same confidence in his ability to beat out Virgil Carter and Bobby Douglass.

Concannon vindicated his faith in himself in 1967, throwing for 1,260 yards and six touchdowns. The ground attack, with Brian Piccolo backing up Sayers, improved. The Bears finished 7-6-1, second place in the newly formed Central Division. Halas, though crippled in both hips with arthritis so painful he sometimes grimaced, gave every appearance of intending to stay on as head coach. But on Monday, May 27, 1968, Papa Bear called a press conference.

Sitting behind his desk in the familiar office at 173 West Madison, he announced his retirement from coaching.

"I would like to have been on the field in 1969 rounding out fifty years as a player and coach," Halas said. "But looking at the practical realities, I am stepping aside now because I can no longer keep up with the physical demands of coaching the team on Sunday afternoons."

It was the end of an era. More accurately, the end of a half-century.

Halas, the all-time winningest coach in football history, compiled a record of 320 wins, 147 defeats, and 30 ties during his forty seasons as an active coach.

Chapter 10

DOOLEY, GIBRON, AND DOLDRUMS

George Halas' choice of a successor upon his retirement in the spring of 1968 was as predictable as the sun coming up in the east over the Rensselaer cornfields. Jim Dooley, the thirty-eight-year-old "boy wonder" of the coaching staff, got the call from his boss the day after Halas announced his retirement.

Papa Bear introduced Dooley at a press conference with the following typically succinct Halas charge:

"Good luck, Kid."

Snappily dressed as always and wearing horn-rimmed glasses, Dooley proved as fast on his feet as he had been when he was an end and made the down-and-out pass a "must" in the playbook of every pro team. Asked what he thought the Bears needed to win a championship, Dooley grinned and replied:

"I'd say we need our 1963 defense and our 1965 offense."

Dooley, always a realist, never minced words with either reporters or players, though sometimes it was hard to understand him. His breathless speech patter was difficult to follow. Sportswriters often had to finish sentences for him. But he never complained of being misquoted. There was no doubting his deep knowledge of football's sophisticated mystique. Dooley built up a strong camaraderie with the press.

Unfortunately, Dooley never had a winning season. The best he did was break even in his maiden year. After a 7-7 season in 1968, he finished 1-13 in 1969, the worst record in Bear history. His 1970 and 1971 teams both posted 7-8 marks.

Dooley's tenure as head coach started badly when he lost his top two quarterbacks, Jack Concannon and Rudy Bukich, with injuries. Virgil Carter was activated to back up Larry Rakestraw and soon moved into the starting job. Carter, who had been a fine college passer at Brigham Young, had Bear fans jabbering with excitement when he came off the reserve squad to earn back-to-back victories over Philadelphia, Minnesota, Green Bay, and San Francisco.

Dooley praised Carter ecstatically. "Virgil was fourth-string quarterback," the Bear coach reminded. "That's like being the last guy in the stag line at the senior prom. You never get to dance with the girls. But the kid never lost hope.''

The 27-19 victory over the 49ers was a costly one for the Bears. Fans who were present in Wrigley Field that afternoon will never lose the memory of Sayers being carried off the field with the first of his knees injuries.

It happened when Sayers took a pitchout from Carter and ran to his left on an attempted sweep. Kermit Alexander, the 49ers' right cornerback, hit Sayers with a low-rolling shoulder tackle just as the Kansas Comet had planted his right leg on the turf to make his cut.

''It's gone! It's gone!'' Sayers screamed instantly. His right knee had been bent ninety degrees sideways, tearing all the ligaments. He underwent surgery the same day by Dr. Theordore Fox, the team's orthopedic specialist. He was, of course, through for the season.

Dooley's Bears, miraculously, went into the final game of the season against Green Bay with a chance for the divisional crown. But they lost to the Packers, 28-27, despite Concannon's two touchdown passes to Dick Gordon.

Concannon and Carter were the Bear quarterbacks in 1969, after the retirement of Bukich. Sayers, back from knee surgery, had an amazing year, especially astounding because he was playing on a repaired leg. Lacking his former speed and finesse, Sayers nevertheless gained 1,032 yards to lead the league in rushing despite the fact his longest gain was only twenty-eight yards.

But it was a year of Bear futility. Dooley, watching his team skid to a 1-13 record, had spats with both players and press.

The excitable young Bear coach grabbed sportswriter Ed Stone of *Chicago Today* by the shirt in the Bears' dressing room and chastised him in front of the players for writing: ''Dooley is basically a gentle person. That's not a rap. It's a fact of nature. A man can't be what he isn't. If Dooley suddenly tried to become a stern commander in the Halas-Lombardi mold, the players would laugh at him.''

''I'll show you how gentle I am,'' Dooley bellowed at Stone. ''You're a leech. I don't want you in this locker room any more except on game days.''

Carter paved the way for a hasty exit from the Bears with an indignant dressing room remark to a sportswriter. Virgil had been beaten out by Concannon in a decision Carter claimed was predetermined. After the Bears lost four games, Dooley turned to Bobby Douglass. With a 1-10 record and Bobby performing poorly, Dooley handed Carter the reins against the 49ers without handing him a game plan. The Bears lost, 42-21, but Carter was outstanding. The next week he started against Green Bay, but was lifted at halftime after completing only two of seventeen passes. He didn't appreciate being benched.

"The Bears have screwed me for the last time," he told George Langford of the *Chicago Tribune* afterwards. "That's the last game I'll ever play for the Bears."

When asked whether Halas might not require him to play out his option before he could leave, Carter said: "I hope he wouldn't be chicken bleep enough to do that."

Two days later Carter was suspended and fined $1,000 "because he called me a chicken bleep," said Halas.

When it was pointed out to Halas that Carter actually had suggested the opposite, Papa Bear said, "It's the same thing."

Chicago sportswriters and columnists took Halas severely to task for this treatment of the popular Carter, who was to return to the Bears for a second tour of duty six years later under Abe Gibron.

At the annual Bear alumni party (for former players), Halas had a couple of drinks, then lashed back at the press, declaring he had "deliberately stepped into the Carter affair to take the heat off the coaches."

"What you read last week was bull," he said, "and I'll tell them to stick it up their rear ends. All this fine publicity hasn't spoiled me."

Bear heroes were numerous but victories were few during the last two years of the Dooley administration. Dick Gordon, the discontented wide receiver, led the NFL in pass catching in 1970 with seventy-one receptions for 1,026 yards and thirteen touchdowns. Two other Bear receivers, George Farmer and Jim Seymour, also seemed to have promise.

But something was lacking. And in the opinion of most Chicago fans, the missing commodity, as always, was a top-notch quarterback. The Bears had a chance to land one at the Super Bowl in January, 1970. A coin flip was to determine whether the Bears or the Pittsburgh Steelers, the two worst teams in pro football, would draft first. The prize was Louisiana Tech quarterback Terry Bradshaw.

Bears vice president Ed McCaskey, George Halas' son-in-law, called "heads" as the coin went into the air. The coin came up tails.

"McCaskey," hollered Jack Griffin of the *Chicago Sun-Times* from the back of the room, "you can't even win a coin flip!"

The Bears said good-bye to Wrigley Field in December of 1970 with a 35-17 victory over Green Bay. The following year, after failing in a bid to set up shop in Northwestern's Dyche Stadium, they took up reluctant residence in Soldier Field, redecorated but still musty and rusty.

Dooley's Bears played some impressive games in 1971. Unfortunately, they did not play enough of them. Among their victims were the Pittsburgh Steelers, Minnesota Vikings, Dallas Cowboys, and Washington Redskins. Dick Butkus won the Redskin game, 16-15, by running into the end zone and catching Bobby Douglass' scrambling pass for the winning point after touchdown. Butkus, who had been a member of the blocking wedge for the attempted extra point kick when the holder lost the snap from center, expressed astonishment that anybody considered his feat interesting.

"When I saw Bobby scrambling around," Butkus said, "I knew there was no way I could get back there and help him. So I ran into the end zone and waved for the football. He hit me perfectly."

After the Bears' dreadful performance in a 6-3 loss at Denver, the writing was on the wall. The Bears had finished 6-8 for the second year in a row. Dooley and his staff were fired during the last week in January, 1972.

And finally, after seven years of waiting in the wings, a portly gentleman stepped in front of the TV cameras at the Bears' office and the Abe Gibron show was on the way. As widely predicted, the forty-six-year-old jowled jester of Dooley's staff was named by Halas as Dooley's successor.

Gibron likes to eat. And he likes to talk. He did a lot of talking on the day of his inauguration.

"I'm a Halas man," he told reporters. "And a Bear man, but not a yes man. I am the boss. This is going to be the Abe Gibron show."

After Gibron's remark, Halas made it clear that Gibron's status with the organization would be no different from that of Dooley's except that "Abe may be more forceful than Jim was."

Halas used the occasion to deny that he had interfered with Dooley's coaching.

"Never did I interfere with Jim Dooley's coaching," Papa Bear declared. "Not until the fourth year of his career—this past season. He had such a deplorable game plan for the Denver game that I came into the office the next day and told him, 'I now want to be put on record as interfering with the offense.' And I made some changes for the next game."

Halas was asked if he had ever issued Dooley instructions as to the use of quarterback Bobby Douglass. "That's the only thing I ever told Dooley as far as players are concerned," said Halas. "I told him that Bobby Douglass is not going to be converted into a running back under any circumstances."

Gibron was tremendously excited with his appointment as head coach. "I've really been sweating this out," he said. "It's the first time in a long time I've weighed under 300 pounds."

Even though Gibron, like Dooley, never produced a winner, the Gibron years went by pleasantly. The big fellow was tremendously popular in Chicago. He had a host of friends, most of whom were his guests at one time or another at the dinner table.

If anything, Abe may have been too close to his players. Like Dooley, he was an excellent assistant coach. But he may have been miscast for the head job. He tended to lose control of both the game and his emotions on the sidelines. It was perhaps this factor more than Gibron's record which prompted Jim Finks to replace Gibron in 1975 with Jack Pardee, who practically never lost control.

Gibron received bad news at his first training camp as head coach. Gale Sayers, the Kansas Comet, was through. The news was hardly a surprise. Sayers, recovered though slowed after the operation on his right knee, had been struck down again in the summer of 1970 in a game against the St. Louis Cardinals. He suffered ligament damage, this time in his left knee.

Sayers delayed an operation and attempted to play, but could manage only fifty-two yards on twenty-three carries in two games that year. In mid-October and again in February, he underwent corrective surgery. Still determined, he tried once again in the fall of 1971, but lasted only two games. Finally, after giving it one more try at Gibron's training camp, Sayers told his old mentor and friend, George Halas, that he was through.

Linebacker Dick Butkus, also afflicted with impossible knee problems after multiple surgery, made it through the 1973 season before he, too, was forced to retire. Butkus later sued the Bears for permitting his injury to be aggravated and shortening his career.

Gibron's Bears flubbed their league debut in 1972, losing, 37-21, to the Atlanta Falcons. The only bright spot was the play of Jim Harrison, a 235-pound sophomore fullback from Missouri who had been one of the flops of the 1971 season. Harrison, enjoying his finest afternoon, battered the Falcon defense twenty times for 113 yards.

The Bears finished 4-9-1 in Gibron's maiden campaign, and it was a long, agonizing season with only occasional binges of exhilaration for Big Abe. Sample postgame Gibron quotes:

After a 20-17 loss in Green Bay: "Sure, we played a nice game. Nice games are for losers. But don't write off this football team. We're still going to show some people."

After a 13-10 victory over Minnesota in the Howard Cosell Monday night game at Soldier Field: "We just played football."

After a 14-0 defeat in Detroit: "Blame it on me. We just weren't sharp and that's the coach's fault. My game plan was the same as the Lions' except mine didn't work."

After a 23-17 loss to the Packers in Soldier Field: "Let me tell you about this [Bear] team. They're growing up. I'm proud to walk into the dressing room with them. The Packers went off the field like flies."

One of the men who helped keep Gibron proud of his failing Bears in 1972 and the two years to come was linebacker Doug Buffone, the pride of Louisville. Buffone launched his Bear career in 1966 when George Halas was still coach. Throughout his sparkling career he was a super pro and a sportswriter's delight.

After the Bears had busted the Broncos, 33-14, in Denver for their first victory of 1973, Buffone came up with one of his typical quips. "I thought maybe I was going to faint from the altitude," he said, "and then I realized I was just getting bored."

The 1973 Bears were bad enough (3-11) so that Buffone's candid observations often were essential comic relief. Only a few times during the season did Gibron's men play well enough to merit sensible conversation in the postgame locker room. One of those times was in Green Bay on November 4, when Bobby Douglass led a 31-17 victory over the Packers.

Gibron called it "Bobby's greatest game as a Bear." Even the often surly Carl Garrett was lavish with praise after the rawboned quarterback from Kansas had run for 100 yards, scored four touchdowns, and completed ten of fifteen passes to five different receivers for 118 yards.

That's some production for a man whose credentials as a quarterback had been challenged ever since he came out of college in 1969.

Douglass, who once threw an eighty-yard touchdown pass to Jim Seymour with a broken wrist, may be the most popular failure in the history of Chicago sports. When he walks into a room, he still has instant recognition. It says a lot for Bobby that three top football men like George Halas, Abe Gibron, and even Jim Finks thought he could play quarterback despite frequent evidence to the contrary. It tooks Finks so long to make up his mind about Douglass that the Bears got nothing in return when the Kansas product was released at the beginning of the 1975 season. He signed with San Diego, then the following year with New Orleans, and finished his career as a short-lived Green Bay Packer.

But if Douglass enjoyed popular acclaim during his six-year stint in Chicago, he also received abuse. In the second quarter of a 1973 game in which the Bears were scrambled by the Detroit Lions, 30-7, a few of the freaks among the Soldier Field crowd cheered as the blond quarterback lay prostrate on the field.

The incapacitation of Douglass signalled the entrance of Gary Huff, a rookie from Florida State. Huff, true to Gibron's predictions, tossed up four interceptions. "It was a tough day for Gary," Abe said afterwards. "It was a damned shame we had to put him into a situation like that."

The following Sunday in Bloomington, Minn., the cops were hustling a drunk out of Metropolitan Stadium, one policeman on each arm.

"I've got to tell you fellows—you're overdoing this thing," bubbled the happy fan.

The Bears must have felt exactly the same way about the Vikings after absorbing a 31-13 pounding from Coach Bud Grant's playoff-bound club. The defeat assured the Bears of a sixth consecutive losing season going back through Jim Dooley's four-year tenure. Abe Gibron might have been playing a tape recording when he said, "a lot of guys on our team gave a great effort."

The 1974 season, Gibron's last, mercifully need not be detailed. There is no point, even though Jim Finks says he watched Gibron's erratic Bears that year with an open mind.

"I honestly didn't know when I came in whether 1974 would be Abe's last year or not," Finks declares. "As the season progressed, it became obvious a change was in order."

The 4-10 finish brought Gibron's three-year record at the Bear helm to 11-30-1. Abe made no excuses when he was fired. Predictably, he said, "We gave it a hell·of a shot. Let's go get a steak."

Chapter 11
THE JIM FINKS HOUSECLEANING

When Jim Finks was summoned by George Halas in 1974 to resurrect the stumbling, fumbling Bears, the one-time Minnesota Miracle Man moved dramatically. He fired just about everybody in sight, including gargantuan, lovable coach Abe Gibron, replacing the great gourmet with a sleek new mentor out of the modern mold—tough, taciturn Jack Pardee.

Only five members of the old-line Bears organization escaped the Finks housecleaning.

Everybody either quit or was fired. Through it all, Finks kept a ready smile on his face as he handed out pink slips along with handshakes to old-timers Halas had tolerated for years. Many were quietly kept on the payroll.

"I didn't feel bad about it at all when I was letting people go," Finks says candidly. "It didn't take any genius to figure out what had to be done here. If you're honest and aboveboard, I don't think you have to apologize to anybody. Let me tell you this: By replacing Abe Gibron, it doesn't mean he was a failure. Or getting rid of a lot of players who were here didn't mean they were bad players or bad people. It merely meant an attitude had developed whereby some very capable people had to be replaced."

"To create new attitudes," Finks continues, "we had to replace people with fresh, bright people. We had to change facilities when possible. We wanted a whole new look, one that creates a positive, upbeat atmosphere rather than one of negativism and defeat. You know what happens in sports, in all kinds of business. Things go in cycles. Once you get down, it's hard to get back up."

Finks' official Bears title was executive vice president and general manager. But he did almost everything. His scope of responsibilities exceeded that of most other general managers, reflecting a shockingly abrupt change of posture by an organization which has been family oriented through its 65-year history.

Veteran Bear followers and intimates of the Halas family could scarcely believe it on that September day in 1974 when the seventy-nine-year-old Halas dramatically turned over the reins to Finks, a rawboned Southern Illinoisan who once quarterbacked the Pittsburgh Steelers.

Was the move for real? Or would Finks, who had fought the Players Association tooth-and-nail during a three-month period as a consultant to the NFL Management Council during the 1974 summer of discontent, become simply another Halas "yes man"?

Finks let the world wait and wonder. For three months after accepting Halas' summons, Finks simply sat back and observed, carefully making notes and accumulating a vast file on Bear malfeasances, miscreants, and misfortunes as Abe Gibron's men shuddered to a 4-10 record.

When the 1974 season ended with a 42-0 loss to the Washington Redskins, Finks' ax swung. On December 27, two days after the Redskin debacle, Gibron announced his "resignation." Along with Abe went his six-man coaching staff. And out went Bobby Walston, the one-time Philadelphia Eagles place kicker who had been vice president and director of player personnel. Walston was regarded by sportswriters close to the club as the source of many of the Bears' problems in recent years.

The Jim Finks housecleaning had begun.

On December 31, while most of the nation was getting warmed up for New Year's Eve festivities, Finks called a press conference. He had hired a head coach. Jack Pardee, a quiet, affable gentleman who had played linebacker for thirteen seasons at Los Angeles and two at Washington and had conquered cancer in 1964, was the man designated to lead the Bears back to respectability.

"I didn't know Jack too well—not nearly as well as I knew Neill Armstrong when I hired him three years later," Finks now admits. "But I had learned enough about Jack so I felt, 'this is my kind of guy. A guy who can do the job that has to be done. Confident, solid, tough, and mature. He has no hangups.' "

Pardee had retired as a player following the 1972 season and remained with the Redskins as an assistant to Coach George Allen. Pardee's leadership qualities received national focus when he accepted his first coaching assignment in the financially troubled World Football League. His Florida (Orlando) Blazers, playing without pay because of loyalty to their coach, posted a 14-6 record in 1974 to wind up in the championship game.

Now Pardee, at age thirty-nine, was to become the first non-Bear apprentice to coach Halas' team in more than forty years and only the ninth head coach in the Bears' fifty-five-year history. Pardee's predecessors were Halas, Dutch Sternaman, Ralph Jones (the only non-Bear), Hunk Anderson, Luke Johnsos, Paddy Driscoll, Jim Dooley, and Abe Gibron.

Pardee's freshman Bear year was not stunning. He finished 4-10 in 1975, no better and no worse than had the maligned Gibron Bears of the previous year. But even in defeat there was something special about Pardee's Bears.

On a late October Sunday in 1975, veteran *New York Times* football observer William N. Wallace squinted at the Soldier Field gridiron from the press box. The Bears were playing the Minnesota Vikings and playing them very well indeed, en route to a heartbreaking 13-9 defeat.

"By jove, there's something different going on here, something I haven't seen for years in Chicago," lectured the scholarly Wallace. "The Bears are playing like—I don't know how else to put it—they're playing like they know what they're doing!"

Pardee's Bears continued to play as if they knew what they were doing in 1976. The team was still far short of championship quality. But the potential was there. And the direction and rhythm and the feeling. A feeling which had not been present during the dreary years of confusion when first Jim Dooley, then Abe Gibron succeeded only in making chaos out of confusion.

Under Pardee there suddenly was cohesion on the sidelines. Suddenly, the players began listening while the coaches were talking. And the coaches listened to each other!

"I will never fault the way Jack ran the team," Finks has said since Pardee's departure. "He was in control."

Pardee began the 1976 season by outwitting his old coach, George Allen, in the season opener. The Bears, accurately diagnosing the Washington Redskins' defensive coverage, changed some formations and came out passing to receiver Brian Baschnagel. When quarterback Bob Avellini, famous for his cast iron posterior, actually RAN for a touchdown, the writing was on the wall.

The Bears beat the Redskins, 33-7, drew a standing ovation from the Soldier Field crowd, and were so dominant they were miffed at losing a shutout on the last play of the contest.

"I have to give the Bears credit," Allen said afterwards, gritting his teeth before heading for the ice cream parlor. "They were a superbly coached team."

The Bears were superbly coached all season as they suffered through a schedule heavily weighted with five playoff qualifiers. When it was all over, Pardee was named coach-of-the-year in the National Football Conference even though the Bears finished with a modest 7-7 record.

The game everybody will remember in that 1976 season was played on November 7, 1976, a chilly, windy day on Chicago's lakefront. That was the day when Johnny Madden guffawed. The portly coach of the Oakland Raiders was moved to hysteria because he had just seen a touchdown taken away from the Bears as the Raiders made a pit stop en route to their very first Super Bowl championship.

The Raiders shouldn't have won the game at all; that's why Bear fans will always remember it. Improving week after week despite an impossibly tough schedule, the Bears had the Raiders on the ropes. But the referee blew a call. It was one of the most incredible blunders in the history of officiating, and the word "inadvertent" became an instant addition to the lexicon of sports.

Referee Chuck Heberling, a National Football League official for twelve years, admitted he blew the whistle "inadvertently" and nullified a fourth quarter Bears touchdown. The spectacular snafu cost the Bears a 28-27 defeat, their fifth loss in nine brutal games, and all but extinguished the playoff hopes of Pardee's scrappy young ball club.

The "inadvertent whistle" occurred with the Bears leading, 27-21, early in the final period. Chicago's Wally Chambers dumped Oakland quarterback Ken Stabler for an eleven-yard loss at the Raider 39-yard line. Stabler lost the ball as he was falling and Bears defensive end Roger Stillwell fielded it on the run and headed for the end zone.

When Stillwell crossed the goal line, he heard no cheers, only a referee's whistle. But he spiked the ball anyway.

"I couldn't figure it out," Stillwell said. "I thought I was the hero. I thought I had won the game. But when the fans didn't yell, I knew something was wrong."

Heberling, interviewed by Don Pierson of the *Chicago Tribune* after the game, gulped and admitted, "It was an inadvertent whistle. I blew it when I shouldn't have. So the only thing I could do was give Chicago the ball."

The Bears had a chance to pull the game out with twenty seconds left when Bob Thomas missed a thirty-one-yard field goal. The kick hit the right upright and bounced back, as if to symbolize the almost-there-but-not-quite Jack Pardee Bears.

The 1976 Bears, reflecting Pardee's conservatism and underscoring the lack of talent at skilled positions, had few surprises. As offensive tackle Jeff Sevy said, "We're so basic. Run on first down, run on second down, pass on third down. Our whole theory is to blow people off the line."

But the new Pardee Bears had hustle. They had a sense of direction and planning lacking since their last championship season of 1963. And they had Walter Payton.

Walter Payton puts on one of his patented stutter-steps against Denver Broncos in Soldier Field. Bears walloped Denver for second year in a row, 27-0, prompting Bronco coach Dan Reeves to moan, "I don't know what always happens to us here."

Ah, yes, Walter Payton. Having Payton on your team means never having to say you're sorry. Payton, the 5-foot-11, 205-pounder from Jackson (Miss.) State, began the 1976 season as a marked man after a torrid freshman year. He finished it on his knees, knocked out physically and emotionally.

Lithe, wily Walter was dueling O. J. Simpson of the Buffalo Bills for the NFL rushing championship when the Bears met the Denver Broncos in Soldier Field in the last game of the year.

As Payton toiled in Chicago, The Juice was waging his end of the battle against the Colts in Baltimore, perhaps dreaming of the day in 1978 when he would return to his San Francisco birthplace to finish out his pro football career.

Walter's mother, Eileen Payton, had come to Chicago from her home in Columbia, Miss., for the Bears' finale. She was ready for a celebration. She sat nervously in the stands with David Condon, sports columnist for the *Chicago Tribune*. She had brought along a cake baked the previous day.

Mrs. Payton's cake didn't fall, but her son did. Walter was sent to his knees with a slashing tackle by Bronco linebacker Tom Jackson. Payton's ankle was badly twisted. He wept as he went to the sidelines. He finished the day with forty-nine yards in fourteen carries and wound up the season with 1,390 yards, tops in the National Football Conference. Buffalo's Simpson won the NFL rushing derby with 1,503 yards.

It was several months later, at a banquet in Kansas City, before Payton could bring himself to talk about the way he felt during that time of supreme agony when he felt he had let both the Bears and himself down.

"It was, I guess, the low point of my life," Walter told me before being honored at the banquet. "So much had been made of the fact that I had a chance to beat O.J. out of the rushing title. When I found myself lying there on the field and knew I had failed, it was like I didn't want to get back up.

"My teammates wanted it so much; they were willing to do anything to get it for me. As a result, I became overly aggressive. And that can be just as bad as not putting out enough. What it is, I'm a competitor. Being injured, not finishing the game, was eating inside of me.

"I didn't know how to cope. I talked to people about how I felt. To my wife, Connie, and to (fullback) Roland Harper. To reporters. They were doing most of the talking, putting words in my mouth. I was just going along with it. But deep down inside of me, I never did really express my inner feelings.

"Finally I went home to see my mother. I explained to her how I felt. She told me, 'Don't worry about it, Son. It was God's will. It was probably best for you that it worked out as it did. This may be a disappointment right now. But it may help your career in the long run because you have a target to shoot at.' "

Mrs. Payton turned out ot be a prophet many times over, especially in 1984 when Walter eclipsed the NFL rushing record of the great Jim Brown.

Chapter 12

1977: A MIRACLE—ALMOST

It was a miracle, for sure, that the Bears were there at all.

But there they were in East Rutherford, N.J. The date was December 18, 1977, and Giants Stadium was as cold as a player agent's heart. As icy as a Siberian martini. As eerie as a close encounter of the first and most frantic kind.

The plot was worthy of Cecil B. DeMille. Or of Pete Rozelle. There were the Bears, counted out at midseason after a 47-0 humiliation by the Houston Oilers had dropped their record to 3 and 5, playing the New York Giants in the regular season finale.

The stakes couldn't have been bigger, the pressure greater, the fan interest more intense. A wild card berth in the postseason playoffs was at stake for the unbelievable Bears, who had put together five straight victories since the Houston debacle.

Time after time during the five-game streak, the Bears had been counted out. But they kept heeding the old cliché and played them one game at a time. And now the whole zany season boiled down to one game with the Giants.

Win it and the Bears were in the playoffs as the wild card team in the National Football Conference. Lose it and the wild card berth would go to George Allen and the Washington Redskins.

A victory would bring the Bear record to 9-5 and eliminate Washington, also 9-5. Under the league's complex system for breaking ties, the Bears would get the nod for the Super Bowl tournament because of a better point differential in conference games than the Redskins.

Not a creature was stirring far from the television set in Chicagoland on this Sunday a week before Christmas when the Bears and Giants teed it up on the ice in East Rutherford.

What followed during the next three frigid hours was one of the most incredible and suspenseful football games ever played, a melodrama which would have been rejected by Hollywood as too implausible.

Coach Jack Pardee's men did almost everything they could to lose the game. Everything except forget to hustle. They forgot to bring the right shoes. They fumbled eight times, recovering seven of them. They let the

Giants' receivers get loose for two touchdown passes—and drop both of them.

Not to mention four failures by placekicker Bob Thomas, only one of which was his fault. He hit the left upright from 23 yards in the first quarter, but New York kicker Joe Danelo matched that malfeasance with a miss from 29.

"People just took turns screwing up for Bob," said quarterback Bob Avellini. "One time I set the ball up wrong, another time there was too much penetration, another time I set up too far back."

With the help of *Chicago Tribune* columnist Bob Markus, who ferreted out a sporting goods store that was open Sundays, the Bears frantically purchased 34 new pairs of shoes by halftime (tied 3-3) and found the traction better.

"If we hadn't changed shoes, we wouldn't have had a chance," said wide receiver Bo Rather.

Chicago hopes soared when the Bears took a 9-6 lead with 6:02 left in regulation time on Robin Earl's 4-yard run. But Thomas' extra point kick was blocked.

Later, Thomas missed a field goal try early in overtime and couldn't kick another when the snap from center went astray.

With the clock running out in overtime the Bears had one last chance to move the ball over the slippery terrain and set up what had to be their last field goal opportunity.

Forty-two seconds remained with Avellini tossed the ball to Walter Payton.

"I was thinking of throwing a turn-in," Avellini said, "but I realized the Giants hadn't taken away the outside. I threw to Walter hoping he'd get out of bounds. Why he cut back, I have no idea."

But Payton did cut back, scampering 14 yards to the 11. "I figured there was plenty of time to kick a field goal even with no timeouts left," Walter explained.

Avellini tried to set up for a "quick out" to stop the clock. But, to his consternation, he saw the field-goal team running onto the field.

"You can't send them back," he said.

The clock was ticking off the final half-minute when Avellini, the holder, had to guess at where to set up for the field goal since all identifying markers had been obliterated. Thomas hadn't the faintest idea how far he had to kick.

"I saw an exit sign to the left," Thomas later recalled. "If I had missed, I would have had them forward my mail to Asia."

The official timer said nine seconds were left when Thomas' kick split the uprights from 28 yards out.

"Bears Win 12-9 In Sudden Death," screamed sports bulletins around the country.

"Bears Reach Playoffs—Miraculously," headlined the *Chicago Tribune*.

Bedlam reigned in East Rutherford and in homes and watering spas throughout Bear country.

"Nobody can say we backed into this," cracked linebacker Doug Buffone. "Maybe we slipped in sidewise a little."

In the dressing room, Thomas' eyes filled with tears as he revealed he was wearing Brian Baschnagel's shoe on his left foot. "It was the only one that would grip the ice."

"This is the reason I chose this profession," coach Jack Pardee shouted to reporters. "It's the most exciting thing in the world to be in a game like this in December, knowing you have to win. I just thank the Lord he gave me the guys he gave me."

For much of the 1977 season, there was good reason to believe neither the Lord nor general manager Jim Finks had given Pardee enough front-line players to reach the Bears' avowed goal of qualifying for postseason play for the first time since their NFL championship of 1963.

As the Bears faltered through the first half of the season, much of the attention of their fandom was riveted upon Walter Payton's pursuit of the league's single season rushing mark of 2,003 yards set by Buffalo's O.J. Simpson in 1973.

And upon all-pro defensive tackle Wally Chambers' verbal spats with Finks while trying futilely to get his ailing knee into shape.

A comment by Pardee after the Bears had opened the season with a 30-20 victory over Detroit underlined the Bears' problems with injuries and lack of depth in key spots. It was an observation destined to be made time and again by Pardee in one form or another as the fall campaign progressed.

"Anytime a team gains 360 yards on you like the Lions did on us," the Bear coach pointed out, "there is room for improvement. With Doug Plank out, and Wally Chambers hurting, and Waymond Bryant having a sore shoulder, and Doug Buffone's foot getting better, we're scrambling around."

Et cetera, et cetera, et cetera, as Yul Brynner might have said.

The Bears' lack of individual skills, particularly on defense, was accented the second week of the season when quarterback Jim Hart set a Cardinal record with 12 straight pass completions in leading St. Louis to a 16-13 victory in Busch Stadium.

"Maybe we should have set up a machine gun arsenal back there," Doug Buffone quipped.

Bob Avellini passed for 238 yards, Walter Payton ran for 140 and scored three touchdowns, and Bo Rather snared a half dozen passes for 113 yards the following Sunday against the supposedly inept New Orleans Saints. But Coach Hank Stram, who was to be fired after the season, had a rare Sabbath of enjoyment as Archie Manning led the Saints to a 42-24 triumph.

The New Orleans QB scampered for three touchdowns and passed for another as the Bears defense collapsed. Manning ran up the middle practically at will, obviously taking note of the absence of the injured Chambers.

"I got no legs," moaned middle linebacker Don Rives, who was hampered by a strained knee ligament. "But I had to play because Tom Hicks has a bad shoulder."

Roger Stillwell, who alternated with Jim Osborne and Ron Rydalch at the two defensive tackle spots, declared flatly, "We miss Wally Chambers He's an intimidating factor, kind of a coach on the field."

The Soldier Field fans got on Pardee after the Bear defeat became inevitable in the second half.

"It's sad, hearing the fans yell at Jack," said Buffone. "It's not his fault, it's our fault. That really gripes me. We had a good game plan. Fans say it's Pardee. It's the ball players. Maybe when we start deciding that, we'll get better. The coach can't block and tackle."

The day after the Saints game, Chambers made a scheduled luncheon appearance at the Playboy Club accompanied by his manager, Jack Childers. Standing at the podium while the bunnies flitted around with food and drink for patrons, Chambers ripped the Chicago press for "negative talk" about his knee injury and said he hoped to return to the lineup the following Monday night against the Los Angeles Rams.

"I'd like to go 100 percent," the Bear tackle said. "It's a showcase game. National TV and all. I want to prove once and for all to fans across the country that I can play and stop all this negative talk by the press. I get tired of reading about my injury all the time."

The Bears' 24-23 victory over the Rams before Frank Gifford, Howard Cosell and Company was noteworthy in several ways.

It marked the last appearance of Ram quarterback Joe Namath, the fabled Broadway Joe who once had predicted a Super Bowl victory for the New York Jets and made good on his promise. Namath, groggy and aching, was replaced by Pat Haden in the fourth quarter against the Bears after an ineffectual performance and never played again. He retired at the end of the season and now resides in the Pro Football Hall of Fame.

The Ram game also marked the first time Bob Avellini called his own plays. The cocky Bear QB hit James Scott with scoring passes of 70 and 72 yards and teamed with tight end Greg Latta for a 20-yard touchdown.

But the Bear-Ram encounter will be most remembered for the hysterical, abrasive postgame tirade by L.A. linebacker Isiah Robertson, who told this reporter (and later denied it):

"Wally Chambers is the poorest excuse for an all-pro I ever saw. He took a cheap shot at Namath that ought to get him kicked out of football. If we ever meet again, I intend to see that he gets his.

"The same thing goes for Walter Payton. He clipped Bill Simpson on one play. There was no excuse for it. If I ever get a chance I'm gonna end his career."

Other Rams joined Robertson in the verbal histrionics. Guard Dennis Harrah, who was ejected by officials after he took out after Waymond Bryant when the Bear linebacker decked Namath, told reporters:

"All I saw was Joe laying there. I just sort of lost my head. It was very stupid to get kicked out of the game. But all the Bears wanted to take cheap shots at Joe. I resented that."

Namath came out of the training room chewing tobacco and trying to look cool. First he minimized the blow to the Adam's apple from Bryant which followed a couple of hard shots to the head by Chambers.

Then Namath blurted: "The Bears were trying to start a war out there.

"What happened to me doesn't make much difference," Joe Willie said. "The Bears won the game; that's all that matters. I played poorly. We lost.

"The thing is, you don't like to let people get away with cheap shots. Chambers hit me in the mouth. Then he hit me in the eye. But I don't think they were late hits. Bryant definitely gave me a late hit. A late hit is a cheap shot."

Robertson was screaming at Payton from the sidelines during the game and Payton was so shaken by the verbal barrage he was near tears in the locker room.

Pardee, himself a former Ram, was incensed by Robertson's mouthings. The Bear coach backed Payton totally.

"No one should make statements like that," Pardee said at the weekly press luncheon. "Robertson was probably frustrated. Walter blocked him hard a few times and it was probably embarrassing to him. The Rams are a veteran team that tries to intimidate through talk."

"What does Pardee know about playing linebacker?" Robertson snorted over the telephone later that day, apparently unaware that the Bear coach played linebacker for 15 years as a Ram and Washington Redskin.

The Monday night victory over Los Angeles left Pardee's Bears with a 2-2 record, with their annual trip to Vikingland coming up. The Bears needn't have gotten on the plane. They could simply have played an old record.

"Same song, second verse," moaned linebacker Don Rives after the Vikings capitalized on Bear goofs to take an early lead, then held off a predictable Chicago rally to win 22-16 in overtime.

"Every year it's the same," safety Doug Plank stewed as he pulled off his shoulder pads. "The Vikings win the first half and we win the second."

Coach Bud Grant's Vikings, who are famous for blocking kicks, did it twice to the Bears, and the results were catastrophic. Linebacker Matt Blair blocked an extra point attempt by Bob Thomas and, with 1:55 left in regulation play, Alan Page blocked Thomas' 41-yard field goal try.

Meanwhile, the Vikings' ancient Fred Cox, who had messed up a 36-yarder on Minnesota's first possession of the game, clicked from 30, 38 and 21 yards. The last of the three field goals knotted the count at 16-16 with 12:24 left in regulation time.

But it was the one Cox didn't even try to kick which finally did in the Bears in overtime. Exactly 6 minutes and 45 seconds into the extra sudden death period, Viking holder Paul Krause set up for Cox on the Bear 11-yard line on first down as Fran Tarkenton glared at Coach Bud Grant for sending in the field goal unit.

Cox never approached the ball. Instead, Krause took the snap, quickly rolled out, and hit tight end Stu Voigt in the end zone. Voigt was all by himself, and the slickly executed touchdown gave the Vikes a 22-16 victory. Tarkenton was as surprised as anybody else.

The Bears dipped down into their mess kit of malfeasances to reach another seasonal low the following Sunday when a combination of holding penalties, dropped passes, messed-up assignments, and fumbles resulted in a 16-10 loss to the Atlanta Falcons.

With the Chicago record 2 and 4, sportswriter Don Pierson all but wrote off the Bears in the *Chicago Tribune*. "Unless the NFL has reached the level of mediocrity some accuse it of desiring," Pierson penned, "the Bears have little chance of reaching the playoffs this time around."

The following day at lunch, middle linebacker Don Rives again made the Bears' weekly press conference a memorable one. Too bad the Soldier Field boo-birds weren't there to hear Rives heatedly label them "the fair-weatherest fans I've ever seen." But the press made certain they got the message.

"Atlanta shouldn't have been on the same field with us, offensively or defensively," Rives fumed. "So why are we 2-4 instead of 6-0? If I knew, I'd be a general manager somewhere.

"We've got to get everybody behind us. Our fans . . . sometimes they make me so sick. When we come on the field for the pregame, you ever hear those silly fans cheer? It's like a morgue out there.

"The only time I've heard them cheer is when we're ahead. When we're down, all we ever get is a bunch of crap . . . When I was walking off the field Sunday, somebody tells me I ought to start looking at films of Butkus, silly things like that. And those people behind the bench, all they tell us is to sit down.

"I just wish one time some of those crackpots would try to come down and play."

Pardee pointed out that "it's a difficult situation to accommodate the fans because of the way Soldier Field is built. A lot of the people who give the players the most abuse are six feet away from us and can't see the field. They question our heritage. Not only us but the Honey Bears, too."

But all was not bitterness in Bearland on that late October Monday. Wally Chambers, the big defensive tackle, had played his first complete game of the season against the Falcons. Chambers was in a good mood as he made another appearance at the Playboy Club. Wally didn't know it, but he had reinjured the surface under his kneecap in the Atlanta game.

Ignoring the pulchritude surrounding him, Chambers said he felt he is "getting in shape, but I'm still not 100 percent." Chambers revealed he had been invited by Muhammad Ali to box one round for a Chicago charity in December and that he planned to accept.

"Ali won't get past the first round," Chambers guffawed. "I got a mean head slap."

Meanwhile, up in Packerland, coach Bart Starr was getting his team ready for an invasion by the Bears. Starr, the wily, former all-pro quarterback, was using one of the oldest propaganda devices known to coaching—the team's bulletin board. Thumb-tacked prominently at the top was an item quoting Don Rives as "guaranteeing" victory over the Packers.

The Bear linebacker had concluded his stirring oratory at the press luncheon by stating, "I guarantee you we'll beat Green Bay. We don't even have to play that good a game because we're so much better than Green Bay."

The *Green Bay Press-Gazette* dutifully and gleefully picked up Rives' quote.

"We've got it plastered all over our locker room," said defensive tackle Dave Roller. "It's an absurd statement. Who is Don Rives?"

The question became academic when Rives and the remainder of the Bears were thrust into the background the following Sunday in Green Bay's Lambeau Field by Walter Payton. Wonderful Walter came dancing out of the tunnel and never stopped until he had waltzed through Packer defenses for 205 yards to tie Gale Sayers' single-game Chicago rushing record.

"It was an easy game to call," grinned quarterback Bob Avellini after Payton, off to his greatest year, had run 23 times and scored two touchdowns in leading a 26-0 Bear rout. It was, remarkably, the first shutout for the Bears since 1972, when they whitewashed Cleveland 17-0 as Abe Gibron rang up his first NFL coaching win.

Symbolically, it was on this same field that Sayers entered the Bears' record book. The Kansas Comet gained 205 yards at Green Bay on Nov. 3, 1968. Payton didn't get a chance to break the record, only to tie it. He carried for eight yards on his final rush, then trotted to the sideline with a share of the record. He missed the last 10:36.

"We weren't going to send him in on that final series," Pardee said, "but he wanted a personal goal of 200."

Payton's personal goal turned out to be modest. He was to far eclipse this performance at a later date during the season.

The Wally Chambers saga reached a pivotal point the week after the Packer game when the big fellow finally decided to go under the knife and have his injured knee repaired. Wally would never put on another Bear jersey. A soothsayer might have told him that he was destined to be traded to the Tampa Bay Buccaneers the following April.

Following his knee surgery, Chambers joined offensive tackle Lionel Antoine in a rehabilitation program. Antoine underwent knee surgery of a different type earlier in the season.

"I hope and pray it's not too late for either one of them," general manager Jim Finks said, not meaning to sound ominous.

And then followed what has come to be known as the Houston debacle. Few times since the Alamo has the state of Texas been witness to a rout of the magnitude of the Oilers' 47-0 slaughter of the Bears.

General Custer never had it so good.

Coach Jack Pardee called the loss "the worst thing I've ever been associated with in any form."

It was the Bears' most devastating defeat since they were handed their jockstraps by the Baltimore Colts 52-0 in 1964, back when George Halas was coach.

Papa Bear was grim-faced as he watched the horrible proceedings in the Astrodome. The Bears made every possible mistake. Things got so bad that Pardee finally yanked Bob Avellini, giving Mike Phipps a rare chance to play quarterback.

Phipps was sacked for a safety to build the Oilers' gusher to 40-0. Billy "White Shoes" Johnson returned the ensuing free kick 75 yards for a touchdown, and the Bears limped home 3-5, downtrodden, disgusted, and hopelessly out of the playoff picture.

Hopelessly?

Well, weren't the Bears one of the worst teams in pro football? Certainly, at this point of the 1977 campaign, they were. Seventeen of the 28 teams in the NFL had better records.

Something happened to turn the Bears around. Something happened to stem the tide of disaster. The Bears were on the gangplank, ready to take the final, watery plunge to oblivion. In the crazy game of NFL Russian roulette, they had the gun pointed to their helmets, and the bullet was in the chamber.

But something happened.

It almost didn't happen soon enough. Before the miracle transpired, the Bears had fallen behind the Kansas City Chiefs 17-0 in game No. 9. The crowd of 49,543 in Soldier Field yelled hysterically as the Bears continued to screw up, blowing two easy field goals and incurring unnecessary penalties. Where was Houdini? The Bears clearly needed a magic trick.

But Walter Payton was running. And when Walter is running, there is always the germ of a hope. Payton, en route to a 192-yard performance, writhed through the Chiefs' defenses from 12 yards out for his third touchdown of the afternoon.

The clock showed 2:02 when Payton sliced into the end zone. But the Chiefs struck back, manhandling the Chicago defenders. With 24 seconds remaining, Ed Podolak sprinted 14 yards to a TD and Kansas City led 27-21.

Brian Baschnagel returned the kickoff to the Bears' 43. Avellini tossed to fullback Robin Earl for 20 yards. Then it happened. Something happened. Houdini turned in his grave. The goddess of fortune smiled on the Bears.

Greg Latta, the Bears' oft-maligned tight end from the World Football League, shook free behind the Chiefs secondary. Avellini reared back and fired. Latta pulled in Avellini's perfect 37-yard pass over his shoulder for a touchdown. Bob Thomas kicked the extra point in a 28-27 victory. "Heck, it was a prayer, really," Avellini said of the bomb to Latta.

And the Bears' incredible surge to the playoffs had begun.

It didn't escape the attention of reporters on the Bear "beat" that assistant coach Fred O'Connor started calling plays in the second half of the win over Kansas City.

In the first half, with Avellini calling plays, Payton carried 13 times and the Bears trailed by 17 points. After O'Connor took over the masterminding, Payton carried 20 times and tallied three TDs.

Payton's total of 33 carries was his high for the season up to that point.

"When you have a Walter Payton," Avellini said, "you better get him the ball 30 times."

Fortified with a one-game "winning streak," the Bears resolutely awaited the annual invasion by the powerful, perennial divisional champion Minnesota Vikings the following weekend.

Going into the Viking game, Pardee did his best to soft-peddle the disablement of quarterback Francis Tarkenton, who was shelved for the season with a broken leg.

"I don't see where Chuck Foreman is hurt," the Bear coach said dryly, "and he's the one you have to stop."

Sunday, November 20, 1977, was a day which will be remembered forever by Bear fans, who watched the greatest performance by a runner in National Football League history. The runner was Walter Payton and

Soldier Field was Payton's Place on this dramatic November afternoon. His powerful legs churning as he alternately danced and drove, Wonderful Walter gained 275 yards in 40 rushes as he carried the Bears to a 10-7 triumph.

Payton's performance eclipsed O.J. Simpson's single-game NFL rushing record, set the previous Thanksgiving against Detroit, by two yards. Walter accomplished his spectacular feat despite a flu bug which kept him feeling queasy with hot and cold flashes through midweek.

But on game day, Walter was perfect.

"You put your faith in God and he'll take care of you," Payton said after leading the Bears to their second straight win.

While Payton was praising the Lord, he didn't forget his six personal apostles, offensive linemen Ted Albrecht, Noah Jackson, Dan Peiffer, Revie Sorey, Dennis Lick, and Greg Latta. Walter invited all six to accompany him to a postgame television appearance just as they had shepherded him all day.

"Did Walter set a record?" Pardee asked sports editor Joe Mooshil of the Associated Press.

"An NFL record?" asked Avellini, who threw only seven passes (completing four), in following a Bears' game plan which even Viking coach Bud Grant had to admit was a fine way to win a football game.

In outdistancing Simpson's single-game effort, Payton, of course, also broke Gale Sayers' Bear record of 205 yards set in 1968 which Walter had struggled so mightily to tie on an earlier Sunday against Green Bay.

Payton also became only the third runner in NFL annals to carry 40 times in one game. Franco Harris of Pittsburgh set the record of 41 in 1976.

"I had to suck it up a little at times," Payton said. "But I didn't know I carried 40 times. It felt more like about 20."

If Payton ever needed an introduction to the nation's pro football writers, his 275-yard performance gave him a 100 percent entree. He spoke to a nationwide conference telephone hookup of 17 writers the day after his romp against the Vikings.

The Pro Football Hall of Fame called and asked for the jersey Walter wore and the ball he carried on his record day. He got an invitation to appear on the Today Show, another to participate in ABC's Superstars competition, and two Chicago newspapers asked permission to print iron-ons featuring him.

"What's all the fuss?" Payton deadpanned at the weekly press luncheon. "I owe everything I have done to the guys up ahead of me."

Columnist Bill Gleason of the *Chicago Sun-Times* snorted. "Walter, how can you give us all this humble stuff about your offensive line all the time?" Gleason asked.

"But I mean it," Payton insisted.

Later, when Pardee took the stand, columnist Bob Markus of the *Chicago Tribune* asked him, "Jack, do you agree with Walter that just about any back could operate with his efficiency behind the Bears' offensive line?"

"He's the best we've got," Pardee smiled. "I don't see anybody as good as him on the bench."

Payton said Minnesota's ancient defensive end, Carl Eller, told him "that I was the greatest running back he'd ever seen." Sixteen of Walter's 40 rushes were sweeps aimed mainly toward the 17-year-vet Eller.

After their victory over the Vikings, the Bears were 5-5. Four games remained and the Bears were cautiously hopeful of sticking in the playoff picture. They survived a shaky first half Thanksgiving Day in the Silverdome to beat the Lions 31-14, and the playoff picture loomed even brighter. But the postseason still was light years away.

The decision over Detroit was the first time the Bears had won three games in a row since 1972. In pacing the unspectacular win, Payton stayed ahead of Simpson's 2,003-yard pace of 1973 with a 137-yard production. Running back Roland Harper, Payton's best blocker, returned to the lineup after missing four weeks with an ankle injury.

The Bears said thanks not only for the victory, but for the fact they got out of Pontiac alive. Pardee called his team away from the sidelines with 25 seconds remaining because fans were hurling beer cans.

"Full cans of beer were coming out of the third deck," Pardee said. "That's as dangerous as a deer rifle."

Chicago fans watching the game at home on television were pleased when the Bears did exactly what they had been demanding—throw the ball to Payton. Avellini lofted a pass to Payton in front of cornerback James Hunter after a Detroit punt, and Walter scampered 75 yards with only the second TD pass of his pro career.

The Bears had Tampa Bay to get by before playing their home finale with Green Bay. Pardee had a difficult time getting the Bears up for the winless Buccaneers, and there were some nervous moments before the Bucs finally succumbed 10-0.

"When they say 'any given Sunday,' you better believe it," proclaimed linebacker Doug Buffone. "It's the biggest truth since corn flakes."

Tampa Bay nearly made it into the win column because of a strong showing by its terrorist defense which "held" Payton to 101 yards and kept the game scoreless for three quarters before the Bears converted a couple of fluke plays into points on the scoreboard.

"I thought we could play them for a month and a half and they wouldn't score a touchdown," quipped Tampa coach John McKay. "And they wouldn't have if we don't give them the ball and let 'em pass from punt formation.''

The Bears didn't score until the last quarter when safety Gary Fencik intercepted and set up a 32-yard field goal by Bob Thomas. Later, on fourth down, punter Bob Parsons passed for a first down to Steve Schubert, setting up a 3-yard touchdown run by Payton.

Having inflicted the Buccaneers' 26th consecutive loss, the Bears turned their attention to traditional foe Green Bay. The Packers' visit to Soldier Field was hardly a classic football battle. But it served the Bears' purpose.

"When you win five in a row, it's like losing five in a row," Doug Buffone said after the Bears had ground out a 21-10 victory. "It forms a habit. We weren't great today. But we're learning how to win."

Payton scored a pair of TDs to equal Gale Sayers' team mark of 14 in a season. Walter also drew within 198 yards of Simpson's season record with 163 yards against the Pack. Payton became the third runner—along with O.J. and Jim Brown—ever to reach 1,800 yards.

Walter even returned kickoffs against Green Bay, one for 68 yards. And James Scott caught seven Avellini passes, one for a touchdown.

With the victory, the Bears assured themselves of their first winning season since 1967. And they set the stage for the big game with the Giants, the day when the earth stood still in East Rutherford.

From the instant Bob Thomas' kick floated through the uprights in icy overtime to clinch victory over the Giants and a playoff berth for Chicago, the Bears became the No. 1 conversation piece in the Windy City. Such minor matters as Christmas and the approach of a new year were secondary.

Forgotten were the disabling losses of Wally Chambers, Lionel Antoine, Ross Brupbacher and Brian Baschnagel. Forgotten also was the fact that Walter Payton had failed by 151 yards to match O.J. Simpson's record NFL season high of 2,003 yards. In the saloons and office buildings, in the gyms and churches and in private homes throughout Chicagoland, it mattered only that the Bears were in the playoffs.

Six wins in a row did not surprise Jim Finks.

"It is inevitable," the confident, urbane Bears general manager said on Christmas night in Dallas, the eve of the Bears' first postseason appearance since 1963. "If you operate properly, you have a winning football team."

Not many Chicagoans seriously expected the Bears to beat the Cowboys, who had carried the art of computerization to a new level of sports perfection. Oddsmakers said the game wouldn't even be close. The wild card Bears were nine-point underdogs, the longest shots in the playoffs, to a Dallas team which had sailed through the regular season 12 and 2 to win the championship of the NFC East.

For once, the experts were right. The Cowboys shut down Walter Payton, took a 17-0 halftime lead, and turned the game into a 37-7 rout when the

Bears turned over the ball five times in their first six possessions of the second half.

"I'm proud of this team," said coach Jack Pardee as he wound up his three-year Bear coaching career with a 20-23 record by watching Roger Staubach complete 8 of 13 passes for 134 yards and Tony Dorsett score two touchdowns en route to the Super Bowl championship.

"This had to be our best game of the year," said Dallas coach Tom Landry after the rout of the Bears. "Every phase of our game was excellent."

The Bears were obviously impressed—awed would be a better word—by the Cowboys.

"Staubach threw three passes in the first half so perfect I thought I was seeing double," said Doug Buffone.

But the Bears, regardless of the lopsided defeat at Dallas, were not humiliated. They were glad just to be there.

"You have to crawl before you can walk," said Bob Avellini.

"I feel personal satisfaction," Finks said, "because we have damn good people here and we're beginning to see the rewards of our work. It's happened and it will continue to happen."

Chapter 13

WHO'S RUNNING THIS SHOW?

When George Halas named Mike Ditka to lead the Bears back from mediocrity, it climaxed one of the wildest scenarios in the history of the Bears or any other sports franchise.

The team was going nowhere under Neill Armstrong, whose 30-34 record in four seasons seemed to vindicate Leo Durocher's famous baseball credo that nice guys finish last. Nice Neill led great prayer services, but had difficulty inspiring the Bears to play tough.

Principal actors in the bizarre melodrama were George "Mugs" Halas Jr., son of the owner whose untimely death in December, 1979, upset the Bears' timetable and forced the script to be rewritten; general manager Jim Finks, hired by Mugs Halas to run the club and rudely shoved aside by Halas after his son's death; Buddy Ryan, re-signed by Halas late in 1981 as Bears' defensive coordinator without Finks' blessing, and finally, Ditka and Halas themselves.

George Halas, Jr., known as Mugs from the time he was a youth hanging helmets in the locker room and carrying water to his father's players, was elevated by Papa Bear to the club presidency in 1963 after having been general manager since 1960.

The Bears' strange saga of internal turmoil that was to be climaxed by the hiring of Ditka actually began serenely and on an upbeat note in 1974 when Mugs Halas gave up the general manager's post and hired his old friend, Jim Finks, to remake the Bears.

George Halas Sr., smiled benignly and, for once in his life, watched quietly from the background as Mugs turned over operating control of the Bears to Finks, a highly esteemed former Minnesota Vikings executive who had formed a close companionship with the younger Halas while Finks served on the prestigious National Football League Management Council and Mugs was a member of the executive committee.

When Finks was hired by the Halases on Sept. 12, 1974, the three became an unholy trinity, so to speak—father, son and spirit of the Bears. The elder Halas retained his title as chairman of the board and chief executive officer. George Halas, Jr., remained as club president. Finks, in addition to becoming general manager, was named vice president and chief operating officer, and allowed to purchase a 3.23% share of stock in the franchise.

From the moment he walked into the Bears' office, at that time a delapidated building on West Madison Street, for the first time as the power behind the throne, Finks obviously held the reins in virtually all matters involving the operation of the club. In good seasons and in bad throughout his nine-year tenure, Finks was the undisputed monarch. With the backing of Mugs Halas, Finks' decisions were unchallenged by George Halas Sr.

"Papa Bear was a one-man show," reflects the Bears' astute director of player personnel, Bill Tobin. "When Mugs was president of the club and hired Finks, he made Jim a one-man show. Jim would make a decision and tell Mugs what he had done. Mugs would then tell Halas and Halas was satisfied. After Mugs died, Jim lost his clout and it became one-on-one."

It didn't help Finks' status or relationship with the elder Halas when the Bears went into a downhill spin in the years after Mugs Halas died. Coach Neill Armstrong's 1979 Bears finished a respectable 10-6 and went to the playoffs. But the next two years were disasters—7-9 in 1980 and 6-10 in 1981. Armstrong was Finks' hand-picked successor to the departed Jack Pardee. Finks lured the genial Armstrong off the coaching staff of Finks' old pal, Bud Grant of the Minnesota Vikings.

Halas reached the end of his patience during the 1981 campaign. Papa Bear started stepping on Finks' toes when he hired former head coach Jim Dooley as an aide to Armstrong. After the season, Halas rehired defensive coordinator Buddy Ryan, fired Armstrong and hired Ditka—all without Finks' input.

Armstrong was axed on a gray Chicago Monday, Jan. 4. Halas did it simply, sending out a press release announcing Armstrong had been terminated after a meeting with himself and Finks. When Halas was asked about Finks' role in the decision, Halas said, "I hadn't discussed it with him."

"Jim Finks may be my biggest supporter and I his, and I will remain so," said Armstrong, who quickly was snapped up by the Dallas Cowboys as a talent researcher.

Even before he hired Ditka, Halas exploded a bombshell on a Thursday afternoon in January by announcing he was taking over operational command of the Bears but that Finks would remain as general manager under terms of Finks' contract.

When word swept around the country that Halas had seized control of his ball club at the age of 86, the reaction was both amused and indignant.

"It's like Orville Wright coming back to run United Airlines," quipped Stan Jones, a former Bears tackle.

The Chicago Tribune story reporting the weird turn of events led off as follows:

"Unlike Woody Allen, Jim Finks has decided to take the money and stay. And the Bears' scenario remains as wild and crazy as Allen's hit movie, 'Take The Money And Run.' Finks said Thursday he will remain as general manager of the Bears. Whether he likes it or not, he might have added. Even if he has to sweep the floors. Owner George Halas said, in effect, 'Fine, as long as I hold the broom.' "

In an obscurely worded and clumsily typed press release, the Bears announced that Finks, whose stock in the franchise was estimated at close to $1 million in paper value, would remain in his job, though shorn of most of his prior responsibilities.

The press release, prepared by Halas' secretary with a hasty addendum by business manager Rudy Custer ordered by Finks, read as follows: "George Halas and Jim Finks got together today and had a mutual meeting of minds to determine the future of the Chicago Bears. The course of action to improve the fortunes of the Club were [sic] mutually resolved and agreed upon."

But what did it mean?

"It means just what it says," Finks said. "It means that I signed a contract in 1974, and I intend to honor my contract. I so informed Mr. Halas of this. Are my feelings hurt? I don't think my feelings are important at this time."

Finks, who had been all but stripped of his command in the previous couple of months, said he had "no idea" how he would fit into Halas' new scheme. "I await directions as to matters he wishes me to undertake, and I will proceed in a spirit of cooperation," Finks said. "My goal has not changed. I want to see the Chicago Bears become world champions.''

Finks said he ''obviously performed a certain role during the years when Mugs was club president. Obviously, Mr. Halas has a different role for me. Events from November to the present time made it clear my duties have changed.''

And Halas made it doubly clear that Finks would have no part in the choosing of Armstrong's successor as head coach. The two ranking candidates were Ditka and George Allen. The latter called his old boss to make a final pitch for the job the night before Halas announced Ditka as his choice.

Sportswriter David Condon of *The Chicago Tribune* got the scoop a day before Halas' official announcement that he had indeed hired his one-time boozing, bruising brawler to be the 10th head coach of the Bears. Halas confirmed the agreement to Condon on Jan. 19, 1982, after a long session with the hard-nosed former star tight end.

In Dallas, Ditka's wife, Dana, confirmed that ''Mike has accepted the Bears' offer, and it's fantastic.''

The signing of Ditka, then 42, dropped Finks further into limbo. Finks at the time had two years remaining on a long-term contract, plus the lucrative Bears stock.

''Jim is determined to eat crow,'' a friend of Finks confided.

''I will report only to George Halas,'' Ditka said before he took the podium for his formal presentation as head coach. ''I have to be in control. I know where the buck stops. I think the leadership will be there. The discipline definitely is going to be there.''

When he finally was handed the mantle of leadership at a packed press conference in Halas' office, Ditka proclaimed himself a man of destiny. Somehow, the statement didn't seem corny, even to jaundiced members of the media, who perhaps were as tired as Chicago fans of the Bears' perennial losing posture.

''I believe that everyone has a destiny, and mine is with the Chicago Bears,'' Ditka said.

''Jim Finks will be in charge of all information on the draft,'' Halas said. ''And that will be submitted to Mike and me, and we'll go over it. As you can see, this will not be a one-man operation.''

Finks left for home after meeting with Ditka early in the afternoon. Ditka vowed he would not get into a ''word game'' over the office politics that recently had brought the franchise close to disaster. ''I have spoken with Jim Finks, and he told me he would do whatever he could to make my job happy, to make my job easy, that he would help in any way he can,'' Ditka said.

Nineteen months later, Finks quit.

After slightly more than 1½ years of forced cohabitation with Ditka in which the two got along surprisingly well superficially, Finks resigned entirely on his own. The timing of his announcement on Aug. 24, 1983, apparently caught Halas and everyone else in the organization by surprise.

Halas, who immediately named the Bears' capable treasurer and general counsel, Jerry Vainisi, to succeed Finks, expressed sorrow and said he had talked Finks into staying the previous December. "He said he wanted to quit but I asked him to stay on until he signed the players," Halas said.

"The players are signed and it's time for me to move on," said Finks, who became president of the Chicago Cubs baseball team, then resigned in 1984 to take a public relations job. "Now is the ideal time. When the season starts, every GM becomes nothing but a sweater. We sweat out the games. The scouts are scouting, the ticket sellers are selling, the coaches are coaching, the players are playing. And we are just sweating."

The death of George Halas, Sr., at the age of 88 on Oct. 31, 1983, stunned the sports world even though Papa Bear's failing health was well known. When Halas died, pro football was left without the only surviving pioneer among the group of visionaries who sat on the famous running board in an auto showroom in Canton, Ohio, over six decades ago and dreamed up the National Football League.

"George Halas WAS the National Football League," declared commissioner Pete Rozelle. "Perhaps the greatest tribute to him is that our game has assumed many of the characteristics of George himself—wisdom and creativity, vitality and endurance and that singular trait of all athletes—competitiveness."

Halas left bequests of more than $600,000 to relatives, old friends, and past and present employees. But his biggest legacy was to the fans, who would continue to enjoy watching the Bears team Halas had founded and kept alive through the perilous years of the depression and up until his death.

Control of the Bears went to Halas' only surviving child, Virginia Halas McCaskey, who named her husband, Edward W. McCaskey, chairman of the board and her eldest son, Michael, club president. Virginia owns the club in trust for the 13 grandchildren of Halas.

Virginia McCaskey, then 60 and a mother of 11, said she and her father talked frequently about the future of the Bears during the last months of his life. And yet, she said in an exclusive *Chicago Tribune* interview, there was a "gap" in their conversations that left some questions unanswered.

"More than most people, he considered himself immortal," Virginia said. "He kept saying to me, 'I am leaving you in control and I want things to be in good order for you.' And yet there was what I felt was a gap."

The gap was closed, the mystery and the rumors ended, and the Bears' future course was officially charted 13 days after Halas' death when Michael

McCaskey took over his grandfather's club a month before his 40th birthday and 39 years after attending his first Bears' game in the arms of his mother.

McCaskey, a former associate professor at the Harvard School of Business, announced immediately that Mike Ditka would have "complete charge and control" in coaching the Bears. Halas had made certain that Buddy Ryan was returned as defensive coordinator before hiring Ditka as head coach. But McCaskey emphasized there would be no divided authority on the staff.

"The head coach is in charge of the offense and defense," McCaskey said. "It's up to him to set up the dynamics. I won't interfere."

The first impression McCaskey made upon Chicago media persons accustomed to Halas' toughness was the obvious personality contrast between the two. Michael carried an image as an intellectual, thoughtful academician with a wealth of marketing know-how gently nurtured in the Ivy League.

It soon became evident that McCaskey had his own brand of toughness. A Boy Scout leader in the McCaskey parish once told Ed McCaskey, "I used to think your son Michael was a pussycat until we played a game of King of the Hill."

"Do I think Mike McCaskey likes me?" Ditka said only recently. "I think he likes the Bears. Therefore, he's going to appreciate me as long as I keep doing a good job. I don't know how to say it any other way. As long as I continue to produce, I'll be appreciated and probably liked and tolerated. The minute I don't, then a lot of things will come to an end."

McCaskey began restructuring and streamlining the Bears' musty old family operation almost from the moment he dusted off his desk pad. He had owned a management consultant firm in Boston, so retooling the Bears' table of organization came easily to him.

With Ditka entrenched momentarily at least as head coach and Jerry Vainisi winding up a successful rookie season as general manager and successor to Jim Finks, McCaskey turned quickly to the club's antiquated and understaffed scouting department. McCaskey plucked Bill Tobin out of the pack of personnel aides and named him director of player personnel to head an expanded scouting staff. Vainisi, Ditka and Tobin each has a clear area of responsibility and all report directly to McCaskey. The four hold frequent, regularly scheduled meetings similar to the executive board of a giant corporation.

"There had been a perception, whether valid or not," Vainisi says, "that there were two conflicting factions, a Finks faction and a Halas-Ditka faction. My No. 1 job, as I saw it from the beginning, was to remove this impression."

McCaskey also named Bill McGrane, a knowledgeable former journalist who for years served Finks as an aide, as director of marketing and communications. McCaskey then won over the Chicago press corps by removing his own younger brother, Patrick, as coordinator of media relations and replacing him with Ken Valdiserri, son of Roger Valdiserri, the highly respected associate athletic director at Notre Dame. Patrick was assigned an important but prosaic role of director of community involvement.

"When my grandfather was ill the last couple of years," McCaskey confided, "it wasn't always clear who was running things. When he was healthy and strong, obviously it was he. But later, it was unclear. Now that I'm here, it is absolutely clear who is running the organization."

Obviously, it doesn't bother McCaskey to follow a football legend like George Halas.

"People keep asking me if I feel intimidated by it," he says. "Maybe I should be, but I am not. He was my grandfather, and I knew him in a much warmer and more personal way than fans have the opportunity to. I look on his accomplishments as absolutely singular. There is not and never will be another George Halas. Case closed."

Chapter 14
1985: HAS 'TOMORROW' ARRIVED?

"Wait 'til next year."

The Bears hope to invoke the ancient rallying cry of frustrated sports teams and turn the future into the present in 1985. "Wait 'til next year" is a losers' lament. The Bears, from Mike McCaskey through Mike Ditka through Walter Payton and Jim McMahon and all those wonderful brutes on defense, plan to convert the plaintive old losers' wail into a winners' refrain.

"Our appetite has been whetted," Ditka says. "There's no reason why we shouldn't play with just as much intensity as last year. That was basically what it was. We just played a little tougher than we had played in the past."

"If we're healthy," and here Ditka hedges just a bit, "we're capable of going all the way. We can't have key people sitting on the bench or lying in the hospital."

You also can't have them sulking over money matters. One key dimension in the Bears' 1985 prospectus is the attitude and availability of players, some of whom haggled over money during the off-season after last year's stunning campaign. Tight end Emery Moorehead, one of Ditka's favorite players who had been a free agent, signed two one-year contracts June 19 and expressed the hope that some disgruntled teammates would follow his lead.

"Everybody feels he's the most important person in our success," Ditka says. "Who's to say who was more important to the defense—Hampton, Singletary, or Otis, or Bell?"

In 1984, general manager Jerry Vainisi had every Bear signed by May. But times have changed. With the United States Football League on the skids, McCaskey has vowed to hold the line on spending.

"I have no oil wells," George Halas' grandson declares.

National Football League owners, seeking to reduce costs, cut four players off their rosters for 1985. At their May meeting in Chicago, the NFL moguls voted to cut back to the pre-strike limit of 45 players on each active squad. A 49-man limit had been in effect since the 1982 player strike.

McCaskey drew snickers when he asserted that the cutback would "improve the quality of the game. Fans will have an easier time identifying with smaller squads."

Fan identification has never been a problem in the National Football League. But player morale has. The loss of 112 jobs predictably drew an outburst from Gene Upshaw, executive director of the NFL Players Association, who labeled the decision "a tragedy for the fans." Upshaw hinted that collective bargaining for 1987 may be militant.

Beyond his unenviable job of cutting the Bear roster to its final 45-man limit, Ditka isn't interested in lengthy debate on such matters. He's more concerned with keeping the Bears on an even keel emotionally and mentally.

"The most important thing for this team to realize," says Ditka, squinting into the sunshine encompassing the Lake Forest practice field, "is that what you do one year has nothing to do with what you'll do the next year.

"Everybody has the tendency to say, 'Well, you were successful in '84 to a degree, so therefore, you automatically have to be successful in '85.' That just doesn't hold water. You've got to be willing to pay the price to collect the rewards."

The biggest key to the Bears' 1985 chances, of course, is quarterback Jim McMahon, who easily passed the first test of his rehabilitated kidneys at the Bears' May minicamp. Rolling his jersey up to expose a bare midriff with no visible scars, McMahon threw his first pass since the previous November when he was hurt in the victory over the Los Angeles Raiders.

"I threw a lot better today than last year at this time. Proves I need six months off," McMahon quipped.

"McMahon is fine," Ditka said with a relieved sigh. "He's got a few more things to learn, trial and error. He's got to throw the ball away more. If I were a quarterback, I'd pattern my whole style after Joe Montana (San Francisco QB whom Ditka coached in the Pro Bowl last winter).

"Joe is so selective. He hurts you so badly when he does certain things. He knows when to dump it off, when to throw it away, when to fall down or run out of bounds.

"Jim can learn those things. The two quarterbacks are very similar. I didn't know Montana's arm was so strong. He has a boyishness about him. He thinks the game is still fun. I think that's what we had last year. The guys were having fun. McMahon has fun when he plays."

Ditka feels the Bears need improvement in the passing game, third down efficiency, turnover ratio and overall special teams play.

"We controlled the ball for almost 35 minutes a game last season," Ditka pointed out. "I'd like to see us continue that. But we've got to throw more efficiently and put more points on the board."

Bear fans will drink to that!

While the 1984 Bears were leading the league in rushing for the second year in a row paced by Payton's 1,684 yards, the Bears were never able to develop a consistent passing attack, finishing 26th in the NFL in passing.

The Bears compensated with a defense that zonked rival quarterbacks with a league-leading 72 sacks, an NFL record. Coordinator Buddy Ryan's defensive unit led the league in fewest yards allowed (241.3 per game) and fewest rushing yards permitted (86.1). The Bears' pass defense was second in the league.

Even with defensive tackle Dan Hampton hurting following rehabilitation from knee surgery, Ryan's 1985 defense should mimic its predecessor in both fury and competence. Ditka and Ryan know they need more backup strength in the defensive line. With this in mind, they amused and startled the nation by making a huge, apparently immobile defensive tackle their No. 1 draft choice.

It was a luxury few other teams would have been able to afford—taking a chance on squandering a top draft choice on a player like William Perry of Clemson, whose weight had been reported at somewhere between 300 and 400 pounds, give or take a hundred pounds or so.

"Gut feeling," said Ditka after making Perry the 22d player taken in the annual draft.

"I've been big since I've been little," Perry told sportswriter Don Pierson of *The Chicago Tribune*.

Back in February, the Bears put the so-called "Refrigerator Man" on a scale that only registered 350 pounds and the scale went into orbit. When he showed up for minicamp in May, however, Perry, who used to eat three chickens at one meal before he went on a diet, was down to 318 pounds.

"This was a risky choice," McCaskey said after the Bears plucked Perry. "We knew it. The scouts went out on a limb. Nobody can say for sure if Perry is going to be a terrific choice in the NFL or not."

"Cheeseburgers," said Perry, when asked his principal weakness.

"He'll look good in that navy blue uniform," Ditka quipped. "Or two uniforms."

"I don't know if I can crack the lineup and help contribute right away," Perry said. "I just want to go out there and help the Bears get that Super Bowl ring."

Hampton was dumbfounded when the Bears picked Perry. "I thought we needed a cornerback," Hampton said.

So did Ditka and Ryan. They named a cornerback in the second round, choosing SMU ace Reggie Phillips. Phillips immediately predicted he would win a starting job.

"I wish I could bump and run on every play," Phillips said. "I've seen the Bears play several times. I love that aggressive play. That's how I was taught at SMU."

Another priority position, which appears to have improved depth with Ken Margerum back from knee surgery after missing all the 1984 season, is wide receiver. Ditka never has been totally happy with the wide receiving corps. Even though he has high regard for Willie Gault's big-play capability, Ditka can't conceal the fact that he regards Gault basically as a track man trying to play pro football. This despite the fact Gault was both a kickoff returner and wide-out at Tennessee.

"Willie can break up a game on any given play, with that great speed of his," Ditka declares, pointing to Gault's six touchdown catches last year. "He has a quality you can't teach in speed. It's just a matter of him dedicating himself to football."

The Bears' third round draft choice was a wide receiver, James Maness of Texas Christian, whose 97 career catches rank fourth in Horned Frog history. Like Gault, Maness also was an All-American sprinter.

"A lot of receivers don't like to go across the middle," Maness said after learning the Bears had drafted him. "They're in the wrong sport if they don't want to get hit."

"Speed was the biggest thing we liked about him," Ditka said of Maness. "Courage was the second thing. He will sacrifice his body."

Place kicker Bob Thomas, who keeps having to prove himself to Ditka every year, was "shocked" (disgusted would be a better word) when the Bears picked Georgia kicker Kevin Butler on the fourth round.

"I don't think kicking is a need," Thomas said bluntly. A Notre Dame graduate, Thomas originally was acquired on waivers from the Los Angeles Rams and commuted between the Bears and Detroit Lions before Ditka finally decided in December, 1982, that Thomas was his kicker—apparently. Thomas kicked 22 field goals in 28 attempts last year even though, as Ditka admits, "it's not easy to kick in Soldier Field." Ditka obviously is still looking for a place kicker who can put the ball in the seats behind the end zone on kickoffs.

Ditka has sworn to place a big emphasis on special teams in 1985. He feels that, with rosters whittled from 49 to 45 men, the kicking and kick return units will be more important than ever.

"We have to win two games by special teams," Ditka declares.

With this in mind, Ditka has named Gault to return kickoffs, a job Willie took over in the thrilling playoff victory over Washington last Dec. 30, and another wide receiver, tough-guy Dennis McKinnon, to return punts.

"We have to get our most skilled people in there on special teams," Ditka explains.

The Bears of 1985 will be as skilled as their 1984 predecessors, and perhaps more so. But will they be as tough? The answer to this question will decide the Bears' fate, believes free safety Gary Fencik, ringleader and unofficial spokesman of Ryan's rugged defense.

"I have a couple of concerns," Fencik says. "In 1977 and 1979, the two previous playoff years in which I participated with the Bears, we had real lackluster years the following season. There was a definite tendency to let up.

"This year we'll be one of the teams other people are pointing for. It's important for people on our team to realize how difficult it was to achieve what we did last year.

"There is more pure talent on this team than any past team I've been on. More talent and better coaching overall. But we have to have a real strong hunger, as we did last year."

Ditka agrees totally.

"I've never been fainthearted," Ditka says, referring to the drafting of Perry. But Ditka's statement actually could have applied to his entire philosophy of coaching.

He's not fainthearted. And he's looking foward to the future, more breathlessly than any Bear fan. But he's trying to play it cool.

"My biggest problem is myself," Ditka admits. "I take things too seriously. I guess it's just my job. But more than that, it's pride.

"What's happened in our whole league is that everybody worries about each individual week too much. It's the big picture that counts. You have to look at what the 16-game season is going to bring you.

"To maintain momentum through 16 games is tough. San Francisco did it last year, but that's unusual. The main thing to remember is, when you let your guard down, don't get thrown off the track. Just remember what's at the end."

And what's at the end for Mike Ditka and the 1985 Bears? Well, how about Super Bowl XX?

"That's our objective," Ditka says. "And it's not a remote dream. First, we have to win the NFC Central. Then, to win the Super Bowl, a lot of things have to happen.

"But basically, it's a three-game series. If you're playing good football at that point and you have the hot hand, you're gonna win it. It's not all that much of a miracle."

Ditka believes what he says. His players believe it. And, certainly, so does every Bear fan.

"I believe it, too," declares Mike McCaskey, sounding every bit like his combative grandfather. "A Super Bowl title really isn't that far away."

BEARS IN PRO FOOTBALL HALL OF FAME

With the induction of Doug Atkins and George Musso in 1982, 20 Bears have been enshrined in the Pro Football Hall of Fame in Canton, Ohio. The Bear immortals:

1963 (charter members)

George Halas, end-owner-coach, Illinois.
Harold (Red) Grange, halfback, Illinois.
Bronko Nagurski, fullback, Minnesota.

1964

Ed Healey, tackle, Dartmouth.
Roy (Link) Lyman, tackle, Nebraska.
George Trafton, center, Notre Dame.

1965

John (Paddy) Driscoll, halfback,
   Northwestern.
Danny Fortmann, guard, Colgate.
Sid Luckman, quarterback, Columbia.

1966

George McAfee, halfback, Duke.
Clyde (Bulldog) Turner, center-linebacker,
   Hardin-Simmons.

1967

Joe Stydahar, tackle, West Virginia.

1971

Bill Hewitt, end, Michigan.

1974

Bill George, linebacker, Wake Forest.

1975

George Connor, tackle-linebacker,
   Holy Cross-Notre Dame.

1977

Gale Sayers, halfback, Kansas.

1979

Dick Butkus, linebacker, Illinois.

1981

George Blanda, quarterback-place kicker,
   Kentucky.

1982

Doug Atkins, defensive end, Tennessee.
George Musso, guard, Millikin.

SECTION 2

The
New
Bears

Jim McMahon, who suffered a lacerated kidney against the Raiders last season, is coach Mike Ditka's kind of quarterback. "We can win with him," Ditka says. "McMahon has fun when he plays."

1984 AT A GLANCE
PRESEASON GAMES (1-3)

	Location	BEARS	Opp.	Att.
Aug. 4 St. Louis	Chicago	10	19	34,399
Aug. 11 Green Bay	Milwaukee	10	17	48,233
Aug. 18 Cincinnati	Chicago	17	25	53,194
Aug. 26 Buffalo	Indianapolis	38	7	60,500
	TOTALS	75	68	196,326

REGULAR SEASON (10-6)

	Location	BEARS	Opp.	Att.
Sept. 2 Tampa Bay	Chicago	34	14	58,789
Sept. 9 Denver	Chicago	27	0	54,335
Sept. 16 Green Bay	Green Bay	9	7	55,942
Sept. 23 Seattle	Seattle	9	38	61,520
Sept. 30 Dallas	Chicago	14	23	63,623
Oct. 7 New Orleans	Chicago	20	7	53,752
Oct. 14 St. Louis	St. Louis	21	38	49,554
Oct. 21 Tampa Bay	Tampa	44	9	60,003
Oct. 28 Minnesota	Chicago	16	7	57,517
Nov. 4 L.A. Raiders	Chicago	17	6	59,858
Nov. 11 L.A. Rams	Anaheim	13	29	62,021
Nov. 18 Detroit	Chicago	16	14	54,911
Nov. 25 Minnesota	Minneapolis	34	3	56,881
Dec. 3 San Diego	San Diego	7	20	45,470
Dec. 9 Green Bay	Chicago	14	20	59,374
Dec. 16 Detroit	Pontiac	30	13	53,252
	TOTALS	325	248	906,802

POSTSEASON (1-1)

	Location	BEARS	Opp.	Att.
Dec. 30 Washington	Washington	23	19	55,431
Jan. 6 San Francisco	San Francisco	0	23	61,040
	TOTALS	23	42	116,471

TEAM STATISTICS

	Bears	Opponent
TOTAL FIRST DOWNS	297	216
Rushing	164	72
Passing	115	122
Penalty	18	22
3rd Down: Made/Att.	105-256	55-209
4th Down: Made/Att.	9-23	2-11
TOTAL NET YARDS	5437	3860
Avg. Per Game	339.8	241.3
Total Plays	1100	885
Avg. Per Play	4.9	4.4
NET YARDS RUSHING	2974	1377
Avg. Per Game	185.9	86.1
Total Rushes	674	378
NET YARDS PASSING	2463	2486
Avg. Per Game	153.9	155.4
Tackled/Yards Lost	36-232	72-583
Gross Yards	2695	3069
Attempts/Completions	390-226	435-197
Pct. of Completions	57.9	45.3
Had Intercepted	15	21
PUNTS/AVERAGE	85-39.2	100-41.3
NET PUNTING AVG.	35.3	34.3
PENALTIES/YARDS	114-851	86-698
FUMBLES/BALL LOST	31-16	33-13
TOUCHDOWNS	37	29
Rushing	22	10
Passing	14	14
Returns	1	5

SCORE BY PERIODS	1	2	3	4	OT	Total
BEARS TOTAL	91	107	62	65	0	325
Opp. Total	33	73	53	89	0	248

1984 GAME BY GAME

GAME 1—BEARS 34 BUCCANEERS 14
Soldier Field—58,789—9/2/84

TAMPA BAY	0	7	0	7	—	14
CHICAGO	3	10	14	7	—	34

BEARS—Thomas 29-yd FG, 4 plays/5 yards. BUCCANEERS—Gerald Carter 74-yd pass from Jack Thompson (Ariri kick), 6 plays/80 yards; BEARS—Thomas 32-yd FG, 14 plays/65 yards. BEARS—Jim McMahon 9-yd run (Thomas kick), 5 plays/55 yards. BEARS—Willie Gault 21-yd pass from McMahon (Thomas kick) 3 plays/20 yards. BEARS—Matt Suhey 1-yd run (Thomas kick), 3 play/4 yards. BEARS—Anthony Hutchison 1-yd run (Thomas kick), 1 play/1 yard. BUCCANEERS—James Owens 4-yd pass from Steve DeBerg (Ariri kick), 6 plays/81 yards.

Team Statistics	BUCCA-	BEARS
First Downs	NEERS	20
Total Net Yards	11	327
Rushes/Net Yards	254	49/183
Net Passing	18/89	144
Pass Attempts/Completions	165	23/17
Had Intercepted	27-9	1
Punts/Average	6	5-42.0
Return Yardage	5-46.0	152
Penalties/Yards	135	10/69
Fumbles/Lost	7/44	2/1
Sacks/Yards	2/2	4/36
Possession Time	2/11	40:44
	19:16	

RUSHING

BEARS—Payton 16-61; Suhey 14-57; C. Thomas 4-25; McMahon 3-21; Jordan 3-18; Gentry 7-5; Hutchison 2-4 BUCCANEERS—Wilder 16-73; Thompson 1-13; Armstrong 1-3

RECEIVING

BEARS—Payton 6-18; Suhey 4-30; Gault 2-40; McKinnon 2-23; Saldi 1-20; Baschnagel 1-17; Gentry 1-7 BUCCANEERS—Carter 2-86; Wilder 2-56; Giles 2-41; House 1-12; Owens 1-4; Armstrong 1-2

PASSING

BEARS—McMahon 16-22-138, 1 TD, 1 int; Avellini 1-1-17 BUCCANEERS—Thomspon 4-17-105, 1 TD, 4 int; DeBerg 5-10-96, 1 TD, 2 int.

INTERCEPTIONS

BEARS—Fencik 2-64; Harris 1-34; Singletary 1-4; Richardson 1-0, Schmidt 1-0 BUCCANEERS— Brown 1-14

SACKS

BEARS—Keys 1-15, Hampton 1-11, Hartenstine 1-10, Singletary 1-0 BUCCANEERS—Washington 1-8, Green 1-3

GAME 2—BEARS 27 BRONCOS 0
SOLDIER FIELD—54,335—9/9/84

DENVER	0	0	0	0	—	0
CHICAGO	10	17	0	0	—	27

BEARS—Bob Thomas 38-yd FG, 7 plays/24 yards. BEARS—Willie Gault 61-yd pass from Jim McMahon (Thomas kick), 2 plays/67 yards. BEARS—Walter Payton 72-yd run (Thomas kick), 3 plays/80 yards. BEARS—Thomas 26-yd FG, 13 plays/55 yards. BEARS—Matt Suhey 4-yd run (Thomas kick), 5 plays/27 yards

TEAM STATISTICS	BRONCOS	BEARS
First Downs	8	15
Total Net Yards	130	406
Rushes/Net Yards	22/53	50/302
Net Passing	77	104
Pass Attempts/Completions	9/27	10/17
Had Intercepted	2	1
Punts Average	9/39.0	5/39.6
Return Yardage	126	127
Penalties/Yards	3/17	9/65
Fumbles/Lost	5/2	2/2
Sacks/Yards	1/8	3/32
Possession Time	23:54	36:06

RUSHING

BEARS—Payton 20-179; Suhey 12-59; Hutchison 7-25; C. Thomas 4-21; Gentry 3-8; McMahon 2-8; Jordan 2-2 BRONCOS—Willhite 12-32; Winder 7-16; Lang 1-6; Elway 1-0; Parros 1-1

RECEIVING

BEARS—Suhey 2-9; Payton 2-7; Baschnagel 2-1; Gault 1-61; McKinnon 1-17; Gentry 1-13; Moorehead 1-6 BRONCOS—Summers 2-30; Watson 2-21; Sawyer 1-17; B. Johnson 1-16; Willhite 1-14; Samson 1-7; Lang 1-4

PASSING

BEARS—McMahon 5-8-93, 1 TD; Avellini 5-9-19, 1 int. BRONCOS Stankavage 4-18-58, 1 int; Kubiak 3-6-40, 1 int Elway 2-3-11

INTERCEPTIONS

BEARS—Frazier 2-42 BRONCOS—Foley 1-0

SACKS

BEARS—Bell 1-12; Keys 1-7; Wilson 1-13 BRONCOS—Ryan 1-8

GAME 3—BEARS 9 PACKERS 7
Lambeau Field—55,942—9/16/84

CHICAGO	3	3	0	3	—	9
GREEN BAY	0	7	0	0	—	7

BEARS—Bob Thomas 18-yd FG, 10 plays/41 yards. BEARS—Thomas 49-yd FG, 10 plays/34 yards. PACKERS—Jessie Clark 1-yd run (Garcia kick), 3 plays/45 yards. BEARS—Thomas 28-yd FG, 17 plays/65 yards

TEAM STATISTICS	PACKERS	BEARS
First Downs	10	15
Total Net Yards	154	345
Rushes/Net Yards	19-32	47-180
Net Passing	122	165
Pass Attempts/Completions	25/11	24/15
Had Intercepted	1	1
Punts/Average	8-42.6	6-39.8
Return Yardage	75	88
Penalties/Yards	3/24	11/94
Fumbles/Lost	0-0	1-0
Sacks/Yards	1-7	3-20
Possession Time	19:10	40:50

RUSHING

BEARS—Payton 27-110; McMahon 4-44; Suhey 11-25; C. Thomas 2-11; Finzer 1-5; Avellini 2-5 PACKERS—Ellis 7-18; Clark 4-11; Huckelby 6-5; Crouse 1-0; Dickey 1-2

RECEIVING

BEARS—Suhey 4-23; Payton 3-29; McKinnon 3-29; Moorehead 2-65; Saldi 2-19; Gault 1-7 PACKERS—Lofton 4-89; Clark 4-29; G. Lewis 2-14; Ellis 1-10

PASSING

BEARS—Avellini 11-17-133, 1 int.; McMahon 4-7-39 PACKERS—Dickey 11-23-142, 1 int.

INTERCEPTIONS

BEARS—Frazier 1-0 PACKERS—T. Lewis 1-9

SACKS

BEARS—McMichael 2-13; Hampton 1-7 PACKERS—Murphy 1-7

GAME 4—SEAHAWKS 38 BEARS 9
Kingdome—61,520—9/23/84

CHICAGO	7	0	0	2	—	9
SEATTLE	7	3	21	7	—	38

BEARS—Matt Suhey 3-yd pass from Walter Payton (Thomas kick), 7 plays/80 yards. **SEAHAWKS**—Keith Simpson 39-yd interception return (Johnson kick). **SEAHAWKS**—Norm Johnson 27-yd FG, 4 plays/2 yards. **SEAHAWKS**—Dave Krieg 3-yd run (Johnson kick), 9 plays/74 yards. **SEAHAWKS**—Eric Lane 55-yd pass from Krieg (Johnson kick), 1 play/55 yards. **SEAHAWKS**—Joe Nash fumble recovery in endzone (Johnson kick). **BEARS**—Seattle penalized for holding in end zone **SEAHAWKS**—Terry Jackson 62-yd interception return (Johnson kick)

TEAM STATISTICS	SEAHAWKS	BEARS
First Downs	12	20
Total Net Yards	203	301
Rushes/Net Yards	35/93	35/136
Net Passing	110	165
Pass Attempts/Completions	16/6	39/20
Had Intercepted	0	3
Punts/Average	9-40.6	7-36.4
Return Yardage	156	95
Penalties/Yards	11/105	11/76
Fumbles/Lost	2/1	4/3
Sacks/Lost	4/34	4/36
Possession Time	27:42	32:18

RUSHING

BEARS—Payton 24-116; Lisch 2-13; Suhey 6-11; Avellini 1-0; C. Thomas 2-4 **SEAHAWKS**—Lane 17-50; Harris 14-23; Krieg 3-18; Doornink 1-2

RECEIVING

BEARS—Gault 6-73; McKinnon 4-35; Suhey 3-11; Moorehead 2-33; Payton 2-12; Saldi 1-19; Baschnagel 1-10; C. Thomas 1-6 **SEAHAWKS**—Lane 1-55; Pratt 1-30; Largent 1-29; Doornink 1-25; Johns 1-5; Turner 1-2

PASSING

BEARS—Avellini 13-26-119, 1 int; Lisch 6-12-77, 2 int; Payton 1-1-3, 1 TD **SEAHAWKS**—Krieg 6-16-146, 1 TD

INTERCEPTIONS

BEARS—none **SEAHAWKS**—T. Jackson 1-62; Simpson 1-39; Brown 1-0

SACKS

BEARS—Dent 1-16; Keys 1-8; Osborne 1-6; McMichael 1-6 **SEAHAWKS**—Green 1-10; Jackson 1-10; Simpson 1-10; Fanning 1-10

GAME 5—COWBOYS 23 BEARS 14
Soldier Field—63,623—9/30/84

DALLAS	10	7	3	3	—	23
CHICAGO	7	7	0	0	—	14

COWBOYS—Raphael Septien 44-yd FG, 4 plays/−4 yards. **BEARS**—Jim McMahon 16-yd run (Thomas kick), 13 plays/72 yards. **COWBOYS**—Tony Dorsett 68-yd pass from Gary Hogeboom (Septien kick), 2 plays/80 yards. **BEARS**—Walter Payton 20-yd run (Thomas kick), 7 plays/53 yards. **COWBOYS**—Tim Newsome 2-yd run (Septien kick), 7 plays/81 yards. **COWBOYS**—Septien 32-yd FG, 9 plays/59 yards. **COWBOYS**—Septien 23-yd FG, 10 plays/61 yards.

TEAM STATISTICS	COWBOYS	BEARS
First Downs	17	26
Total Net Yards	313	400
Rushes/Net Yards	25/59	47/283
Net Passing	254	117
Pass Attempts/Completions	29/18	23/11
Had Intercepted	0	1
Punts/Average	5-42.6	3-39.3
Return Yardage	68	130
Penalties/Yards	8-115	8-55
Fumbles/Lost	1-0	4-1
Sacks/Yards	2-5	1-11
Possession Time	24:37	35:22

RUSHING

BEARS—Payton 25-155; Suhey 15-48; McMahon 5-45; Lisch 1-31; C. Thomas 1-4 **COWBOYS**—Dorsett 18-51; Newsome 5-8; Hogeboom 2-0

RECEIVING

BEARS—McKinnon 4-53; Suhey 2-24; Payton 2-16; Gault 2-7; Moorehead 1-22 **COWBOYS**—Dorsett 4-80; Renfro 4-72; Newsome 4-54; Cosbie 4-48; Donley 1-22

PASSING

BEARS—McMahon 6-14-79; Lisch 5-8-43, 1 inst.; Suhey 0-1 **COWBOYS**—Hogeboom 18-29-265, 1 TD

INTERCEPTIONS

BEARS—none **COWBOYS**—Clinkscale 1-9

SACKS

BEARS—McMichael 1-11 **COWBOYS**—Jeffcoat 1-5, Clinkscale 1-0

GAME 6—BEARS 20 SAINTS 7
Soldier Field—53,752—10/7/84

NEW ORLEANS	0	7	0	0	—	7
CHICAGO	6	7	0	7	—	20

BEARS—Bob Thomas 48-yd FG, 7 plays/27 yards. **BEARS**—Thomas 46-yd FG, 4 plays/−5 yards. **SAINTS**—Wayne Wilson 15-yd pass from Richard Todd (Anderson kick), 6 plays/40 yards. **BEARS**—Walter Payton 1-yd run (Thomas kick), 10 plays/80 yards. **BEARS**—Dennis McKinnon 16-yd pass from Jim McMahon (Thomas kick), 8 plays/75 yards.

TEAM STATISTICS	SAINTS	BEARS
First Downs	14	20
Total Net Yards	321	343
Rushes/Net Yards	31/176	49/246
Net Passing	145	97
Pass Attempts/Completions	26/7	14/10
Had Intercepted	0	0
Punts/Average	7-45.7	7-40.1
Return Yardage	60	62
Penalties/Yards	10/68	5/35
Fumbles/Lost	1/1	0/0
Sacks/Yards	4-31	1-13
Possession Time	24:50	35:10

RUSHING

BEARS—Payton 32-154; Suhey 11-44; McMahon 4-25; McKinnon 1-21; Gentry 1-2. **SAINTS**—G. Rogers 16-99; Gajan 7-51; W. Wilson 6-19; Todd 2-7

RECEIVING

BEARS—Suhey 3-45; Gault 2-33; Payton 2-11; Moorehead 1-18; McKinnon 1-16; Saldi 1-5. **SAINTS**—T. Young 2-93; W. Wilson 2-27; Brenner 1-19; Tice 1-17; Gajan 1-2

PASSING

BEARS—McMahon 10-14-128, 1 TD **SAINTS**—Todd 7-26-158, 1 TD

INTERCEPTIONS

BEARS—none **SAINTS**—none

SACKS

BEARS—McMichael 1-13 **SAINTS**—Paul 1-10; Geathers 1-9; Jackson 1-8; Warren 1-4

GAME 7—CARDINALS 38 BEARS 21
BUSCH STADIUM—49,554—10/14/84

CHICAGO	7	7	7	0	—	21
ST. LOUIS	10	7	7	14	—	38

CARDINALS—Neil O'Donoghue 44-yd FG, 8 plays/53 yards. **BEARS**—Willie Gault 28-yd pass from Jim McMahon (Thomas kick), 5 plays/77 yards. **CARDINALS**—Randy Love 5-yd run (O'Donoghue kick), 8 plays/68 yards. **BEARS**—Walter Payton 1-yd run (Thomas kick), 4 plays/53 yards. **CARDINALS**—Ottis Anderson 9-yd run (O'Donoghue kick), 6 plays/75 yards. **BEARS**—Suhey 1-yd run (Thomas kick) 14 plays/79 yards. **CARDINALS**—Ottis Anderson 1-yd pass from Neil Lomax (O'Donoghue kick), 6 plays/70 yards. **Cardinals**—Lomax 9-yd run (O'Donoghue kick), 3 plays/11 yards. **CARDINALS**—Willard Harrell 1-yd run (O'Donoghue kick), 6 plays/32 yards.

TEAM STATISTICS	CARDINALS	BEARS
First Downs	23	20
Total Net Yards	354	370
Rushes/Net Yards	28/124	37/178
Net Passing	230	192
Pass Attempts/Completions	24/14	26/13
Had Intercepted	1	1
Punts/Average	3-35.3	4-34.3
Return Yardage	122	126
Penalties/Yards	4-30	10-74
Fumbles/Lost	0-0	2-2
Sacks/Yards	2-10	5-41
Possession Time	28:55	31:05

RUSHING

BEARS—Payton 23-100; McMahon 6-60; Suhey 8-18 **CARDINALS**—Anderson 19-82; Lomax 2-29; Love 2-6; Mitchell 1-5; Ferrell 2-2; Harrell 2-0

RECEIVING

BEARS—Suhey 5-42; Gault 3-84; McKinnon 3-65; Saldi 2-11 **CARDINALS**—Green 6-166; Mitchell 3-31; Tilley 2-57; Anderson 2-10; Marsh 1-7

PASSING

BEARS—McMahon 13-23-202, 1 TD; Lisch 0-2; Payton 0-1 **CARDINALS**—Lomax 14-24-271, 1 TD, 1 int.

INTERCEPTIONS

BEARS—Gayle 1 – 1 **CARDINALS**—Washington 1-10

SACKS

BEARS—Hampton 2-20; Bell 1-10; Dent 1-9; Wilson 1-2 **CARDINALS**—Greer 1-6; Galloway 1-4

GAME 8 BEARS 44 BUCCANEERS 9
Tampa Stadium—60,003—10/21/84

CHICAGO	14	6	7	17	—	44
TAMPA BAY	0	3	0	6	—	9

BEARS—Walter Payton 8-yd run (Thomas kick) 6 plays/57 yards **BEARS**—Payton 3-yd run (Thomas kick), 6 plays/45 yards **BUCCANEERS**—Obed Ariri 46-yd FG, 12 plays/47 yards. **BEARS**—Dennis McKinnon 32-yd pass from Jim McMahon (kick failed) 8 plays/78 yards. **BEARS**—Willie Gault 10-yd pass from McMahon (Thomas kick), 4 plays/23 yards. **BEARS**—Bob Thomas 49-yd FG, 11 plays/43 yards **BUCCANEERS**—Gerald Carter 4-yd pass from Steve DeBerg (kick failed), 9 plays/32 yards. **BEARS**—Brad Anderson 49-yd pass from McMahon (Thomas kick) 2 plays/45 yards. **BEARS**—Dennis Gentry 5-yd run (Thomas kick) 3 plays/37 yards.

TEAM STATISTICS	BUCCANEERS	BEARS
First Downs	17	23
Total Net Yards	292	427
Rushes/Net Yards	15-45	39-169
Net Passing	247	258
Pass Attempts/Completions	39-23	19-13
Had Intercepted	1	0
Punts/Average	3-47.7	2-40.5
Return Yardage	190	88
Penalties/Yards	15-104	16-114
Fumbles/Lost	4-1	0-0
Sacks/Yards	1-3	6-41
Possession Time	28:39	31:21

RUSHING

BEARS—Payton 20-72; Jordan 2-25; Suhey 5-24; McMahon 6-24; C. Thomas 2-9; Gentry 2-8; Hutchison 2-7 **BUCCANEERS**—Wilder 13-44; DeBerg 2-1

RECEIVING

BEARS—Payton 3-25; McKinnon 2-51; Moorehead 2-40; Gault 2-27; Anderson 1-49; McMahon 1-42; Dunsmore 1-20; Saldi 1-7 **BUCCANEERS**—Carter 10-109; House 5-61; Giles 4-63; T. Bell 2-26; Wilder 2-12; Dixon 1-17

PASSING

BEARS—McMahon 12-18-219, 3TD; Payton 1-1-42 **BUCCANEERS**—DeBerg 24-39-288, 1 TD, 1 int.

INTERCEPTIONS

BEARS—Frazier 1-14 **BUCCANEERS**—none

SACKS

BEARS—Dent 3-29; Hartenstine 2-11; Fencik 1-1 **BUCCANEERS**—Cotney 1-3

GAME 9—BEARS 16 VIKINGS 7
SOLDIER FIELD—57,517—10/28/84

MINNESOTA	0	0	0	7	—	7
CHICAGO	6	10	0	0	—	16

BEARS—Matt Suhey 2-yd run (kick failed), 14 plays/61 yards **BEARS**—Dennis McKinnon 18-yd pass from Jim McMahon (Thomas kick), 12 plays/71 yards. **BEARS**—Bob Thomas 19-yd FG, 6 plays/69 yards **VIKINGS**—Leo Lewis 22-yd pass from Wade Wilson (Stenerud kick), 6 plays/71 yards.

TEAM STATISTICS	VIKINGS	BEARS
First Downs	16	18
Total Net Yards	167	307
Rushes/Net Yards	16-41	40-129
Net Passing	126	178
Pass Attempts/Completions	36-20	27-16
Had Intercepted	2	0
Punts/Average	8-36.9	6-36.2
Return Yardage	74	72
Penalties/Yards	2-10	4-53
Fumbles/Lost	4-0	1-1
Sacks/Yards	1-2	11-101
Possession Time	26:16	33:44

RUSHING

BEARS—Payton 22-54; McMahon 6-39; Suhey 9-31; Finzer 1-5; C. Thomas 1-2; Moorehead 1 – 2 **VIKINGS**—Manning 4-20; Anderson 5-19; Brown 3-17; Nelson 4- – 15

RECEIVING

BEARS—Moorehead 3-64; Gault 3-36; Suhey 3-21; Payton 3-18; McKinnon 2-23; Dunsmore 1-16; C. Thomas 1-2 **VIKINGS**—Jordan 5-43; Lewis 3-71; White 3-51; Senser 3-28; Nelson 3-16; Jones 2-9; Brown 1-9

PASSING

BEARS—McMahon 16-26-180, 1 TD; Payton 0-1 **VIKINGS**—Manning 14-24-138, 1 int; Wilson 6-12-89, 1 TD, 1 int.

INTERCEPTIONS

BEARS—Richardson 1-7; Bell 1-7 **VIKINGS**—none

SACKS

BEARS—Dent 2½-20; Bell 2-15; Wilson 1½-17; Hampton 1½-13; McMichael 1½-17; Hartenstine 1-11; Harris 1-8 **VIKINGS**—Johnson 1-2

GAME 10—BEARS 17 RAIDERS 6
Soldier Field—59,858—11/4/84

L.A. RAIDERS	0	3	3	0	—	6
CHICAGO	7	7	0	3	—	17

BEARS—Walter Payton 18-yd run (Thomas kick) 4 plays/76 yards **BEARS**—Payton 8-yd run (Thomas kick) 3 plays/11 yards **RAIDERS**—Chris Bahr 44-yd FG, 6 plays/18 yards **RAIDERS**—Bahr 40-yd FG, 8 plays/40 yards. **BEARS**—Bob Thomas 29-yd FG, 4 plays/8 yards

TEAM STATISTICS	RAIDERS	BEARS
First Downs	12	13
Total Net Yards	181	259
Rushes/Net Yards	23-75	47-175
Net Passing	106	84
Pass Attempts/Completions	28-12	16-7
Had Intercepted	3	1
Punts/Average	5-44.4	7-41.1
Return Yardage	128	130
Penalties/Yards	1-5	4-40
Fumbles/Lost	4-2	2-0
Sacks/Yards	1-11	9-58
Possession Time	26:07	33:53

RUSHING

BEARS—Payton 27-111; C. Thomas 5-23; Suhey 8-17; Fuller 4-14; McMahon 3-10 RAIDERS—Allen 15-42; King 3-20; Hawkins 3-12; Wilson 1-3; Humm 1 −2

RECEIVING

BEARS—Payton 3-18; Moorehead 2-19; Gault 1-50; Suhey 1-11 RAIDERS—Christensen 5-61; Allen 4-53; Williams 3-50

PASSING

BEARS—McMahon 3-11-68, 1 int.; Fuller 4-5-27 RAIDERS—Wilson 7-19-70, 2 int.; Humm 4-7-56, 1 int.; Allen 1-2-38

INTERCEPTIONS

BEARS—Fencik 2-19; Frazier 1-33 RAIDERS—McElroy 1-31

SACKS

BEARS—Dent 4½-31; Wilson 1½-3; Hartenstine 1-10; Singletary 1-8; Harris 1-6 RAIDERS—Nelson ½-5½; Long ½-5½

GAME 11—RAMS 29 BEARS 13
Anaheim Stadium—62,021—11/11/84

CHICAGO	7	6	0	0	—	13
L.A. RAMS	0	6	6	17	—	29

BEARS—Steve Fuller 1-yd run (Thomas kick), 13 plays/63 yards BEARS—Bob Thomas 20-yd FG, 8 plays/49 yards. RAMS—Mike Lansford 21-yd FG, 11 plays/66 yards. BEARS—Thomas 52-yd FG, 8 plays/56 yards. RAMS—Lansford 45-yd FG, 4 plays/57 yards. RAMS—Henry Ellard 63-yd pass from Jeff Kemp (kick failed), 4 plays/74 yards. RAMS—Eric Dickerson 1-yd run (Lansford kick), 12 plays/95 yards. RAMS—Dickerson 4-yd run (Lansford kick), 2 plays/19 yards. RAMS—Lansford 29-yd FG, 6 plays/18 yards

TEAM STATISTICS	RAMS	BEARS
First Downs	17	15
Total Net Yards	370	321
Rushes/Net Yards	35-195	25-94
Net Passing	175	227
Pass Attempts/Completions	15-7	27-21
Had Intercepted	0	0
Punts/Average	2-44.5	3-39.7
Return Yardage	40	117
Penalties/Yards	3-10	8-63
Fumbles/Lost	0-0	3-1
Sacks/Yards	2-13	0-0
Possession Time	29:22	30:38

RUSHING

BEARS—Payton 13-60; Fuller 6-29; Suhey 3-11; C. Thomas 1-3; Baschnagel 1-0; McKinnon 1- −9 RAMS—Dickerson 28-149; Crutchfield 5-44; Kemp 1-2; Redden 1-0

RECEIVING

BEARS—Payton 7-78; Moorehead 3-44; McKinnon 3-39; Suhey 3-14; Dunsmore 2-33; C. Thomas 2-14; Gault 1-18 RAMS—Ellard 3-93; Brown 3-71; Farmer 1-11

PASSING

BEARS—Fuller 21-27-240 RAMS—Kemp 7-15-175, 1 TD

INTERCEPTIONS

BEARS—none RAMS—none

SACKS

BEARS—none RAMS—Wilcher 1-10; Owens ½-1½; Collins ½-1½

GAME 12—BEARS 16 LIONS 14
Soldier Field—54,911—11/18/84

DETROIT	0	7	7	0	—	14
CHICAGO	7	3	0	6	—	16

BEARS—Pat Dunsmore 1-yd pass from Steve Fuller (Thomas kick), 16 plays/77 yards. BEARS—Bob Thomas 24-yd FG, 6 plays/43 yards. LIONS—James Jones 1-yd run, 9 plays/67 yards. LIONS—Jeff Chadwick 7-yd pass from Gary Danielson (Murray kick), 11 plays/55 yards. BEARS—Thomas 52-yd FG, 8 plays/45 yards. BEARS—Thomas 19-yd FG, 10 plays/45 yards

TEAM STATISTICS	LIONS	BEARS
First Downs	11	17
Total Net Yards	167	331
Rushes/Net Yards	26/71	41/175
Net Passing	96	156
Pass Attempts/Completions	16-10	25-14
Had Intercepted	0	0
Punts/Average	5-26.8	3-33.7
Return Yardage	66	41
Penalties/Yards	4-25	1-12
Fumbles/Lost	2-1	2-0
Sacks/Yards	3-15	3-19
Possession Time	23:16	36:44

RUSHING

BEARS—Payton 29-66; C. Thomas 5-52; Fuller 3-37; Suhey 4-20 LIONS—J. Jones 17-42; Jenkins 5-16; D'Addio 3-11; Thompson 1-2

RECEIVING

BEARS—McKinnon 5-83; Payton 4-43; Moorehead 1-27; Gault 1-12; Cabral 1-7; Dunsmore 1-1; C. Thomas 1- −1 LIONS—Chadwick 3-32; Nichols 2-21; J. Jones 2-13; Thompson 1-35; Rubick 1-13; Jenkins 1-1

PASSING

BEARS—Fuller 13-23-164, 1 TD LIONS—Danielson 10-16-115, 1 TD

INTERCEPTIONS

BEARS—none LIONS—none

SACKS

BEARS—Dent 2-14; Hampton 1-5 LIONS—Cofer 1½-8½; Cobb ½-2½

GAME 13—BEARS 34 VIKINGS 3
METRODOME—56,881—11/25/84

CHICAGO	7	10	17	0	—	34
MINNESOTA	3	0	0	0	—	3

VIKINGS—Stenerud 20-yd FG, 11 plays/59 yards. BEARS—Willie Gault 30-yd pass from Steve Fuller (Thomas kick), 5 plays/57 yards BEARS—Bob Thomas 45-yd FG, 9 plays/28 yards. BEARS—Emery Moorehead 13-yd pass from Fuller (Thomas kick), 10 plays/75 yards. BEARS—Thomas 37-yd FG, 5 plays/41 yards. BEARS—Todd Bell 36-yd interception return (Thomas kick). BEARS—Walter Payton 2-yd run (Thomas kick), 7 plays/59 yards.

TEAM STATISTICS	VIKINGS	BEARS
First Downs	9	20
Total Net Yards	161	399
Rushes/Net Yards	19/90	42/229
Net Passing	71	170
Pass Attempts/Completions	31/12	25/16
Had Intercepted	2	0
Punts/Average	8-48.3	5-41.2
Return Yardage	188	137
Penalties/Yards	2-15	2-10
Fumbles/Lost	0-0	0-0
Sacks/Yards	1-8	3-19
Possession Time	23:19	36:41

RUSHING

BEARS—Payton 23-117; Jordan 4-25; Suhey 4-23; C. Thomas 2-20; Gentry 3-17; Hutchison 3-11; Fuller 2-9; Lisch 1-7 VIKINGS—Anderson 10-39; Nelson 4-31; T. Brown 5-20

RECEIVING

BEARS—Gault 3-53; Payton 2-33; Suhey 2-9; Anderson 1-17; Cameron 1-13; Baschnagel 1-13; Moorehead 1-13; Saldi 1-9; Hutchison 1-7; Jordan 1-6; C. Thomas 1-2 VIKINGS—Jordan 2-15; Lewis 2-14; Anderson 2-13; M. Jones 1-16; White 1-15; Collins 1-6; T. Brown 1-6; Senser 1-5; D. Nelson 1-0

PASSING

BEARS—Fuller 12-19-143, 2 TD; Lisch 4-6-35 VIKINGS—Wilson 12-31-90, 2 int.

INTERCEPTIONS

BEARS—Bell 2-39 VIKINGS—none

SACKS

BEARS—Hartenstine 1-3; McMichael 1-6; Singletary 1-10 VIKINGS—Martin 1-8

GAME 14—CHARGERS 20 BEARS 7
JACK MURPHY STADIUM—45,470—12/3/84

CHICAGO	0	0	7	0	—	7
SAN DIEGO	0	6	0	14	—	20

CHARGERS—Rolf Benirschke 48-yd FG, 6 plays/32 yards CHARGERS—Benirschke 27-yd FG, 8 plays/32 yards BEARS—Walter Payton 10-yd run (Thomas kick), 6 plays/34 yards CHARGERS—Bobby Duckworth 88-yd pass from Ed Lutyer (Benirschke kick), 2 plays/88 yards. CHARGERS—Lester Williams 66-yd pass interception (Benirschke kick)

TEAM STATISTICS	CHARGERS	BEARS
First Downs	9	18
Total Net Yards	319	312
Rushes/Net Yards	21/77	33/164
Net Passing	242	158
Pass Attempts/Completions	29-12	37-21
Had Intercepted	0	1
Punts/Average	8-38	11-37.5
Return Yardage	171-	116
Penalties/Yards	2-10	7-46
Fumbles/Lost	5-2	3-2
Sacks/Yards	5-37	4-33
Possession Time	22:51	37:09

RUSHING

BEARS—Payton 23-92; Lisch 5-51; Thomas 3-14; Suhey 2-7 CHARGERS—Jackson 18-59; McGee 1-11; Luther 2-7

RECEIVING

BEARS—Payton 4-38; Suhey 4-36; Gault 5-31; C. Thomas 3-16; Dunsmore 1-20; Anderson 1-11; Moorehead 1-7; Krenk 1-7; Baschnagel 1-14 CHARGERS—Duckworth 3-185; Chandler 3-47; Sievers 3-18; Joiner 1-12; Holohan 1-10; Jackson 1-3

PASSING

BEARS—Lisch 18-33-164, 1 int.; Fuller 3-4-21 CHARGERS—Luther 12-29-275, 1 TD

INTERCEPTIONS

BEARS—none CHARGERS—L. Williams 1-66

SACKS

BEARS—Duerson 2-17; Hampton 1½-11; McMichael ½-5 CHARGERS—Robinson 2-11; Ehin 1-10; B. R. Smith 1-9; L. Williams 1-7

GAME 15—PACKERS 20 BEARS 14
SOLDIER FIELD—59,374—12/9/84

GREEN BAY	0	7	6	7	—	20
CHICAGO	0	0	7	7	—	14

PACKERS—Ed West 3-yd pass from Rich Campbell (Del Greco kick), 4 plays/37 yards. BEARS—Matt Suhey 2-yd pass from Payton (Thomas kick), 4 plays/14 yards. PACKERS—Del Rodgers 97-yd kickoff return (Del Greco kick). BEARS—Payton 7-yd run (Thomas kick), 6 plays/33 yards. PACKERS—Phil Epps 43-yd pass from Campbell (Del Greco kick) 6 plays/71 yards

TEAM STATISTICS	PACKERS	BEARS
First Downs	17	25
Total Net Yards	287	301
Rushes/Net Yards	30-110	51-228
Net Passing	177	73

Pass Attempts/Completions	31-13	25-11
Had Intercepted	2	2
Punts/Average	6-42.5	6-41.8
Return Yardage	155	98
Penalties/Yards	6-59	5-30
Fumbles/Lost	0-0	4-3
Sacks/Yards	5-28	3-23
Possession Time	24:25	35:35

RUSHING

BEARS—Payton 35-175; Suhey 7-26; Lisch 6-23; Gentry 1-2; C. Thomas 1-2 PACKERS—Ivery 12-50; Ellis 9-28; Lofton 1-19; Huckleby 1-10; Campbell 2-2; Crouse 2-1; Wright 3-0

RECEIVING

BEARS—Suhey 5-34; Moorehead 4-53; Dunsmore 2-14 PACKERS—Epps 3-65; Coffman 2-33; Lofton 2-28; Crouse 2-27; Ivery 2-27; Ellis 1-17; West 1-3

PASSING

BEARS—Lisch 10-23-99, 1 int.; Payton 1-4-2, 1 TD, 1 int. PACKERS—Campbell 9-19-125, 2 TD, 2 int; Wright 4-10-75; Ellis 0-1; Scribner 0-1

INTERCEPTIONS

BEARS—Fencik 1-19; Duerson 1-9 PACKERS—Flynn 2-3

SACKS

BEARS—Dent 2-12; Hampton 1-11 PACKERS—Douglass 3-16; Martin 1-12; Carreker 1-0

GAME 16—BEARS 30 LIONS 13
SILVERDOME—53,252—12/16/84

CHICAGO	0	14	3	13	—	30
DETROIT	3	3	0	7	—	13

LIONS—Eddie Murray 52-yd FG, 4 plays/2 yards. BEARS—Calvin Thomas 1-yd run (Thomas kick), 7 plays/46 yards. LIONS—Murray 45-yd FG, 6 plays/14 yards. BEARS—Greg Landry 1-yd run (Thomas kick), 6 plays/14 yards. BEARS—Thomas 30-yd FG, 9 plays/36 yards. BEARS—Thomas 35-yd FG, 6 plays/36 yards. BEARS—Willie Gault 55-yd pass from Landry (Thomas kick), 2 plays/54 yards. BEARS—Thomas 42-yd FG, 6 plays/36 yards. LIONS—James Jones 4-yd pass from Eric Hipple (Murray kick) 9 plays/83 yards

TEAM STATISTICS	LIONS	BEARS
First Downs	13	13
Total Net Yards	196	293
Rushes/Net Yards	15/47	43/94
Net Passing	149	199
Pass Attempts/Completions	38/14	21/11
Had Intercepted	1	3
Punts/Average	9-41.8	5-42.8
Return Yardage	179	168
Penalties/Yards	5-57	3-15
Fumbles/Lost	3-1	1-0
Sacks/Yards	0-0	12-100
Possession Time	25:12	34:48

RUSHING

BEARS—Payton 22-62; Gentry 4-37; C. Thomas 6-4; Suhey 5-3; Landry 2-1; Lisch 3- – 4; LIONS—Jones 4-16; Witkowski 2-13; Jenkins 5-11; Bussey 3-7; Black 1-0

RECEIVING

BEARS—Moorehead 5-86; Payton 2-25; Gentry 2-9; Gault 1-55; Krenk 1-24; LIONS—Chadwick 5-82; Nichols 4-92; Thompson 2-38; J. Jones 2-18; Bussey 1-19

PASSING

BEARS—Landry 11-20-199, 1 TD, 3 int.; Lisch 0-1 LIONS—Hipple 11-27-187, 1 TD, 1 int.; Witkowski 3-10-62; J. Jones 0-1

INTERCEPTIONS

BEARS—Bell 1-0 LIONS—Graham 2-7; Watkins 1-0

SACKS

BEARS—McMichael 2½-18; Hampton 2-13; Wilson 2-28; Waechter 2-7; Dent 1-9; Duerson 1-10; Singletary 1-11; Keys ½-4 LIONS—none

101

DIVISIONAL PLAYOFF
BEARS 23 REDSKINS 19
RFK STADIUM—55,431—12/30/84

CHICAGO	0	10	13	0	—	23
WASHINGTON	3	0	14	2	—	19

REDSKINS—Mark Moseley 25-yd FG, 13 plays/56 yards. **BEARS**—Bob Thomas 34-yd FG, 6 plays/46 yards. **BEARS**—Pat Dunsmore 19-yd pass from Walter Payton (Thomas kick) 6 plays/65 yards. **BEARS**—Willie Gault 75-yd pass from Steve Fuller (kick failed), 2 plays/80 yards. **REDSKINS**—John Riggins 1-yd run (Moseley kick), 10 plays/74 yards. **BEARS**—Dennis McKinnon 16-yd pass from Fuller (Thomas kick) 9 plays/77 yards. **REDSKINS**—Riggins 1-yd run (Moseley kick), 5 plays/36 yards. **REDSKINS**—Finzer safety

TEAM STATISTICS	REDSKINS	BEARS
First Downs	22	13
Total Net Yards	336	310
Rushes/Net Yards	27-93	35-114
Net Passing	243	196
Pass Attempts/Completions	42-22	17-10
Had Intercepted	1	0
Punts/Average	5-36.8	5-39.4
Return Yardage	29	17
Penalties/Yards	7-55	6-34
Fumbles/Lost	3-2	2-1
Sacks/Yards	5-34	7-49
Possession Time	29:36	30:24

RUSHING

BEARS—Payton 24-104; Suhey 7-7; Fuller 2-5; C. Thomas 1-5; Finzer 1--7 **REDSKINS**—Riggins 21-50; Theismann 5-38; Washington 1-5

RECEIVING

BEARS—McKinnon 4-72; Gault 1-75; Suhey 1-33; Dunsmore 1-19; C. Thomas 1-13; Payton 1-12; Moorehead 1-6 **REDSKINS**—Monk 10-122; Muhammad 5-62; Didier 4-85; Washington 2-12; Warren 1-11

PASSING

BEARS—Fuller 9-15-211, 2TD; Payton 1-2-19, 1 TD **REDSKINS**—Theismann 22-42-292, 1 int

INTERCEPTIONS

BEARS—Richardson 1-0 **REDSKINS**—none

SACKS

BEARS—Dent 3-23; Hampton 2-15; McMichael 1-6; Waechter 1-5 **REDSKINS**—Milot 3½-20; Manley 1-6; Grant ½-8

NFC CHAMPIONSHIP GAME
49ers 23 BEARS 0
Candlestick Park—61,040—1/6/85

CHICAGO	0	0	0	0	—	0
SAN FRANCISCO	3	3	7	10	—	23

49ers—Ray Wersching 21-yd FG, 10 plays/73 yards. **49ers**—Wersching 22-yd FG, 13 plays/65 yards. **49ers**—Wendell Tyler 10-yd run (Wersching kick) 5 plays/35 yards **49ers**—Freddie Solomon 10-yd pass from Joe Montana (Wersching kick) 8 plays/86 yards. **49ers**—Wersching 34-yd FG, 8 plays/36 yards

TEAM STATISTICS	49ers	BEARS
First Downs	25	13
Total Net Yards	387	186
Rushes/Net Yards	29-159	32-149
Net Passing	228	37
Pass Attempts/Completions	35-19	22-13
Had Intercepted	2	1
Punts/Average	3-39.0	7-43.1
Return Yardage	84	84
Penalties/Yards	3-20	7-50
Fumbles/Lost	1-0	1-0
Sacks/Yards	9-50	3-8
Possession Time	28:07	31:53

RUSHING

BEARS—Payton 22-92; Fuller 6-39; Suhey 3-16; C. Thomas 1-2 **49ers**—Tyler 10-68; Craig 8-44; Montana 5-22; Harmon 3-18; Ring 2-5; Cavanaugh 1-2

RECEIVING

BEARS—Suhey 4-11; McKinnon 3-48; Payton 3-11; Moorehead 2-14; Dunsmore 1-3 **49ers**—Solomon 7-73; D. Clark 4-83; Wilson 2-25; Tyler 2-22; Francis 2-20; Nehemiah 1-10; Harmon 1-3

PASSING

BEARS—Fuller 13-22-87, 1 int; **49ers**—Montana 18-34-233, 1 TD, 2 int; Cavanaugh 1-1-3

INTERCEPTIONS

BEARS—Fencik 2-5 **49ers**—Hicks 1-0

SACKS

BEARS—Wilson 1-2; Keys 1-0; McMichael ½-3; Hampton ½-3 **49ers**—Carter 2-8; Johnson 2-19; Board 1-8; Dean 1-4; Pillers ½-0; Williamson ½-0; Team 1-9

BEARS COACHES

MIKE DITKA, Head Coach

"I think it's important that this game go to the man who deserves it the most, and that's Mr. Halas. Somewhere, he's smiling pretty good right now." (Mike Ditka after Bears' 34-3 win over Vikings November 25 giving Chicago NFC Central title).

Mike Ditka, who had trod the frozen turf of Wrigley Field in victory as a tight end on the Bears' last championship in 1963, put it into historical perspective when he awarded the game ball to the late "Papa Bear" following the Bears' 1984 NFC Central Division clincher. It was Halas who founded the team and the league, Halas who coached the NFL champions of 1963 and Halas who hired Ditka to be head coach in 1981 to lead the Bears out of mediocrity to their traditional place of respect.

In 1984, Mike Ditka paid back the man who hired him three years ago by leading the Bears to their first divisional title and first championship of any kind in 21 years. Their 11-7 record included a divisional playoff win over the Washington Redskins (23-19) and an appearance against the world champion San Francisco 49ers in the NFC championship game (23-0 loss). But more important, 1984 was a year in which Mike Ditka silenced the critics who openly questioned his style of coaching, his inexperience and leadership ability.

The 45-year old Ditka, the Bears' 10th head coach, owns a 22-21 record since taking the helm on January 20, 1982. Perhaps the mark that is more indicative of the direction that the Bears have taken in the last two years is his winning 16 of the last 24 games, including nine of the last 11 home games.

Ditka is a 24-year veteran of the NFL as both a player and coach. He has been in league playoffs in 14 of those seasons and been a member of teams that have been NFC champions five times and NFL champions three times. While serving nine years as an offensive coach under Tom Landry at Dallas, the Cowboys were in the playoffs in all but one season and won NFC

championships in 1975, 1977, and 1978 with the NFL crown following the 1977 season.

Born October 18, 1939, in Carnegie, Pennsylvania, Ditka enjoyed a 12-year NFL playing career with the Chicago Bears (1961-66), the Philadelphia Eagles (1967-68), and the Dallas Cowboys (1969-72), as a tight end. During those seasons, the Bears were in the playoffs once and the Cowboys four times. The Bears won the NFL championship over the New York Giants 14-10, a game in which Ditka made a key third quarter catch that set up the winning touchdown. In 1970, the Cowboys were the NFC champs and after the 1977 season, they were NFL Champions.

Ditka's versatility brought him college all-American honors in 1960 at Pittsburgh where he was a solid two-way performer, defensively at end and middle linebacker, offensively as a receiver and blocker. He was also one of the nation's leading collegiate punters with a three-year average of 40 yards per boot. He starred in the East-West game and was voted the outstanding lineman of the Hula Bowl.

The Bears first-round draft choice in 1961 (5th pick), Ditka was the NFL rookie of the Year, all-NFL 1961-64, and played in five Pro Bowls (1962-66). In 1964, he set an NFL record for tight ends by catching 75 passes in a Bear uniform. The mark was broken in 1980 by San Diego's Kellen Winslow.

Ditka joined the Cowboys' coaching staff in 1973. In addition to handling the Dallas special teams, he has coached Pro Bowl performers at each receiver position—wideouts Drew Pearson and Tony Hill plus tight end Bill Joe Dupree.

Mike is actively involved in Little City Foundation, the Fellowship of Christian Athletes and Sports Teams Organized for the Prevention of Drug Abuse. He and his wife Diana have four children: Mike (24), Mark (21), Megan (21) and Matthew (18).

BUDDY RYAN, Defensive Coordinator

Gaining national recognition as one of the most innovative minds in football history, Buddy Ryan enters his eighth season as the Bears' defensive coordinator.

Ryan's 1984 unit developed into one of the best defenses in NFL annals, leading the entire league in fewest yards allowed (241.3 per game) and fewest rushing yards allowed (86.1) while establishing a NFL record 72 sacks. Despite their reputation, as vicious hitters, the Bears defense was the least penalized team in the NFL in 1984. The Bears pass defense ranked second in the league, just 33 yards shy of the top spot and the distinction of leading the league in all three major defensive categories—a feat accomplished by just four teams in NFL history. In Ryan's seven years with the Bears, the defense has ranked in the NFL's top ten five times.

Ryan, who also handles the linebackers in addition to his duties as co-ordinator, is a strategist who employs multiple variations of alignments and coverages. His popular "46" defense is a 5-1-5 set that is named after its original middleman, former safety Doug Plank, who wore uniform number 46. The scheme forces offensive lineman into one-on-one blocking and opens up avenues for blitzing.

A 17-year veteran of NFL coaching, Ryan joined the Bears in 1978 after coaching the Minnesota Vikings defensive line for two years. From 1968 through 1975, he was on the defensive staff of the New York Jets under Hall of Fame coach Weeb Ewbank. Ryan coached in Super Bowls with both teams making him one of just a handful of coaches to have been to Super Bowls with two different teams.

The stocky Oklahoman was a four-year letterman at Oklahoma State from 1952-55 as an offensive guard before beginning his coaching career as defensive coordinator at the University of Buffalo from 1961-1965. He served in a similar role the next two years with Vanderbilt (1966) and the University of Pacific (1967) before joining the Jets.

Born February 17, 1934, in Frederick, Oklahoma, Ryan is an outdoor enthusiast and owner of a horse farm in Kentucky where he spends much of his spare time. He and his wife, Joan, have three children and reside in Lincolnshire.

ED HUGHES, Offensive Coordinator

If there is one thing that Ed Hughes deserves in 1985, it is the opportunity to work with one healthy quarterback. Due to the woes to QBs Jim McMahon and back-up Steve Fuller, the Bears used a total of six different signal-callers at one time or another last season, including the NFL's all-time leading rusher, Walter Payton.

Despite the QB misfortunes, the Bears again led the NFL in total rushing for the second year in a row and finished a respectable seventh in overall offense in 1984. In addition, the Hughes-led offense held the edge in possession time in each of their 18 games and were outgained by opponents only twice during the 1984 campaign. The Bears outgained their opponents by 1,577 yards last season and out-rushed foes by a remarkable total of 1,597 yards. With a healthy Jim McMahon back in the QB saddle, Hughes hopes to have the Bears amongst the league-leading passing attacks.

Hughes, 57, came to the Bears February 1, 1982, from the Philadelphia Eagles and it marked a reunion with head coach Mike Ditka. They were coaching mates in Dallas (1973-76). During those years, the Cowboys made the playoffs three times including a Super Bowl trip.

Prior to joining the Bears, Hughes was an offensive assistant with the Philadelphia Eagles after serving as offensive coordinator for the New Orleans Saints (1978-80), where he was a coaching mate of Dick Stanfel's.

Born October 23, 1927, in Buffalo, New York, Hughes played collegiately at Tulsa and professionally for the L.A. Rams and New York Giants as a defensive back. He began his coaching career with the Dallas Texans (1960-62). He also coached with the Denver Broncos (1963), the Washington Redskins (1964-67), the St. Louis Cardinals (1972), and the Detroit Lions (offensive coordinator, 1977).

Ed and his wife, Nancy, have five children and reside in Libertyville.

JIM DOOLEY, Research and Quality Control

Seeing the Chicago Bears win the NFC Central division title and advance in the playoffs last season was something special for Jim Dooley. Because he was part of the Bears' last successful season in 1963 when the Chicagoans captured the NFL crown. It brought back some fond memories and comparisons for the veteran NFL coach and administrator. Dooley, 55, was an offensive coach on the Bears' last championship team, a squad that like the 1984 Bears, was known for its ball control offense and stout defense.

Dooley enters his 25th season with the Chicago Bears and has worn many hats since joining the organization as a player in 1952. His career with the Bears includes time spent as a player (1952-55, 57, 59-62), offensive coach (1963-65), defensive coach (1966-67), head coach (1968-71) and in his current position since 1981. He is currently in charge of studying and evaluating all players and teams in the league. His reports are used in the development of the Bears' weekly game plan.

After starring as a halfback for Miami (FL), Dooley was a first round draft pick of the Bears in 1952. He was used on defense as a rookie and led the team in interceptions. After shifting to flanker on offense in 1953, he led the team in pass receptions, an achievement he also reached in 1957 and 1959.

Dooley played nine seasons for the Bears and is the club's sixth all-time leading receiver. His playing days were interrupted twice: when he served the Air Force in 1955-56 and in '58 when he was sidelined with a broken ankle.

With Dooley as offensive coach for the Bears' in 1965, the team set an all-time scoring record with 409 points.

Dooley was born February 8, 1930, in Stoutsville, Missouri. He and his wife have five children and reside in Chicago.

DALE HAUPT, Defensive Line Coach

Like photographs, numbers and statistics don't lie. And the statistics and ranking that the 1984 Bears' defense amassed clearly indicate that last season was a year in which the Bears' defense came of age. They finished the season ranked number one in fewest yards yielded in the NFL and on top of that set an NFL standard for most sacks in a season (72). The Bears broke the previous mark of 67 set by the 1967 Oakland Raiders. A principal architect behind this record-setting defense is line coach Dale Haupt. Haupt's front four accounted for 50.5 of the Bears' 72 sacks, were instrumental in the Bears' league-leading yield of 86.1 yards rushing per game, as well as their number one rankings in QB sack percentage, opponent first downs allowed and third down efficiency. The Bears' tenacious front line was also influential in the team finishing second in opponent passing yards per game (155.4), third in average gain per pass play and second in yards yielded per defensive play.

Haupt enters his eighth season with the Bears, and since arriving in 1978, the Bears defense has averaged 45 sacks a year. Born April 12, 1929 at Manitowoc, Wisconsin, the three-time university letterman spent six years tutoring linemen in the Atlantic Coast Conference prior to joining the Bears. His one year at Duke was preceded by a five-year stint at North Carolina State (1972-76). He coached in the 1968 and 1971 Tangerine Bowls, the 1972 and 1975 Peach Bowls, the 1973 Liberty Bowl, and the 1974 Astro-Blubonnet Bowl.

Haupt began his college coaching career at Tennessee where he was head freshman coach from 1960-63. He joined the staff at Iowa State (1964-65) for two seasons before a six-year tour at the University of Richmond.

He and his wife, Francis, have two children and reside in Libertyville.

STEVE KAZOR, Special Teams

The man in charge of assembling the Bears kamikaze units is Steve Kazor, who enters his fourth year on the Bears staff.

Handpicked by Mike Ditka upon the head coach's arrival in 1982, Kazor helped veteran kicker Bob Thomas enjoy his best season in 1984, while rookie Dave Finzer developed into an effective punter. Under Kazor's guidance, Thomas kicked 22 of 28 field goals while Finzer led the NFL with 26 punts inside the 20-yard line. Kazor's challenge this season will be to upgrade the team's effectiveness on punt and kickoff returns—an area that was inconsistent last season partly due to injuries.

Kazor joined the Bears prior to the 1982 season after spending three years in the Dallas Cowboys scouting department where he worked for Gil Brandt. Kazor also has been an assistant coach and recruiting coordinator at Colorado State (1975), Wyoming (1976) and Texas-El Paso (1979-80). He was head coach at Emporia College in 1973 where he was the youngest college coach in the country.

Kazor also held assistant coaching jobs at Texas-Arlington (1974), Texas-

Austin (1976-79) and Westminster College (1970), where he played nose tackle for four years (1966-69) as a collegian.

Born February 24, 1948 in New Kensington, Pennsylvania. Kazor and his wife, Colleen, have two children and reside in Vernon Hills.

JIM LaRUE, Defensive Secondary

Beginning his 35th year of coaching and eighth with the Bears is secondary coach Jim LaRue.

A coach of expertise, having tutored virtually every position in football, LaRue's knowledge has paid dividends for a Bears defense which has ranked among the Best in the NFL including a to-ranked position last season. Both of LaRue's safeties, Gary Fencik and Todd Bell, have made Pro Bowl appearances under LaRue's tenure, while cornerback Leslie Frazier was enroute to that plateau in 1984 before suffering a foot injury which bothered him the remainder of the season. In addition, LaRue has developed a rookie cornerback in each of the past two seasons to assume a starting role—Mike Richardson in 1983 and Shaun Gayle last season.

LaRue joined the Bears in 1978 after serving two seasons as an offensive assistant with the Buffalo Bills. Prior to entering the NFL in 1975, he was an assistant coach at six major colleges and a successful head coach at the University of Arizona.

As the Wildcats boss for eight years (1959-66), LaRue posted a 41-37-2 record and compiled an 8-1-1 mark as independent in '61 and shared the WAC title in 1964. The 8-1-1 mark is the best one-year record in Arizona football history.

A two-way halfback in college at Carson-Newman, Duke and Maryland during WWII years, LaRue is a Duke mathematics graduate, who holds a master's degree in education from Maryland.

Born August 11, 1925 in Clinton, Oklahoma, LaRue and his wife, Betty, have three children and reside in Libertyville.

TED PLUMB, Receivers

Developing the Bears' young wide receivers and utilizing the talents of a veteran corps of tight ends will be Ted Plumb's task in 1985. Plumb, who enters his sixth season as the team's receivers coach, is looking for consistency in the team's aerial attack that showed flashes of brilliance in 1984.

A veteran coach highly respected among his peers in the NFL, Plumb began his pro coaching career in 1974 as offensive backfield coach of the New York Giants. After three years, Plumb left to join Leeman Bennett's Atlanta Falcons as quarterback/receivers coach until joining the Bears in 1980.

Plumb played wide receiver on Baylor teams that played in the 1960 Gator Bowl and 1961 Gotham Bowl where they split with Utah State (24-9) and Florida (13-12 loss).

After playing one season with the Buffalo Bills in 1962, Plumb coached five years in the high school and junior college ranks before joining the TCU staff in 1968. After three years with the Horned Frogs, Plumb coached at Tulsa (1971) and Kansas (1972-73) before joining the Giants.

Raised in northern California, Plumb was born August 20, 1939 at Reno, Nevada. He and his wife, Marianna, have three children and reside in Buffalo Grove.

JOHNNY ROLAND, Offensive Backfield

After an outstanding eight-year career as a player, Johnny Roland begins his seventh year in NFL coaching.

Since joining the Bears in 1983, Roland has directed a ground attack that has paced the NFL in each of his two years with Chicago. Roland has utilized the talents of fullbacks Matt Suhey and Calvin Thomas to complement all-pro Walter Payton.

A fourth-round draft choice of the St. Louis Cardinals in 1965, Roland's playing career included trips to the Pro Bowl in both 1967 and 1968. He finished his career with 3,750 yards on 1,015 carries and 28 TD's; 153 receptions, 1,430 yards and 6 TD's.

Born May 21, 1943, in Corpus Christi, Texas, Roland was a versatile collegian at Missouri, starring as a running back and cornerback from 1963-

BRAD ANDERSON 86

Wide Receiver	Arizona	2nd Year
Ht: 6-2	Wt: 196	Born: 1/21/61,
		Glendale, AZ

Acquisition: Was selected in eighth round (212th player) of the 1984 draft. **1984 SEASON:** Appeared in 13 games as back-up WR including 2 playoff tilts . . . Made 2 starts in place of injured Dennis McKinnon . . . Made first career start vs. Green Bay (12/9) . . . Caught 49-yard TD pass from Jim McMahon @ Tampa Bay (10/21) and earned game ball . . . Was also used as special teamer . . . **Games Played: 13 Games Started: 2.** **COLLEGIATE, PERSONAL:** Was selected All-Pac 1st team senior year at Arizona . . . Was honorable mention All-America . . . Participated in East-West Shrine Game . . . Caught 6 passes for 85 yards and a TD in Blue-Gray game . . . Led Wildcats with 44 catches for 870 yards and 5 TD's in '82 . . . Caught 50-yard TD pass against Washington, a 69-yard TD pass against Pacific, a 72-yard pass against USC and 65-yard TD pass vs. ASU . . . Redshirted in '80 after transferring from BYU . . . Was WR on BYU's '79 WAC championship team . . . Member of National Honor Society . . . Hobbies include golf, tennis and water sports . . . Given name Brad Steward Anderson . . . Has a BA degree in accounting.

ANDERSON'S PRO STATS

		RECEIVING			RUSHING			
YEAR	No.	Yds.	Avg.	TD	No.	Yds.	TD	Gms/Sts
1984	3	77	25.7	1	0	0	0	13/2

ANDERSON'S SINGLE GAME HIGHS

Long Catch: 49 (TD) @ Tampa Bay (10/21). Most Caught: 1 @ TB (10/21), @ Minn. (11/25), @ S.D. (12/3). Most Yds. Rec.: 49 @ TB (10/21) (1 catch).

65. As a senior, Roland earned all-American honors.

In 1974, Roland assisted his former college coach, Dan Devine, on the Green Bay Packers' staff and followed Devine to Notre Dame in 1975. Roland was on the staff of the Philadelphia Eagles from 1976-78 before entering private business until his assignment with the Bears.

Roland has three children and resides in Vernon Hills.

DICK STANFEL, Offensive Line

Few coaches in the NFL have a resume that can match that of Dick Stanfel. Often described by Mike Ditka as "the best offensive line coach in football," Stanfel begins his fifth year with the Bears.

In 1984, Stanfel's line cleared the way for the NFL's top ground attack for the second straight year. Equally impressive is the fact that he did it with a line that had no one with more than four years of experience.

Stanfel joined the Bears in 1981 after serving as the New Orleans Saints interim head coach for the final four games of 1980. He began his coaching career at Notre Dame (1959-62) and spent one season (1963) on the California staff before taking his initial pro coaching assignment with the Philadelphia Eagles in 1964.

After seven seasons with the Eagles, Stanfel joined the 49ers as line coach in 1971 and stayed there until joining the Saints in 1976.

As a player, Stanfel followed a collegiate career at the University of San Francisco with nine years in the pros. A second round draft pick by Detroit, Stanfel played four years with the Lions and was the league's most valuable player in 1954 when the Lions won the NFL Championship. The four-time all-pro guard also played with the Washington Redskins (1956-58).

One of Stanfel's top accolades as a coach came in 1979 when his offensive line at New Orleans allowed a record low 17 sacks during a 16-game season.

Born July 20, 1927 at San Francisco, Stanfel has three children and resides in Libertyville.

Dan Hampton, the hub of the Bear defensive line, fights off a would-be blocker. The seven-year pro from Arkansas is coming off knee surgery and a slow, painful rehabilitation.

BRIAN BASCHNAGEL 84

Wide Receiver — Ohio State
Ht: 6-0 Wt: 193
10th Year
Born: 1/8/54, Kingston, NY

Acquisition: Third round draft choice in 1976.

1984 SEASON: Appeared in all 16 games including 1 post-season affairs . . . Started for injured Dennis McKinnon at Minnesota (11/25) and San Diego (12/3) . . . Finished 2nd in special team tackles with 7 . . . Recovered fumble in loss to Dallas **Games Played: (season)** 16

Games Started: 2

PRO CAREER: Enters 10th season with the Bears . . . Begins the season 14th on the all-time Bears receiving list in catches (134) and 12th on the all-time receiving list in yardage (2,024) . . . Best one-season out-put was '81 when he caught 34 passes for 554 yards and 3 TD's . . . Caught first pro TD pass (54 yards) from Walter Payton (10/21/79) at Minnesota . . . Led Bear kickoff return men in 1st 3 seasons . . . Led NFL in KOR yards as a rookie with 754 . . . Set a Bear standard with 8 KOR's at Houston (11/6/77) . . . Was special team captain as a rookie . . . Voted Brian Piccolo Award by veterans after '76 season . . . 2nd unit PFWA all-rookie selection . . . Began Bear career as cornerback.

COLLEGIATE, PERSONAL: Two-time academic all-America as wingback at OSU . . . Played in 4 Rose Bowls . . . Made 670 rushing yards at OSU, 794 receiving, 406 returning kickoffs and 167 returning punts . . . Owned a 7.8 yard per carry average . . . Played in last college All-Star game won by Steelers 24-0 . . . Also played in Hula and Japan Bowls . . . Given name is Brian Dale Baschnagel . . . Married (Mindy) . . . NCAA Football Foundation Hall of Fame Scholar Athlete . . . Involved in Big Brothers, Sports Teams Organized for Prevention of Drug Abuse, Red Cloud Athletic Fund, Chicago Board of Education, Chicago Boys Club, Brian Piccolo Cancer Research Fund and Multiple Sclerosis Society . . . Was named one of top 10 outstanding Young men in Illinois in 1984 by the Jaycees . . . Graduated from Pittsburgh North Allegheny High School where he was prep all-America . . . Appointed Bears alternate player representative to FNLPA . . . BA degree in finance.

BASCHNAGEL'S PRO STATS

Year	Gms/Sts	Receiving No.	Yds.	TD	Punt Returns No.	Yds.	TD	Kickoff Returns No.	Yds.	Avg.	TD
1984	16/3	6	53	0	0	0	0	0	0	0	0
1983	16/4	5	70	2	0	0	0	3	42	14.0	0
1982	9/9	12	194	3	0	0	0	0	0	0.0	0
1981	16/15	34	554	3	0	0	0	2	34	17.0	0
1980	16/15	28	396	2	0	0	0	0	0	0.0	0
1979	16/11	30	452	2	0	0	0	12	260	21.6	0
1978	16/1	2	29	0	1	2	0	20	455	22.7	0
1977	10/4	4	50	0	3	54	0	23	557	24.2	1
1976	14/12	13	226	0	2	2	0	29	754	26.0	0
Career	129/73	134	2,024	9	6	58	0	89	2,102	23.6	1

KURT BECKER 79

Guard — Michigan
Ht: 6-5 Wt: 267
4th Year
Born: 12/22/58, Aurora, IL

Acquisition: Sixth round draft choice in 1982.

1984 SEASON: Steady performer at right guard, where he started all 16 games including both playoff contests . . . Missed all preseason games due to hyperextended foot . . . Earned game ball vs. New Orleans in game which Payton broke Jim Brown's NFL rushing record . . . **Games Started (season):** 16 **Games Played:** 16

PRO CAREER: Begins 4th year with Bears with string of 30 consecutive starts at left guard . . . Played in final 5 games of the '82 season after spending the first 2 games of the year on inactive list.

COLLEGIATE, PERSONAL: Was a consensus All-America and Lombardi Trophy semi-finalist after 4 years at Michigan under Bo Schembechler . . . Was college teammate of current Bear offensive lineman Stefan

Humphries . . . Wolverines were ranked 13th nationally in rushing offense in his senior year . . . Enter Michigan at 216 pounds . . . All-America Strength team member . . . Redshirted in '77 . . . Given name Kurt Frank Becker . . . Was a three-sport standout at Aurora (IL) East High . . . Earned business communications degree at Michigan . . . Involved in Red Cloud Athletic Fund and Brian Piccolo Cancer Research Fund . . . BA degree in business administration.

BECKER'S PRO STATS

TOTAL GAMES: 37; 1982 (5), 1983 (16), 1984 (16). TOTAL STARTS: 30, 1983 14, 1984 (16).

TODD BELL   25   5th Year

Safety	Ohio State	Born: 11/28/58,
Ht: 6-1	Wt: 205	Middletown, OH

Acquisition: Fourth round draft choice in 1981.

1984 SEASON: Made Pro Bowl team as starter for first time in career . . . Names to PFW all-NFC defensive team, AP, UPI second team, Seagram sports All-Pro team . . . Used in various roles in Bear defensive alignments including stint as cornerback in playoffs due to injury to Leslie Frazier . . . Led Bear secondary in sacks (4.5) . . . Earned game ball in win over Minnesota (11/25) including 36-yard TD return (2nd career) . . . Also had interception in season finale at Detroit (12/16) . . . Earned game ball in season opening win over TB (9/2) . . . Finished 3rd on team in tackles (77), 3rd in solos (58), 3rd in intercepts (4); also had 2 fumble recoveries . . .

Games Played: 16 Games Started: 16.

PRO CAREER: Begins 5th year with the Bears . . . Owns 4th longest Bear interception off Eric Hipple 11/11/82 (92 yards, TD) . . . Finished 2nd in special team tackles with 28 in '81 . . . Was 95th player selected in the '81 draft.

COLLEGIATE, PERSONAL: UPI, NEA 2nd team all-America at OSU . . . Was twice selected to the UPI 1st team all-Big Ten . . . National Strength Coaches Association All-Strength Team . . . Played in Hula and Japan Bowls . . . Raced 20 yards with blocked punt to score winning TD in 18-15 win over Michigan in '79 . . . Win sent Buckeyes to Rose Bowl . . . Stripped Charles White of ball to save TD in '80 Rose Bowl (USC 17, OSU 16) . . . Made 3 interceptions including 1 for a TD return . . . Given name Todd Anthony Bell . . . Father is minister . . . Was prep all-America linebacker at Middletown (OH) High . . . Track star and state long jump champ for 3 straight years . . . Broke Jesse Owens' '33 prep record in long jump with 25' 5" leap . . . Finished 3rd in state 100-yard dash with a time of 9:07 . . . Working on degree in physical education major.

BELL'S PRO STATS

Year	Interceptions			Tcks/Solo	Fum. Rec.	Pass Def.	Force Fum.	Sack/-Yds.	Games/Starts
	No.	Yds.	TD						
1984	4	46	1	77/58	2	5	1	4.5/-37	16/16
1983	0	0	0	115/92	1	6	1	3/-30	15/15
1982	0	0	0	13/12	;	4		1/9	9/0
1981	1	92	1	32/22		5	2	0/0	16/0
Career	5	138	2	237/184	4	20	5	8.5/-76	56/31

BELL'S SINGLE GAME HIGHS

Most Tackles: 8 (twice) vs. Minnesota (10/28); vs. Redskins (10/11/81).
Most Solos: 7 (twice) vs. Minnesota (10/28); vs. Redskins (10/11/81). Long
Interceptions: 92 (TD) vs. Lions (11/22/81) off Eric Hipple.

MARK BORTZ   62   2nd Year

Guard	Iowa	Born: 2/12/61
Ht: 6-6	Wt: 271	Pardeeville, WI

Acquisition: Was second choice in eighth round of 1983 draft.
1984 SEASON: Started in 15 of Bears' 16 games and also both playoff games at left guard . . . Was converted from defensive lineman to guard prior to the final preseason game in 1983 . . . Played extremely well against Randy White of Dallas (9/30) . . . Earned game ball vs. New Orleans when Payton broke rushing mark . . . Sprained ankle @ Tampa Bay and missed Minnesota game (10/28) . . . **Games Played: 15 Games Started: 15.**
PRO CAREER: Begins only 3rd season with Bears . . . Has bright future as offensive lineman . . . Played all 16 games in rookie season . . . Is big, fast, strong and agile . . . Mike Ditka says about Bortz: "He has a great future as offensive guard"
COLLEGIATE, PERSONAL: Was 219th player selected in the draft . . . Was defensive co-captain and standout at Iowa . . . Played in East-West Shrine game . . . College stats show: 231 total tackles, 126 solo tackles; 1 forced fumble, 6 recovered fumbles, 8 passes deflected, 1 blocked kick . . . Was All-America . . . Given name is Mark Steven Bortz . . . Was all-state in football and basketball . . . Conference Champion and school record-setting for shot-put and discus at Pardeeville (WI) High School . . . General studies major.

BORTZ'S PRO STATS

Total Games: 31; 1984 (15), 1983 (16). Total Starts: 15; 1984 (15). Playoff Games: 2, 1984 (2). Playoff Starts: 2; 1984 (2).

BRIAN CABRAL   54

Linebacker	Colorado	7th Year
Ht: 6-1	Wt: 227	Born: 6/23/56, Ft. Benning, GA

Acquisition: Signed as free agent 9/1/81.
1984 SEASON: Valuable special teamer who appeared in all 16 regular season games and both playoff tilts . . . Finished 4th on the team in special team tackles . . . Only Bear who plays on every special team . . . Played in some short yardage and goal line situations **Games Played: 16 Games Started: 0**
PRO CAREER: Begins 7th year in NFL and 4th with Bears . . . Bears are fourth NFL club he's played with—also Packers, Colts, Falcons . . . Original team was Atlanta . . . Originally joined Bears as free agent 8/21/81 before being waived on 8/31/81 . . . Signed with Packers in training camp of '81 . . . Also member of Colts in '80, but was waived (9/2/80) . . . Falcons drafted him as their 4th round pick in '78 . . . Sat out that year due to knee injury . . . Made 3 starts for Atlanta in '79 before being traded to Colts.
COLLEGIATE, PERSONAL: Was a 3-year letterman at Colorado . . . Was 2nd team all-Big eight member . . . Played in Blue-Gray game . . . Given name Brian David Cabral . . . Hawaiian surname is Kealihaaheo . . . Married (Becky) . . . One son (Kyle), one daughter (Maile) . . . Prepped at Honolulu St. Louis High . . . Involved in professional athletes Christian Ministry—Athletes for Christ during off-season . . . Hobbies include basketball, racquetball . . . Is involved in FCA, Pro Athletes Outreach Special Olympics, Sports Teams Organized for Prevention of Drug Abuse, Brian Piccolo Cancer Research Fund . . . Has BSR in therapeutic recreation.

CABRAL'S PRO STATS

Year/Club	Interceptions			Tkls/ Solo	Fum. Rec.	Pass Def.	Force Fum.	Sack –Yds.	Gms/ Sts.
	No.	Yds.	TD						
1984 Bears	0	0	0	8/8	0	0	0	0	16/0
1983 Bears	0	0	0	17/15	0	0	0	1/10	16/4
1982 Bears	0	0	0	1/0	0	0	0	0/0	8/0
1981 Bears	0	0	0	33/27	0	2	1	0/0	16/4
1980 Packers	0	0	0	10/8	0	0	0	1/0	7/0
1979 Falcons	0	0	0	69/58	0	2	0	2/10	66/8

CABRAL'S SINGLE GAME HIGHS

Most Tackles: 12, vs. Denver 12/20/81. Most Solos: 9, @ K.C. 11/8/81; vs. Denver 12/20/81

JIM COVERT

		74
Tackle	Pittsburgh	3rd Year
Ht: 6-4	Wt: 271	Born: 3/22/60
		Conway, PA

Acquisition: First round selection in 1983 draft.

1984 SEASON: Youngest captain in the NFL . . . Made key block on Walter Payton's 72-yard run vs. Denver (9/9) . . . Earned game ball vs. New Orleans (10/7) . . . Member of offensive unit that for two years in a row has been instrumental in Bears' league-leading ground game . . . Started in both Bear playoff games . . . **Games Played:** 16 **Games Started:** 16.

PRO CAREER: Has now started all 32 games since joining Bears as #1 draft choice in '83 . . . Was consensus all-rookie selection (Football Digest, UPI, PFW).

COLLEGIATE, PERSONAL: Two-year All-America at Pittsburgh . . . Lombardi Trophy semi-finalist . . . Gave up only 3 sacks in 3 years; none his senior year . . . Is a dedicated weight lifter . . . Was redshirted in '79 . . . Played in Senior and Hula Bowls . . . Given name James Paul Covert . . . Was teammate of Dolphins QB Dan Marino at Pittsburgh and was best man in his wedding January '85 . . . Was 3-year letterman in football and wrestling and captained both . . . Pinned all but one of his wrestling opponents as senior . . . Enjoys jazz, Hemingway . . . English major . . . Is a member of Chicago Boys Club, FCA, Lake Forest Chamber of Commerce, Brian Piccolo Cancer Research Fund and Better Boys Foundation . . . Was recipient of Piccolo award voted by Bear veterans in his rookie year.

COVERT'S PRO STATS

Total Games: 32; 1984 (16), 1983 (16). Total Starts: 32; 1984 (16), 1983 (16). Playoff Games: 2; 1984 (2). Playoff Starts: 2, 1984 (2).

RICHARD DENT

		95
Defensive End	Tennessee State	3rd Year
Ht: 6-5	Wt: 253	Born: 12/13/60,
		Atlanta, GA

Acquisition: First selection in the eighth round of 1983 draft.

1984 SEASON: Made first Pro Bowl appearance as a starter and recorded 3 sacks . . . Led NFC in sacks with 17½ . . . Slowed early in season with bruised thigh suffered in Tampa game (9/2) . . . Had 3 sacks for −29 yards @ Tampa Bay (10/21) . . . Turned in 4½ sack performance (−31 yards), 7 tackle, 1 fumble recovery performance vs. Raiders (11/4) and earned NFC Defensive Player of the Week honors and game ball . . . Turned in game ball performance vs. Detroit (11/18) after 4 tackles and 2 sacks . . . His 17½ sacks established club record for sacks in a season . . . Earned numerous post-season honors: College and Pro Football Weekly's 1st team defense, All-NFC, AP second team defense, UPI 1st team . . . Recorded 3 sacks in playoff win vs. Washington . . . **Games Played: 16 Games Started: 10.**

PRO CAREER: Emerged as a solid defensive end in '83 while filling in for injured Dan Hampton . . . Was awarded game ball vs. San Francisco (11/27/83) as a substitute . . . Made first pro start vs. Philadelphia (11/13) and contributed with 4 tackles and 1 assist.

COLLEGIATE, PERSONAL: Was 203rd player selected in '83 draft . . . Set Tennessee State record with 39 career sacks . . . College Stats: 158 total tackles, 72 solos, 6 fumble recoveries . . . Given name is Richard Lamar Dent . . . All-state at Atlanta Murphy High . . . Hobbies include racquetball, tennis, swimming, horseback riding . . . Commercial arts major.

DENT'S PRO STATS

	Int./Yds.	Tkls./Solo	Fum. Rec.	Pass Def.	Force Fum.	Blk. Kick	Sack/−Yds.	Games/Starts
1984	0/0	39/31	1	1	4	0	17.5/140.5	16/10
1983	0/0	12/9	0	0	1	1	3/28	16/3
Total	0/0	51/40	1	1	5	1	20.5/168.5	32/13

Acquisition: Third round draft choice in 1983.

1984 SEASON: Valued special teamer who finished year leading the club in special team tackles (11) . . . Saw considerable amount of playing time in playoff game vs. SF due to injury to Les Frazier . . . Had 5 tackles against 49ers . . . Had game ball performance at Green Bay (9/16) . . . Was used in nickel-back defensive situations . . . Had game ball performance vs. L.A. Raiders (11/4) . . . Had 3 kickoff returns for 44 yards at San Diego (12/9) . . . Picked off first pass of career vs. Packers (12/9) . . . **Games Played: 16, GAMES STARTED: 0.**

PRO CAREER: Started 6 of last 7 games at free safety in '83 due to injury to Gary Fencik . . . Made 12 tackles vs. Packers (12/4/83) and 8 tackles vs. Rams (11/6/83) . . . Finished 9th on team in tackles with 49 (41 solos) and 3rd on team in special team tackles . . . Finished year with/best KOR average (22.0).

COLLEGIATE, PERSONAL: Four-year starter at Notre Dame . . . Set school record with 256 career interception yards and had 12 career pickoffs . . . Set ND record with 103 punt returns for 2nd best (869 yards) . . . Was captain and MVP in '82 . . . Given name is David Russell Duerson (Chase Anthony) . . . All-America at Muncie Northside High . . . Plays all brass instruments . . . Toured 38 countries in 34 days with US Ambassador Band in summer of '75 . . . National Honor Society member . . . Spent summer of '81 as a law clerk in Miami, FL . . . Spent summer of '82 in Indiana Senator Richard Lugar's Washington D.C. office . . . Last year formed Damco Corporation, a drug and alcohol awareness camp for youngsters . . . Involved in Brian Piccolo Cancer Research Fund and Red Cloud Athletic Fund . . . BA degree in economics/communications.

22

DAVE DUERSON

Safety	Notre Dame	3rd Year
Ht: 6-1	Wt: 205	Born: 11/28/60, Muncie, IN

DUERSON'S PRO STATS

	Interceptions			TD	Tkls./Solo	Fum./Rec.	Pass Def.	Force Fum.	Blk. Kick	Sack/Yds.
	No.	Yds.	Avg.							
1984	1	9	9.0	0	32/28	0	4	0	0	3/−27
1983	0	0	0.0	0	49/41	0	4	1	0	0/0
Total	1	9	9.0	0	81/69	0	8	1	0	3/−27

113

	KICKOFF RETURNS				PUNT RETURNS				
	No.	Yds.	Avg.	TD	No.	Yds.	Avg.	TD	Gms/Sts
1984	5	95	19.0	0	1	4	4.0	0	16/0
1983	3	66	22.0	0	0	0	0.0	0	16/6
Total	8	161	20.1	0	1	4	4.0	0	32/6

DUERSON'S SINGLE GAME HIGHS

Longest Kickoff return: 26 vs. Dallas (9/30/84). Most Tackles: 12 @ Green Bay (12/4/83). Most Solos: 11 @ Green Bay (12/4/83).

PAT DUNSMORE   88

Tight End	Drake	3rd Year
Ht: 6-3	Wt: 237	Born: 10/2/59, Duluth, MN

Acquisition: Fourth round draft choice in the 1983 draft.
1984 SEASON: Injured groin in training camp and was placed on IR until Sept. 28 . . . Alternated with Moorehead as play messenger last 10 games . . . Caught first career TD pass vs. Detroit (11/18) . . . Caught 19-yard TD pass from Payton in Bears' 23-19 playoff win over Redskins **Games Played: 14 Games Started: 1**
PRO CAREER: Played in all 16 games in '83 and made first pro start vs. Philadelphia (11/13) . . . Made first pro reception vs. Minnesota (10/9/83) . . . Had best game of career vs. Detroit (10/16/83) when he caught 5 passes for 73 yards.
COLLEGIATE, PERSONAL: Was 107th player selected in the '83 draft . . . Was All-America at Drake . . . Switched from wide receiver to tight end . . . Bulldog's 3rd leading career receiver with 128 receptions for 1,771 yards, 7 TD's . . . Given name Patrick Neil Dunsmore . . . Married (Bianca) . . . All-conference in football and all-area in basketball at Ankeny (1A) High . . . Involved in Brian Piccolo Cancer Research Fund . . . BS degree in education.

DUNSMORE'S PRO STATS

		Receiving			Games/
Year	No.	Yds.	Avg.	TD	Starts
1984	9	106	11.8	1	14/1
1983	8	102	12.8	0	16/1
Total	17	208	12.2	1	30/2

DUNSMORE'S SINGLE GAME HIGHS

Long Catch: 25 @ L.A. Rams (11/11/84). Most Yards Rec: 73 @ Detroit (10/16/83). Most Caught: 5 @ Detroit (10/16/83) (5-73).

GARY FENCIK   45

Safety	Yale	10th Year
Ht: 6-1	Wt: 193	Born: 6/11/54, Chicago, IL

Acquisition: Signed as Free Agent 9/15/76.
1984 SEASON: Turned in one of finest seasons of career . . . Is now second on all-time Bear interception list with 30 (Richie Petitbon, 37) . . . Had 2 intercepts in season opener vs. Tampa (9/2) including 61-yard return . . . Also picked off two Montana passes in playoff vs. SF (1/6/85) . . . Had two intercepts vs. L.A. Raiders (11/4) . . . Finished 2nd on team in tackles with 103 and first in solos with 82 . . . Was 2nd on club in passes defended (9) . . . Earned NFC Defensive "Player of Week" honors vs. Tampa Bay (9/2) . . . Turned in 9-tackle performance vs. Green Bay (12/9) **Games Started: 16 Games Played: 16.**
PRO CAREER: Enters '85 season needing 7 interceptions to tie club leader Rich Petitbon . . . Is now 2nd on all-time list having surpassed Ben-

nie McRae in 1984 . . . Turned in fine all-around year in '84 following injury hampered '83 season . . . Missed 8 games that year due to groin injury . . . Was PFW all-NFL in '82 . . . AP, TSN all-NFL, UPI all-NFC in '81 . . . Voted to NFC Pro Bowl squad for 2nd time after '81 season, first time as starter . . . Scored first NFL TD with 69-yard interception return vs. Broncos (12/20/81) . . . Underwent knee (left medial ligament) and ankle (left) surgeries following all-pro '79 season when he made career high 6 pick-offs . . . Owns 7 game ball trophies: Tampa Bay (9/2/84), Minnesota (12/11/83), Detroit (11/21/82), Denver (12/20/81), Detroit (11/4/79), Washington (12/16/78), Tampa Bay (12/4/77) . . . Has played in 121 of 132 games since joining club as free agent . . . Made first pro interception off Joe Namath . . . Was Miami's 10th round pick in '76 but training camp injury/illness forced cut.

COLLEGIATE: Wide receiver who set Yale record with 82 receptions for 1,435 yards, 7 TD's—since broken by Curt Grieve . . . All-Ivy League in '75 with 42 catches for 729 yards (3 TD's) . . . Owned 99-yard TD reception in '75 vs. Princeton . . . Caught 11 passes for 187 yards vs. Harvard in '74 . . . Given name John Gary Fencik . . . Father is assistant principal of Barrington (IL) High School . . . Has vacationed in Kenya . . . This past off-season vacationed in Tahiti, Australia and New Zealand . . . Took seminar from Howard Cosell as collegian . . . Captained Barrington High football and basketball teams . . . Spent '75 spring studying in London . . . Has BA in history from Yale . . . Involved in YMCA, Brian Piccolo Cancer Research Fund and Lake Forest Chamber of Commerce.

FENCIK'S PRO STATS

Year	Interceptions No.	Yds.	TD	Tkls/Solo	Fum. Rec.	Pass Def.	Force Fum.	Sack -Yds.	Gms/Sts.
1984	5	102	0	103/82	1	9	0	1/1	16/16
1983	5	34	0	36/25	1	5	1	0/0	8/7
1982	2	2	0	82/52	0	5	0	0/0	9/9
1981	6	121	1	135/112	2	17	2	1/9	16/16
1980	1	8	0	125/95	3	8	0	1/0	15/15
1979	6	31	0	103/73	1	9	0	0/0	14/14
1978	4	77	0	130/95	2	10	0	0/0	16/16
1977	4	33	0	133/93	0	7	0	0/0	14/14
1976	0	0	0	15/9	1	0	1	0/0	13/0
Career	30	408	1	862/636	10	70	6	3/10	121/107

FENCIK'S SINGLE GAME HIGHS

Long Intercept: 69t vs. Broncos 12/20/81 off Craig Morton (1-69). Most Deflections: 4 vs. L.A. Raiders 11/4/84. Most Intercepts: 5 times; last 11/4/84 vs. Raiders. Most Solos: 12 at St. Louis 9/25/77. Most Total Tackles: 17 at St. Louis 9/25/77. Last interception: vs. Green Bay 12/11/84.

JEFF FISHER   24

Defensive Back
Ht: 5-11
Wt: 190
Southern Cal

5th Year
Born: 2/25/58,
Culver City, CA

Acquisition: Seventh round draft choice in 1981.
1984 SEASON: Became Bears all-time leading punt returner with 123 . . . Also set club record for returns in season with 58 . . . Returned 8 punts vs. Detroit (12/16) to establish club record for single game returns . . . Earned game ball vs. Denver (9/9) after 4 PR's for 65 yards, 21 LG . . . Best return was 28-yards effort vs. Detroit (12/16) . . . Also saw action in passing situations as extra defensive back . . . Had four tackles in reserve role vs. Denver (9/9) . . . Recovered fumble vs. San Diego (12/3).
Games Played: 16 Games Started: 0.
PRO CAREER: Suffered broken leg midway through '83 season (10/23/83) and missed final eight games . . . Still finished second on team in PR's in '83 (13 for 71 yards) . . . Record 29 tackles including 22 solos in '83 . . . Finished second on club with 3 interceptions in '82 . . . Led team in punt returns in '81 and '82 . . . Earned game ball vs. Vikings (12/6/81) after picking off pass, recovering fumble, forcing fumble and returning 5 PR's for 49 yards . . . 88-yard punt return for TD vs. Bucs (9/20/81) was longest by Bear in Soldier Field, longest vs. Bucs, and longest Bear since

Scooter McLean raced 89 yards vs. Cardinals (10/11/42) . . . 177th player selected in '81 draft.

COLLEGIATE, PERSONAL: All-Pac 10 academic team as senior (3.36 GPA) . . . Made 12 tackes, 1 interception in '79 win over Notre Dame . . . USC stats show: 5 interceptions, 108 tackles, 3 fumble recoveries, 11 passes broken up . . . Also served as backup, barefoot placekicker . . . Given name Jeffrey Michael Fisher . . . Prepped at Woodland Hills High . . . Scholastic Coach all-America WR as senior . . . Set L.A. prep record with 13 catches for 284, 2 TD day . . . Also had 6 interceptions as senior . . . Favorite book, "The Choir Boys" by Joseph Wambaugh . . . Sells computer soft-ware during off-season . . . Has BS degree in Public Administration . . . Involved in Sports Teams Organized for Prevention of Drug Abuse, Lake Forest Chamber of Commerce and the Brian Piccolo Cancer Research Fund.

FISHER'S PRO STATS

Year	Interceptions			Tkls Solo	Fum. Rec.	Pass Def.	Force Fum.	Blk Kick	Sack/Yds.	Gms/Sts.
	No.	Yds.	TD							
1984	0	0	0	4/3	1	0	0	0	0/0	16/0
1983	0	0	0	28/22	1	1	0	0	0/0	8/3
1982	3	19	0	29/23	0	2	0	0	0/0	9/0
1981	2	3	0	21/18	1	3	1	0	0/0	16/0
Career	5	22	0	82/66	2	6	1	0	0/0	49/3

Year	Kickoff Returns				Punt Returns			
	No.	Yds.	Avg.	TD	No.	Yds.	Avg.	TD
1984	0	0	0	0	58	492	8.5	0
1983	0	0	0	0	13	71	5.5	0
1982	7	102	14.6	0	9	65	7.2	0
1981	6	96	16.0	0	43	509	11.8	1
Career	13	198	15.2	0	123	1,137	9.2	1

FISHER'S SINGLE GAME HIGHS

Long Punt Return: 88t vs. Bucs 9/20/81 (2-93). Most Punt Return: 8 at Detroit 12/16/84 (8-103). Most Solos: 7 at Detroit 10/19/81. Long Int. Return: 19 at Los Angeles 12/26/82 (1-19).

LESLIE FRAZIER   21

Cornerback	Alcorn State	5th Year
Ht: 6-0	Wt: 189	Born: 4/3/59
		Columbus, MS

Acquisition: Signed as Free Agent 7/18/81.

1984 SEASON: Played at all-pro level before injury foot and missing five regular season games . . . Started first 10 games of season and had five interceptions before damaging nerve in right foot vs. Raiders (11/4) . . . Returned to start season finale vs. Lions (12/16) and played extensively in two playoff games . . . Game ball vs. Denver (9/9) after two interceptions and four tackles . . . Tied Fencik for team lead in thefts . . . Had 6 tackles and interception (which set up TD) vs. Tampa Bay (10/21) . . . Acrobatic interception at Green Bay (9/16) deep in Bear territory halted potential scoring drive and preserved 9-7 win; Ditka said "One of the greatest plays I've ever seen." Games Played: 11 Games Started: 11

PRO CAREER: Had 7 interceptions in '83 tying him (with 8 others) for 3rd in NFL . . . Picked off John Elway pass vs. Denver (10/2/83) and returned for TD . . . Game ball vs. Philadelphia (11/13/83) after picking off a pass, recovering a fumble and making four solos . . . Recorded seven tackles at New Orleans (9/18/83) and at Green Bay (12/4); also had two interceptions vs. Green Bay and returned for 1 for 56 yards . . . Led team in '83 in passes defensed (21) . . . Started 6 of 9 games in '82 . . . Deflected 12 passes to lead team . . . Played in 12 games in '81, when he was one of four rookie DB's to make team.

COLLEGIATE, PERSONAL: Three-year letterman at Alcorn

State . . . Two-year all-Southwestern Conference; MVDB '81 . . . Kodak All-America . . . Played in Sheridan College All-Star game . . . Most valuable defensive back for Alcorn State in '80 . . . Also MVP on baseball team . . . All-conference in baseball and two-year letterman . . . Captained in '79 . . . Given name Leslie Antonio Frazier . . . Married (Gale) . . . Prepped at Columbus (MS) High . . . Hobbies include music, basketball, ping-pong . . . Favorite book: Bible . . . BA degree in business administration . . . Involved in Red Cloud Athletic Fund, Fellowship of Christian Athletes, Lake Forest Chamber of Commerce and Brian Piccolo Cancer Research Fund.

FRAZIER'S PRO STATS

Year	Interceptions No.	Yds.	Tkls Solos	Fum. Rec.	Pass Def.	Force Fum.	Blk Kicks	Sack/ Yds	Gms/ Sts
1984	5*	89	30/24	0	5	1	0	0/0	11/11
1983	7*	135	60/52	1	21*	0	0	0/0	16/16
1982	2	0	31/28	1	12	1	0	1/7	9/6
1981	0	0	2/2	0	0	0	0	0/0	12/0

*Led team. Also had 6 KOR's for 77 yards in 1981.

FRAZIER'S SINGLE GAME HIGHS

Long Intercept: 56 at Green Bay (12/4/83). Most Deflections: 5 vs. Patriots (12/5/82). Most Interceptions: 2 at Green Bay 12/4/83 (2-75); vs. Denver 9/9/84 (2-42). Most Solos: 8 at Minnesota 11/28/82. Most Tackles: 8 (twice) at Minnesota 11/28/82; at New Orleans 9/18/83. Last Interception: vs. Raiders 11/4/84 (1-33).

ANDY FREDERICK

71

Tackle   New Mexico   9th Year
Ht: 6-6   Wt: 269   Born: 7/25/54   Oak Park, IL

Acquisition: From Cleveland Browns in exchange for past considerations (Gerry Sullivan) April 28, 1983.

1984 SEASON: Dependable backup at tackle who saw action in every game . . . Replaced injured Van Horne vs. Dallas (9/30) and started following two games vs. New Orleans (10/7) and St. Louis (10/14) . . . Received game ball vs. Saints (10/7) as part of line that paved way for record breaking day for Payton . . . Preseason starter at RT. **Games Played:** 16 **Games Started:** 2.

PRO CAREER: Started 6 games in '83 after joining team in trade prior to season . . . Played 7 games for Browns in '82 after being claimed on waivers from Cowboys (9/8/82) . . . Reserve tackle in Cleveland at right tackle after playing left tackle as Cowboy reserve for 5 years . . . Played for Dallas when Ditka was there as assistant . . . Resigned by Cowboys (8/31/79) after being waived (8/21/79) . . . 5th round draft choice by Cowboys in '77.

COLLEGIATE, PERSONAL: Defensive tackles at New Mexico and played in East-West Shrine game . . . Native of Broadview (IL) and played at Westchester St. Joseph High . . . Given name Andrew Brian Frederick . . . Married (Danita) . . . Hobbies include golf, singing dalmatian, wood working . . . Resides in Libertyville, IL . . . Involved in Sports Teams Organized for Prevention of Drug Abuse and Brian Piccolo Cancer Research Fund.

FREDERICK'S PRO STATS

TOTAL GAMES: 117; Cowboys 1977 (14), Cowboys 1978 (16), Cowboys 1979 (16), Cowboys 1980 (16), Cowboys 1981 (16), Browns 1982 (7), Bears 1983 (16), Bears 1984 (16). TOTAL STARTS: 14: Cowboys 1978 (5), Cowboys 1980 (1), Bears 1983 (6), Bears 1984 (2).

STEVE FULLER

4

Quarterback   Clemson   7th Year
Ht: 6-4   Wt: 195   Born: 1/5/57   Enid, OK

Acquisition: From Los Angeles Rams in exchange for an 11th round pick in '84 and a 6th round choice in '85.

1984 SEASON: Led Bears to NFC Championship after Jim McMahon suffered season ending injury . . . Started four regular season games and both playoff contests . . . Relieved McMahon vs. Raiders (11/4) and completed 4 of 5 passes in 17/6 win . . . Started next four games and rated as NFL's top passer during that time . . . Separated shoulder in preseason opener vs. Cards (11/4) and placed on injured reserve until 10/1 . . . Separated same right shoulder again vs. Chargers (12/3) and sat out until playoffs . . . Made first start vs. Rams (11/11) and completed 21 of 27 passes for 240 yards . . . Connected on 9 of 15 for 211 and 2 TD's in playoff win over Redskins . . . Threw 2 TD passes in division clinching win over Vikings (11/25). **Games Played: 6 Games Started: 4.**

PRO CAREER: Did not throw pass for Chiefs in '83 after being obtained in trade with Chiefs for CB Lucius Smith and Rams 5th round choice in '85 (8/20/83) transaction . . . Shared QB duties with Bill Kenney at K.C. in '81-82 . . . Started 3 games in '82 and threw for 665 yards completing 49 of 93 passes in '82 . . . Best outing at Pittsburgh where he completed 18 of 31 attempts for 249 yards, the best passing output of the season for Chiefs . . . It was his 7th 200-yd. performance of career . . . Rushed for 712 yards and 5 TD's as Chief . . . Had arthroscopic right knee surgery in '81 after injury in first preseason game . . . Passed for 934 yards in '81 hitting 77 of 134 for 3 TD's . . . Enjoyed best year in '80 when he started first 13 games before arthroscopic knee surgery sidelined him for final 3 games . . . Finished as AFC's 4th rated QB that year, throwing for 2,250 yards and 10 TD's . . . Chiefs 2nd choice in first round of '79 draft . . . Made first start in 3rd game of rookie campaign.

COLLEGIATE, PERSONAL: ACC Player of Year in '77 and '78 . . . Clemson stats: 287 of 554 for 4,359, 22 TD's, 21 interceptions . . . Led Tigers to 11-1 record and Gator Bowl win over Ohio State as senior . . . Finished 6th Heisman Trophy balloting . . . Set Clemson records for career passing yardage, single-season passing (1,655 as junior) and single season total offense (2,164 as senior) . . . Rhodes Schol-

arship candidate . . . History major . . . Attended Spartanburg, H.S. (SC) and graduated as class valedictorian . . . Offered scholarships in four different sports: gold, tennis, baseball and football . . . Given name Stephen Ray Fuller . . . Married (Anna).

FULLER'S PRO STATS

Year/Club	Att	Comp.	Yds.	TD	Int.	Comp. %
1984 Bears	78	53	595	3	0	.679
1983 L.A. Rams	0	0	0	0	0	0
1982 Kansas City	93	49	665	3	2	.527
1981 Kansas City	134	77	934	3	4	.575
1980 Kansas City	320	193	2,250	10	12	.603
1979 Kansas City	270	146	1,484	6	14	.541
Career	895	518	5,928	25	32	.579

FULLER'S SINGLE GAME HIGHS

Most Completions: 21 (three times); 11/30/80 vs. Cin (21 of 37); 12/13/81 vs. Miami (21 of 37); 11/11/84 vs. Rams (21 of 37; Most Pass Atts: 37 (twice); 11/30/80 vs. Cin (21 of 37) and 12/13/81 vs. Miami (21 of 37) Most Yards Passing: 261; 12/6/81 at Denver (18 of 34) Most TD's Passing: 2 (three times) 10/19/80 at Denver; 11/9/81 at Seattle; 11/25/84 at Minnesota Highest % Passing: .900, 10/25/81 at Oakland (9 of 10) Most Interceptions: 4; 9/16/79 at Houston Longest Pass: 77 yards 11/2/80 vs. Baltimore Most Sacks: 10; 11/2/80 vs. Baltimore (66 yds.) Most Sack Yards: 66; 11/2/80 vs. Balt (10 sacks)

WILLIE GAULT   83

Wide Receiver	Tennessee	3rd Year
Ht: 6-0	Wt: 178	Born: 9/5/60
		Griffin, GA

Acquisition: Second selection in the first round of the 1983 draft.

GAULT'S PRO STATS

		RECEIVING		
Year	No.	Yds.	TD	Gms/Sts
1984	34	587*	6*	16/15
1983	40	836*	8	16/13
Career	74	1423	14	32/28

* Lead team.
Also in '83 13 KOR's for 276, 21.2 avg. 9 PR's 61 yds. 1 KOR for 12 yds. in '84.

GAULT'S SINGLE GAME HIGHS

Long Catch: 87 at Green Bay 12/4/83, from McMahon. Most Caught: 6 at Seattle 9/23/84. Most Yards Rec.: 130, at Baltimore 9/25/83 (5-130). Long KOR: 38 vs. Falcons 9/4/83. Most Yards, KOR: 52, vs. Falcons 9/4/83. Long PR: 12 vs. Broncos 10/2/83. Most Yds. PR's: 29 vs. Broncos 10/2/83 (3-29). Combined yards: 174 vs. Broncos 10/2/83 (Rec. 98, Rush 22, PR 29, KOR 25).

SHAUN GAYLE   23

Cornerback	Ohio State	2nd Year
Ht: 5-11	Wt: 191	Born: 3/8/82
		Hampton, VA

Acquisition: Selected in the 10th round of 1984 draft after Bears gained right from Cleveland Browns.
1984 SEASON: Emerged as third cornerback and started 6 games filling in for injured Richardson and Frazier . . . Proved to be surprise of '84

1984 SEASON: Displayed "big play" capabilities by leading team in TD receptions (6) and yards per catch (17.3) . . . Started 15 of 16 games, missing start of San Diego game (12/3) with hamstring pull . . . Made key 75-yard TD catch vs. Redskins in playoff win . . . Had 6 catches for 73 yards vs. Seattle (9/23) in best outing of '84 . . . Caught 61-yard TD pass from McMahon vs. Denver (9/9) . . . Finished season with 34 catches for 587 yards. **Games Played: 16 Games Started: 15.**
PRO CAREER: Selected to Football Digest, UPI, PFW, PFWA all-rookie teams in '83 . . . His 40 receptions in '83 were most by Bear rookie since Harlon Hill caught 45 in '54 . . . Led club in receiving yards (836) and yards per catch (20.9) . . . 87-yard TD catch at Green Bay (12/4/83) was longest in NFC in '83 . . . Had 3 100+ yard games in '83 (at New Orleans 9/18, at Baltimore 9/25, at Green Bay 12/4) . . . Became only 7th player in team history to catch 3 TD passes in one game (at N.O.) . . . Became 1st Bear to have 2 consecutive 100+ yard games (9/11-18) since Dick Gordon (11/15-22/70) . . . Led Bear kickoff returners in yardage (276) and had longest KOR of season (38 yards vs. Atlanta, 9/4).
COLLEGIATE, PERSONAL: Set SEC mark with 5 career KOR's for TD's at Tennessee, one shy of NCAA record holder Anthony Davis (USC) . . . Led SEC as senior in KOR's with 23.9 average (23-549) . . . Finished 2nd in SEC and 18th nationally while leading Vols in combined yards with 124.2 yards per game . . . Had 50 catches for 668 yards and 4 TD's . . . 13.6 in 110-meter high hurdles was second best in world in '82 . . . '83 Indoor Champion in 60-yard dash and high hurdles . . . Made '80 U.S. Olympic team as sprinter . . . Finished third in 100 meter hurdles in 1983 World Championships in Helsinki . . . Ran second leg in world record 400-meter relay . . . Given name Willie James Gault . . . Married (Dainnese) . . . Prepped at Griffin High (GA) . . . Track team won state championship in 3 of his 4 years . . . Marketing major.

Some say Mike Singletary (50) already plays the middle linebacker post as tough as Dick Butkus, who will be in the WGN radio booth critiquing Singletary this season.

training camp as bargain 10th round choice . . . Recorded only interception of season in first professional start at St. Louis (10/14) when he replaced Richardson (broken wrist) . . . Also had season-high four tackles and blocked kick vs. Cardinals . . . Started five of last six games for Frazier (foot) before breaking high right ankle in game 15 vs. Green Bay (12/9) . . . Placed on injured reserve for final regular season game and playoffs . . . Played extensively in passing situations when not starting . . . Suffered broken hand in preseason vs. Green Bay (11/11).
Games Played: 15 Games Started: 6.
COLLEGIATE, PERSONAL: Led Buckeye defensive backs in tackles (74), passes defended (8) and forced fumbles (3) as senior . . . Started all 12 games in '83 . . . Had 60 tackles in '82 including 2 lost yardage stops . . . Also broke up 11 passes as junior . . . Had 4 interceptions in OSU career . . . Bench presses 325 pounds and squats 650 pounds . . . Runs 40 in :04.59 . . . All-state and all-America at Bethel High (VA) . . . Team compiled 206-3 record in this three varsity seasons . . . Hobbies include basketball and music . . . Father is retired Army officer.

GAYLE'S PRO STATS

Year	Interceptions No.	Yds.	TD	Tkls Solo	Fum. Rec.	Pass Def.	Force Fum.	Blk Kick	Sck Yds	Gms Sts
1984	1	-1	0	19/14	0	7	0	1	0/0	15/6

DENNIS GENTRY

#29

Running Back   Baylor   4th Year
Ht: 5-8   Wt: 184   Born: 2/10/59, Lubbock, TX

Acquisition: Selected in the fourth round of the 1983 draft.
1984 SEASON: Scored first career touchdown at Tampa Bay (10/21) . . . Had best day of year in season finale at Detroit with 4 rushes for 37 yards . . . Also had 2 receptions in that game and four for the year . . . Was 2nd on team in kick returns (11) and return yards (209) while leading team in return average (19.0) . . . Had 4 kick returns for 58 yards vs. Dallas (9/30) . . . Had 3 kick returns for 49 yards in NFC Title game vs. 49ers (1/6/85) **GAMES PLAYED: 16 GAMES STARTED: 0.**
PRO CAREER: Led club with 18 special team tackles in '83 . . . Was 3rd on team in KOR's with 130 yards including 18.6 average . . . Scored a TD in all four '83 preseason games . . . Was 3rd on club in special team tackles in '82 . . . 2nd in kickoff and punt returns that year . . . Was 89th player selected in '82 draft.
COLLEGIATE, PERSONAL: Was the number two rusher in Baylor history (behind Ambercrombie) . . . Was redshirted in '78 . . . Was 3-year starter at Baylor . . College stats show: 414 rushes, 2,213 yards, 14 TD's . . . Played in Senior Bowl . . . Given name is Dennis Louis Gentry . . . All-South Plains at Lubbock (TX) Dunbar High . . . Physical education major.

GENTRY'S PRO STATS

Year	RUSHING				RECEIVING				Gms/Sts
	Att.	Yds.	Avg.	TD	No.	Yds.	Avg.	TD	
1984	21	79	3.8	1	4	29	7.3	0	16/0
1983	16	65	4.1	0	2	8	4.0	0	15/0
1982	3	25	8.3	0	1	9	9.0	0	9/0
Career	40	169	4.2	1	7	46	6.8	0	40/0

Year	KICKOFF RETURNS				PUNT RETURNS			
	No.	Yds.	Avg.	TD	No.	Yds.	Avg.	TD
1984	11	209	19.0	0	0	0	0	0
1983	7	130	18.6	0	0	0	0.0	0
1982	9	161	17.9	0	15	77	5.1	0
Career	27	500	18.1	0	15	77	5.1	0

DAN HAMPTON

99

Defensive Tackle   Arkansas   7th Year
Ht: 6-5   Wt: 266   Born: 1/19/57
Oklahoma City, OK

Acquisition: First selection in first round of '79 draft.

1984 SEASON: Pro Bowl selectee for third time in career . . . Also named to Sporting News, PFW, AP and NEA all-pro first teams . . . Started 15 games, missed Rams game (11/11) with hyperextended elbow . . . Also missed part of Seattle game (9/23) with hyperextended knee . . . Third on team in sacks (11-95.5) and 6th in tackles (54) . . . Recorded sacks in 9 of 15 games in which he played . . . Season-high two sacks vs. Detroit (12/16) and St. Louis (10/14) . . . Also had 2 sacks (−19 yds.) in play-offs . . . 8 tackles vs. Green Bay (12/9) was also season-best . . . Deflected two passes in season opener vs. Bucs (9/2) . . . Had surgery on knee in off-season **Games Played:** 15 **Games Started:** 15.

PRO CAREER: Started just 11 games in injury-plagued '83 season but still finished 4th on team in sacks with 5 . . . Selected to several all-pro teams following '82 season in which PFW named him NFL most valuable player . . . Played in Pro Bowl in '80 and '82 . . . Led team in sacks in '82 with 7; second in tackles with 71 while starting all 9 games at DRE . . . Finished 5th on team in tackles (11.5) and defensive line in tackles (73) in '80 . . . Made first pro sack on former Buc Doug Williams as rookie . . . 1st rookie to start on Bears defense since '75 . . . Had pair of sacks on Eagles Ron Jaworski in '79 playoff loss . . . 4th player selected in '79 draft behind LB Tom Cousineau (Browns), DT Mike Bell (Chiefs) and QB Jack Thompson (Bengals) . . . Bears obtained that pick plus TE Bobby Moore from Tampa Bay for DE Wally Chambers . . . Voted '79 Brian Piccolo Award by veterans.

COLLEGIATE, PERSONAL: Coaches All-America pick after senior year at Arkansas . . . Won Houston Post SWC Defensive Player of Year at DT . . . Four-year letterman . . . Twice all-SWC . . . Had 18 sacks as senior . . . Became starter as sophomore . . . Played in Senior, Fiesta, Orange and Cotton Bowls . . . Made 32 tackles behind line in college career . . . Given name Daniel Oliver Hampton . . . Nickname: Danimal . . . Married (Terry) . . . Prep all-America at Jacksonville (AR) High after playing in school band until junior year . . . Grew up on 42-acre farm near Cabot (Ark) . . . Music buff who plays 6 instruments: Bass guitar, classical guitar, drums, saxophone, piano and organ . . . Favorite book: "The World According to Garp" by John Irving . . . Mother Joan (father deceased) still lives on farm . . . Resides in north suburban Lake Bluff . . . Business major.

HAMPTON'S PRO STATS

Year	Int. Yds.	Tks Solo	Fum. Rec.	Pass Def.	Force Fum.	Blk Kick	Sacks/ Yards	Gms/ Sts.
1984	0/0	54/40	3	2	1	0	11.5/95.5	15/15
1983	0/0	47/40	0	4	0	1	5/27	11/11
1982	0/0	71/62	0	0	0	0	7/57	8/7
1981	0/0	68/56	0	4	1	0	9/77	16/16
1980	0/0	73/58	0	1	2	0	11.5/108.5	16/16
1979	0/0	70/48	2	3	1	0	4.5/28	16/16
Career	0/0	383/304	5	14	5	1	48.5/393	83/83

HAMPTON'S SINGLE GAME HIGHS

Most Sacks: 3 (34 yards) vs. Saints 9/14/80. Most Tackles: 16 vs. Saints 9/19/82. Most Solos: 13 vs. Saints 9/19/82.

AL HARRIS

90

Linebacker   Arizona State   7th Year
Ht: 6-5   Wt: 253   Born: 12/31/56
Bangor, ME

Acquisition: Second selection in the first round of 1979 draft.
1984 SEASON: Enjoyed best season of pro career in first full-year at

linebacker . . . Started all 16 games and finished as team's fourth leading tackler (68) . . . Game ball vs. Minnesota (10/28) after 10-tackle, 1 sack performance . . . Graded 100% by Bear coaches in second Vikings game (11/25) in 7-tackle effort . . . Had interception in season-opener vs. Tampa Bay (9/2) . . . Strong performance vs. Raiders (11/4) included six tackles and sacks . . . Season-high 10 tackles vs. Green Bay (12/9). **Games Played: 16 Games Started 16.**

PRO CAREER: Has overcome injury problems and changing positions to become solid performer . . . Started 8 games at DRE, 3 at LB in '83 . . . Finished 8th on club in tackles (57) despite missing three games with turf toe . . . Started 7 games at DRE in '82 and last 11 games there in '81 . . . Earned game ball at K.C. (11-8-81) after 11 tackles, 7 solos, and 2 fumble recoveries . . . Scored TD on 44-yard interception return vs. Broncos (12/20/81) . . . Capped 1980 comeback season with game-saving block of 32-yard FG at Tampa (12/20) to preserve 14-13 win with 40 seconds left and received game ball . . . Left knee cartilage surgery (7/28/79) . . . Notched first pro sack on former Lions' Jeff Komlo . . . 9th player selected in '79 draft—five picks after Bears took Dan Hampton.

COLLEGIATE, PERSONAL: Consensus All-America pick and finalist for Lombardi and Outland Trophies after senior year with Sun Devils . . . First unanimous pick in ASU history . . . All-WAC as junior . . . All 11 tackles in '78 Fiesta Bowl vs. Penn State . . . Finished senior year with 19 sacks and 22 other tackles behind scrimmage . . . Given name Alfred Carl Harris . . . With father in Air Force, Al grew up in Maine, North Carolina, New Jersey, West Virginia and Hawaii . . . Finished senior year at Leilehua Valley High in Wahiawa, Hawaii . . . Hawaii "Player of the Year" as senior . . . Also basketball center, track long jumper . . . Hobbies include bowling and horseback riding . . . B.S. degree in communications.

Year								
1983	57/49	0/0	1	0	5*	1	5/25	13/11
1982	27/23	0/0	0	1	0	0	2.5/19.5	8/7
1981	61/47	1/44t	3	5	1	0	2/17	16/11
1980	11/9	0/0	0	0	0	0	0/0	16/0
1979	1/1	0/0	0	0	0	0	1/7	4/0
Career	225/181	2/78	4	12	6	2	12.5/82.5	73/45

HARRIS' SINGLE GAME HIGHS

Most Solo Tackles: 9 vs. Lions 11/22/81; vs. Packers 12/9/84. Most Tackles: 11 at Kansas City 11/8/81.

MIKE HARTENSTINE   73

Defensive End	Penn State	11th Year
Ht: 6-3	Wt: 254	Born: 7/27/53, Allentown, PA

Acquisition: Second round draft choice in '75.

1984 SEASON: Enters '85 with a streak of 147 consecutive games played . . . Only played on kick-blocking team in final two regular season games due to sprained right knee . . . Was able to start both playoff games . . . Received game balls in both Tampa Bay games in which he got three of his 6 sacks in '84 . . . Finished 5th on team in sacks (6) . . . Missed part of Dallas game (10/30) due to cartilage tear in ribs . . . Had string of 145 consecutive starts broken vs. Green Bay (12/9) . . . Among NFL's strongest defensive lineman . . . **Games Played: 16, Games Started: 14.**

PRO CAREER: His streak of 147 consecutive games is 2nd only to Bob Parsons' 167 in Bear annals . . . Was chosen as second alternate in '83 Pro Bowl . . . Led team in sacks in '83 with 12 . . . Also finished 4th on team in tackles (70) . . . Scored TD at Tampa Bay (11/20/83) on 10-yard fumble return in 4th quarter . . . Owns game ball performances vs. Tampa Bay (thrice; 9/2/84, 10/21/84, 9/11/82), Green Bay (12/10/78), Detroit (11/4/79) . . . Normal off-season day includes four hours of weight work . . . '75 all-rookie consensus selection.

COLLEGIATE, PERSONAL: NCAA-ABC defensive player of

HARRIS' PRO STATS

Year	Int/Yds	Tkls/Solos	Fum. Rec.	Pass Def.	Force Fum.	Blk Kick	Sack Yds	Gms Sts
1984	1/34	68/52	0	6	0	0	2/14	16/16

'74 . . . Also consensus All-America as 220-pound defensive tackle . . . 2-year letterman, 3-year regular . . . 212 tackles, 15 sacks as starter . . . Lions were 32-4 in his seasons . . . Played in Sugar, Orange and Cotton Bowls . . . Give name Michael Albert Hartenstine . . . Married (Donna), two sons (Michael, Beau), one daughter (Jill) . . . Resides in Lake Bluff, IL . . . All-state linebacker at Bethlehem (PA) Liberty High . . . Also participated in basketball and track . . . General arts and sciences major.

HARTENSTINE'S PRO STATS

YEAR	Tkls/Solo	Fum. Rec.	Pass Def.	Blk. Kick	Force Fum.	Sack/Yds.	Games/Starts
1984	36/24	2	0	0	2	6/45	16/14
1983	70/56	1	4	0	3	12/91.5	16/16
1982	24/21	0	1	0	0	4.5/38	9/9
1981	34/29	1	2	0	2	2/12	16/5
1980	66/54	0	4	0	1	6/61	16/16
1979	60/40	1	1	0	1	8/74	16/16
1978	70/44	3	2	0	2	6/57	16/16
1977	55/34	3	4	0	1	1/0	14/11
1976*	86/56	3	5	0	1	3/32.5	14/14
1975*	61/36	2	3	0	1	5/61	14/14
Career	562/394	16	26	1	14	53.5/472	147/131

*Scored TD on 12-yard lateral run @ Dalls 10/24/76. *Scored safety with 22-yard sack of Vikings' Fran Tarkenton 10/27/75. #Scored TD on 10-yard fumble return @ Tampa Bay 11/20/83.

HARTENSTINE'S SINGLE GAME HIGHS

Most Solo Tackles: 10 vs. Den. 12/12/76. Most Sacks: 3 vs. Sea. 12/12/82.
Most Total Tackles: 12 vs. Den. 12/12/76.

JAY HILGENBERG　　**63**

Center	Iowa	5th Year
Ht: 6-3	Wt: 258	Born: 3/21/59, Iowa City, IA

Acquisition: Signed as Free Agent 5/8/81.
1984 SEASON: Emerged as one of league's most consistent centers in first year as full-time starter . . . Started all 16 games . . . Earned game ball vs. New Orleans after Payton broke Jim Brown's rushing mark . . . Also had flawless year as kick snapper. **GAMES PLAYED:** 16 **GAMES STARTED:** 16.
PRO CAREER: Has played in all 58 games since joining team as free agent in '81 . . . Started final 8 games in '83, making first professional start vs. Detroit (10/30/83) . . . Graded 100% on special teams play vs. Bucs (1/2/83) . . . Regarded as one of top deep snappers in league.
COLLEGIATE, PERSONAL: Two-year honorable mention All-America at Iowa . . . Two-year all Big-Ten . . . Four-year letterman . . . Played in Blue-Gray game, Hula and Japan Bowls . . . Given name Jay Walter Hilgenberg . . . Prepped at Iowa City High . . . Nephew of former Viking Wally Hilgenberg . . . Brother Joel is second year center with Saints . . . Favorite book: "The Postman Always Rings Twice" . . . Completed general studies degree at Iowa in '85 off-season.

HILGENBERG'S PRO STATS

Total Games: 58; Bears 1981 (16), 1982 (9), 1983 (16), 1984 (16). Total Starts: 24; Bears 1983 (8), 1984 (16).

STEFAN HUMPHRIES　　**75**

Guard	Michigan	2nd Year
Ht: 6-3	Wt: 263	Born: 1/20/62, Broward, FL

Acquisition: Selected in third round of 1984 draft.
1984 SEASON: Played in 12 of first 14 games before being placed on injured reserve with knee injury . . . Had earlier injured knee vs. St. Louis (10/14) and missed following game against Tampa Bay (10/21) . . . Capable

back-up and special teams player. **GAMES PLAYED: 12 GAMES STARTED:** 0.

COLLEGIATE, PERSONAL: Personified "student-athlete"... Nominated by UM for Rhodes Scholarship while receiving numerous All-America honors... UPI, Football Writers, Football News and TSN first team All-America... Maintained 3.77 GPA in Bio Engineering... Earned academic All-America and all-league laurels as junior and senior... Began career on defensive front but switched to offense midway through freshman year... Three-year starter... Stood out as sophomore while playing on the same line as more heralded teammates and current NFLers Bubba Paris (49ers) & Kurt Becker (Bears)... Heavily recruited out of St. Thomas Aquinas High... Prep-Athlete-of-the-Year and team MVP... Class Valedictorian and National Merit finalist... Earned seven letters in football, basketball and track... Father is school principal... Active in Fellowship of Christian Athletes... Plans to attend Northwestern Medical School in spring of '86.

TYRONE KEYS 98

Defensive End | Mississippi State | 3rd Year
Ht: 6-7 | Wt: 267 | Born: 10/24/59
Brookhaven, MS

Acquisition: From N.Y. Jets for 5th round draft choice in 1985 (7/13/83).
1984 SEASON: Valuable lineman who can play either tackle or end... Started first six games at end before suffering back injury vs. Saints (10/7)... Missed Cardinal game (10/14) and played reserve role remainder of season except for Rams game (11/11) when he replaced injured Hampton at tackle... Recorded five tackles in Rams game... Had 2.5 sacks in first four games of season... Also had sack in playoff loss at San Francisco. **Games Played: 14. Games Started:** 7.
PRO CAREER: Saw action 14 games in '83 including 4 as starter... First career start at L.A. Rams (DRE) and made 7 tackles while knocking down pass (11/6/83)... Started next three games at DLT... Strained lower back in SF game (11/27) and used as sub in last 3 games... 5th round draft choice of N.Y. Jets in '81 but elected to play for British Columbia in CFL '81-'82.

COLLEGIATE, PERSONAL: Three-year all-Southeastern Conference at MSU... Played in Senior Bowl... Given name Tyrone P. Keys... Married (Bessie Ruth)... Mississippi co-defensive "player of year" with Hugh Green at Jackson (MS) Callaway High... Uncle Lee Calhoun won 2 gold medals in '56 and '60 Olympics for hurdles... Hobbies include photography... Has B.S. degree in physical education.

KEYS' PRO STATS

Year	Tkls Solos	Fum. Rec.	Pass Def.	Blk Kick	Force Fum.	Sack –Yds.	Games/ Starts
1984	18/14	0	0	0	0	2.5/26	14/7
1983	17/14	0	2	0	0	0/0	14/4
Career	35/28	0	2	0	0	2.5/26	28/11

KEYS' SINGLE GAME HIGHS

Most Tackles: 7 vs. Rams (11/6/83). Most Solos: 5 vs. Rams (11/11/84).

MITCH KRENK 89

Tight End | Nebraska | 2nd Year
Ht: 6-2 | Wt: 233 | Born: 11/19/59
Crete, Neb.

Acquisition: Claimed on waivers from Dallas 8/28/84.
1984 SEASON: Played in 8 games as well as both playoff tilts... Had 2 catches for 31 yards including 24-yard catch at San Diego (12/3)... Played with Cowboys in preseason and had 5 receptions for 67 yards before being waived (8/26)... Played in two tight end situations and special teams with Bears... Injured back at Seattle (9/23) and placed on injured reserve until being activated (10/28). **Games Played: 8 Games Started:** 0.

PRO CAREER: Spent '83 preseason with Seattle before being waived in final cutdown . . . Played in '83 preseason with Cowboys. **COLLEGIATE, PERSONAL:** Three-year letterman at Nebraska who earned a scholarship after joining team as walk-on . . . Caught 18 passes in four years at Nebraska . . . Two-way all-league lineman at Nebraska City High . . . Married (Judy) . . .

KRENK'S PRO STATS

		Receptions	
Year	No.	Yds.	TD
1984	2	31	0

KEN MARGERUM 82

Wide receiver	Stanford
Ht: 6-0	Wt: 180

4th Year
Born: 10/5/58
Fountain Valley, Cal.

Acquisition: Selected in 3d round of '81 draft.
1984 SEASON: Spent the entire year on the physically unable to perform list after tearing a ligament in his left knee during mini-camp (5/16) . . . Had surgery 5/24. **Games played: 0. Games started: 0.**
PRO CAREER: Played in 15 games, including 9 starts, in 1983 . . . 5th on team in receptions (21) and yards receiving (336) . . . Had 3rd longest reception of year (60 yards) at New Orleans . . . Best game was at Detroit (6 catches, 82 yards, TD) . . . Named to PFWA, UPI, PFW all-rookie teams . . . First career TD was 22-yard catch from Vince Evans at Oakland (12/13/81) . . . Led Bears in receptions (30) and reception yardage (584) in '81.
COLLEGIATE, PERSONAL: Consensus All-America . . . Broke Cardinal records for catches, yards, TD catches set by Tony Hill, James Lofton, Gene Washington . . . Finished 3rd on all-time Pac-10 receiving list . . . 4 TD catches vs. Oregon State in '80 set conference record for single-game TD catches . . . Played in Hula and Senior Bowls . . . All-state at Fountain Valley High School . . . 2nd in state in 120-yard hurdles (13.7) . . . Also triple jumper and low hurdler . . . Has BA in communications/psychology.

MARGERUM'S PRO STATS

	RECEIVING				RUSHING				
	No.	Yds.	Avg.	TD	Att.	Yds.	Avg.	TD	Gms/Sts
1984		DNP				DNP			
1983	21	336	16.0	2	1	7	7	0	15/9
1982	14	207	14.8	3	0	0	0	0	9/9
1981	39*	584*	15.0	6	1	11	11	0	16/6
Career	74	1127	15.2	6	2	18	9	0	40/24

MARGERUM'S SINGLE GAME HIGHS

Long Catch: 60 at New Orleans 9/18/83, from McMahon. Most Caught: 10 at Minnesota 10/4/81. Most Yds. Rec.: 140 at Minnesota 10/4/81.

WILBER MARSHALL 58

Linebacker	Florida
Ht: 6-1	Wt: 225

2nd Year
Born: 4/18/62,
Titusville, FL

Acquisition: First round draft choice (11th player in '84 draft).
1984 SEASON: Made first NFL start vs. Dallas (9/30) after Otis Wilson pulled hamstring—made 8 tackles . . . Played in short yardage and certain passing situations . . . Also a valuable special teamer who forced key fumble in Dallas game on punting team . . . Missed St. Louis game (10/16) with pulled hamstring **Games Played: 15 Games Started: 1.**
COLLEGIATE, PERSONAL: Was Lombardi Award finalist . . . '83 honors included: AP, UPI, NEA, Football Coaches, Walter Camp 1st team All-America . . . Was responsible for 95 tackles, 2 INT's, team-leading 8 tackles behind the line of scrimmage and 6 QB sacks in his senior year . . . Was only junior among 12 finalists for Lombardi

Award . . . Credited with 123 (70 solos, 53 assists), 11 tackles for losses (behind line) and 6 QB sacks . . . Greatest tribute came from former USC and current Ram coach John Robinson, who said: "Wilber is the finest outside linebacker I've seen in my seven years at USC." . . . As a sophomore broke school single season record for sacks (11, –109 yards) and tackles for losses (16) . . . Equally impressive career at Astronaut High . . . Selected 1st team all-America by Parade Magazine and National High School Athletic Coaches . . . All-Southern Player-of-the-Year and Academic all-America as a senior . . . Teammate of Bengal WR Chris Collinsworth for 1 year . . . Excellent tennis and basketball player . . . Given name Wilber Buddyhia Marshall . . . 1 of 13 children . . . Father is Bahamian . . . Criminal justice major.

MARSHALL'S PRO STATS

Year	Interceptions No.	Yds.	TD	Tks/ Solo	Fum. Rec.	Force Fum.	Pass Def.	Blk. Kick	Sack –Yds.	Gm./ Sts
1984	0	0	0	19/17	0	0	0	0	0	15/1

MARSHALL'S SINGLE GAME HIGHS

Most Tackles: 8 vs. Dallas (9/30). Most Solos: 7 vs. Dallas (9/30)

JIM McMAHON   9

Quarterback
Ht: 6-1

B.Y.U.
Wt: 190

4th Year
Born: 8/21/59.
Jersey City, NJ

Acquisition: Was the Bears' number one selection in the 1982 draft.
1984 SEASON: Injury plagued season which forced him to miss seven games including playoffs . . . Suffered hairline fracture in throwing hand and severely bruised back in Denver game (9/9) . . . Reinjured back following week at Green Bay (9/16) and did not play at Seattle (9/23) . . . Hand injury forced him out of Dallas game in fourth quarter (9/30) . . . Played

entire game vs. New Orleans and started next four games before suffering season-ending kidney laceration vs. L.A. Raiders (11/4) . . . Began season with strong performance vs. Bucs with 16 completions in 22 attempts, 138 yards and 1 TD . . . Threw 61-yard TD pass to Gault vs. Denver; play in which Rulon Jones made hit to force hand and back injury . . . Earned game ball at Tampa when he threw for three TD's, completing 12 of 18 for 219 yards . . . Was placed on IR November 10th and remained there for rest of season **GAMES STARTED: 9 GAMES PLAYED: 9.**
PRO CAREER: Set three Bear passing records in '83; highest passing rating (78.5); highest completion percentage (58.4); lowest percentage, passes had intercepted (3.96) . . . Passed for career-high 298 yards at Green Bay (12/4) . . . Had game ball performance vs. 49ers (11/19/83) which included 11 of 19 completions for 159 yards, 1 TD, 9 carries, 74 yards . . . Threw career high 38 passes at Green Bay (12/4) . . . Completed career high 20 passes vs. Atlanta (9/4) vs. Atlanta and at Green Bay (12/4) . . . Caught 18-yard TD pass from Payton at L.A. Rams (9/16) . . . Had 3 200+ yard passing games . . . Threw longest pass in NFC in '83; 87 yards (TD) to Willie Gault at Green Bay (12/4) . . . Was voted UPI, NFC "Rookie of the Year" in '82 . . . PFWA, PFW, Football Digest all-rookie . . . 80.1 passing rating in '82 was 4th in NFC, 9th in NFL, 8th best in Bear history, best in NFL for a rookie . . . Game ball performance vs. Lions (12/21/82) included 16 of 27 for 233 yards, 2 TD . . . Started last 7 games of '82 . . . 5th player selected in draft, 2nd QB . . . Brian Piccolo winner in '82.

McMAHON'S PRO STATS

Year	Gms./Sts.	PASSING Att.	Com.	Pct.	Yds.	Int.	TDs	Rating	RUSHING Att.	Yds.	Avg.
1984	9/9	143	85	59.4	1,146	2	5	97.8	39	276	7.1
1983	14/13	295	175	59.3	2,184	13	12	77.7	55	307	5.6
1982	8/7	210	120	57.1	1,501	7	9	80.1	25	105	4.4
Career	31/29	648	380	58.6	4,831	22	29	82.0	119	688	5.7

McMAHON'S SINGLE GAME HIGHS

Most Yards, Game: 298 at Green Bay 12/4/83 (20-38). Most Pass Att., Game: 38 at Green Bay 12/4/83 (20-38, 298 yards). Most Passes Completed, Game: 20 (twice) vs. Atlanta 9/4/83 (20-29, 254 yards); at Green Bay 12/4/83 (20-38, 298 yards). Most TD's, Game: 2 (5 times); last vs. Green Bay 12/18/84. Completion Pct., Game: 75% at Tampa Bay 12/20/83 (8-12). Long Pass: 87 yards at Green Bay 12/4/83. Most Interceptions, game: 3 vs. Denver 10/2/83. Rushing yards, game: 74 vs. San Francisco 11/27/83 (9-74).

McMAHON vs. NFL

Team	Gms.	Att.	Comp.	Yds.	Int.	TD	Pct.	Rush	Yds.	TD
Atlanta	1	29	20	254	1	1	.690	2	3	0
Baltimore	1	20	8	89	0	0	.400	2	21	0
Dallas	1	14	6	79	1	0	.428	5	4	0
Denver	2	31	20	267	1	4	.645	4	36	0
Detroit	2	43	27	364	3	3	.628	6	36	0
Green Bay	3	70	38	499	3	3	.543	16	75	1
L.A. Rams	1	57	37	458	0	3	.649	12	52	1
L.A. Raiders	1	11	3	68	1	0	.272	3	10	0
Minnesota	4	73	40	386	3	3	.548	14	66	0
New England	1	21	15	192	2	2	.714	2	7	0
New Orleans	3	53	33	431	1	2	.623	6	38	1
Philadelphia	1	16	10	140	2	2	.625	5	43	0
St. Louis	2	56	29	362	0	2	.518	11	84	0
San Francisco	2	19	11	159	1	1	.579	9	74	0
Seattle	1	29	19	199	1	0	.655	4	16	0
Tampa Bay	5	106	64	889	3	6	.603	18	97	1

DENNIS McKINNON   85

Wide Receiver	Florida State	3rd Year
Ht: 6-1	Wt: 185	Born: 8/22/61
		Quitman, GA

Acquisition: Signed as Free Agent 5/4/83.

1984 SEASON: Proved to be one of the best bargains in Bear history after establishing himself as the team's most consistent receiver . . . Started first 12 games before missing final four after arthroscopic surgery on left knee (11/26) . . . Finished fourth in receptions (30) and third in yards (434) . . . Returned for playoffs and played key role in win over Redskins, 4 rec. 72 yds, 1 TD . . . Finest game of career vs. Detroit (11/18), 5 catches for 83 yards . . . Received game ball vs. New Orleans (10/7), 1 rec. 21 yds, 1 rush, 21 yds, and 5 pt ret for 62 yds. **Games Started:** 12 **Games Played:** 12.

PRO CAREER: Developed into starting receiver as rookie free agent . . . Team's leading punt returner in '83 (34 for 316) . . . Returned punt 59 yards for TD at Green Bay (12/4/83) . . . Had 20 catches for 326 yards in '83 . . . Awarded game ball at Philadelphia (10/23/83) after making 1 catch, 20 yards, TD, 5 punt returns for 48 yards . . . His TD in Philadelphia gave Bears 7-6 win . . . Also scored TD vs. Eagles with :10 left in first half that led Bears to 17-14 win (11/13/83) . . . Made 3 catches for 65 yards and scored only TD vs. San Francisco (11/27/83) in Bears 13-3 win . . . Regarded by Mike Ditka as the best blocking wide receiver in professional football.

COLLEGIATE, PERSONAL: Four-year stats at Florida State: 53 receptions, 888 yards, 16.8 average, 8 TD's, 2 carries, 34 yards . . . Played in '79 and '80 Orange Bowls . . . Also played in '82 Gator Bowl where he had 2 catches for 36 yards, TD and one carry for 65 yards . . . Given name Dennis Lewis McKinnon . . . Prepped at Miami (FL) South Miami High . . . Has B.A. degree in Criminology . . . Boyhood idol was Paul Warfield.

McKINNON'S PRO STATS

Year	Gms/Sts	Receiving			Punt Returns			Kickoff Returns		
		No.	Yds.	TD	No.	Yds.	TD	No.	Yds.	Avg.
1984	12/12	30	434	3	5	62	0	0	0	0
1983	16/3	21	236	4	34*	316*	1*	2	42	21.0
Career	28/15	51	670	7	39	378	1	2	42	21.0

* Led team.

McKINNON'S SINGLE GAME HIGHS

Long Catch: 49, vs. S.F. (11/27/83). Most Caught, Game: 5, vs. Lions (11/18/84). Most Yards, Game: 83, vs. Lions (11/18/84). Most KOR's Game: 2, at L.A. Rams (2-42) (11/6/83). Long KOR: 25 at L.A. Rams (11/6/83). Most PR's, Game: 7, at Green Bay (12/4/83) (78 yards). Long PR: 59 (TD) at Green Bay (12/4/83). Combined Yards: 106, vs. Detroit (10/16/83) 42 rec, 64 pt ret.

STEVE McMICHAEL   76

Defensive Tackle	Texas	6th Year
Ht: 6-2	Wt: 260	Born: 10/17/57
		Houston, TX

Acquisition: Signed as Free Agent 10/15/81.
1984 SEASON: Started all season despite knee problems . . . Finished 3rd on team in sacks (10) and 7th in tackles (42) . . . Named NFC Defensive Player of the Week in season finale at Detroit (12/16) after recording 5 tackles and 2½ sacks . . . Had 1½ sacks and 3 tackles vs. Minnesota (10/28) . . . Season-high 6 tackles vs. New Orleans (10/7) . . . Had arthroscopic knee surgery on August 8. **Games Started:** 16
PRO CAREER: Finished 2nd on team in sacks in '83 with 8.5 . . . Game ball at Tampa Bay (11/20) after making 5 tackles, 2 sacks and forcing a fumble . . . Made 6 kickoffs in '83 . . . Had 64-yard run with fumble vs. Bucs (1/2/83) . . . Joined Bears after being waived by Patriots during '81 training camp . . . Replaced Brad Shearer . . . Back injury forced him to injured reserve 11/3/80 through remainder of '80 season . . . New England's 3rd round selection in '80 . . . Played in six games for Patriots.
COLLEGIATE, PERSONAL: Consensus All-America at Texas . . . 372 tackles and 30 sacks over 4 years . . . Led team with 142 tackles as junior, 138 as senior . . . Defensive MVP in '80 Hula Bowl with 14 tackles . . . AP All-America strength team . . . Finalist for '79 Outland Trophy and '80 Lombardi Award . . . Had 9 solos, 4 assists, 2 sacks in Longhorns 16-7 win over Oklahoma . . . Kicked 8 of 10 PAT's and 2 of 3 FG's as sophomore when Russell Erxleben was hurt . . . Given name Steve Douglas McMichael . . . Married (Debra) . . . Prepped at Free (TX) High . . . Hobbies include rattlesnake hunting, fishing . . . Physical education major . . . Involved in Red Cloud Athletic Fund and Lake Forest Chamber of Commerce.

McMICHAEL'S PRO STATS

Year/Club	Tkls. Solo	Fum. Rec.	Pass Def.	Force Fum.	Blk Kick	Sack Yds	Gms. Sts.
1984 Bear	42/30	0	2	0	0	10/91.5	16/16
1983 Bears	37/35	1	2	1	0	8½/86	16/10
1982 Bears	18/17	1	0	0	0	4/36	9/0
1981 Bears	1/1	1	1	0	0	0/0	10/0
1980 Bears	5/3	0	0	0	0	0/0	6/0
1980 Pats	5/3	0	0	1	0	0/0	6/0
Career		3	5	1		22½/213.5	57/26

McMICHAEL'S SINGLE GAME HIGHS

Most Solos: 6 vs. Detroit, 11/6/83. Most Tackles: 7 vs. Detroit, 11/6/83. Most Sacks: 2½ vs. Detroit, 12/16/84.

EMERY MOOREHEAD   87

Tight End	Colorado	9th Year
Ht: 6-2	Wt: 225	Born: 3/22/54,
		Evanston, IL

Acquisition: Signed as Free Agent 10/21/81.
1984 SEASON: Emerged as starter at mid-season and held job through playoffs . . . Started final 9 games and served as play messenger alternating with Dunsmore . . . Finished fifth in receptions (29) and second in reception yards (497) . . . Earned game ball after key 27-yard catch on 4th down vs. Detroit (11/18) set up game winning field goal . . . Also received game ball

after catching 3 passes for 64 yards vs. Vikings (10/28)... Caught 13-yard TD pass from Fuller in division-clinching win over Vikings (11/25)... Season-high 5 catches for 86 yards in season finale at Detroit (12/16)... 50-yard catch clinched 9-7 win over Green Bay (9/16). **Games Played: 16 Games Started: 9.**

PRO CAREER: Started 15 games in '83, finishing 3rd on team in both receptions (42) and reception yards (597)... Scored go-ahead TD vs. Philadelphia (11/13/83) on 2-yard pass from McMahon to lead Bears to 17-14 win... Scored winning TD at Minnesota (12/11/83) on another 2-yard pass from McMahon to give Bears 19-13 win... Had 6 catches for 74 yards and TD in best outing of '83 vs. Detroit (10/30)... Led Bears in receiving yardage in '82 with 363 while starting every game at TE... His 5 TD receptions in '82 were most by Bear TE since Ditka had 5 in '65... Had 65-yard KOR at K.C. (11/8/81)... Awarded to Bears via waivers 8/4/81 from Broncos... Traded to Broncos from N.Y. Giants (5/23/80) for draft pick... On injured reserve list for Giants 11/27/79 through end of season... Giants 6th round choice in '77.

COLLEGIATE, PERSONAL: Running back and flanker at Colorado... 35 receptions for 604 yards in final two season... Given name Emery Matthew Moorehead... Married (Leslee)... One son (Aaron)... One daughter (Kelly)... All-state at Evanston (IL) High... Also starred in basketball and track... Worked for campus TV station as announcer/producer... Also interned at Denver TV station during summers... BA degree in communications.

MOOREHEAD'S SINGLE GAME HIGHS

Long Catch: 50 at Minnesota, 11/28/82; at Green Bay, 9/16/83. Most Catches: 6 vs. Detroit, 10/30/83 (6-74). Most Yards, game: 86 at Detroit, 12/16/83 (5-86).

WALTER PAYTON   34

Running Back	Jackson State	11th Year
Ht: 5-11	Wt: 204	Born: 7/25/54, Columbia, MS

Acquisition: Bears' number one selection in 1975 draft.
1984 SEASON: Made 7th Pro Bowl appearance... Selected All-Pro by TSN, PFW, Football Digest, AP, NEA, UPI, PFWA... Became NFL's all-time leading rusher vs. New Orleans (10/7) surpassing Jim Brown... Accomplished the feat with 154-yard effort and record breaking run came in third quarter (6 yards); mark came in 10th season, 2,795th career rushing attempt... Also broke Brown's combined yardage mark in second game of season vs. Broncos (9/9) with 179-yard effort; his 7th best rushing output for one game (included 72 yd. TD run; 3rd best of career)... Was named NFC Offensive "Player of the Week," following Denver game... Led team in rushing yards and number of receptions... Had second best rushing output of career in '84 (best is 1,852 in '77)... Broke club best rushing output for career receptions, previously held by Johnny Morris... Had 9 100+ yard games in '84 including 6 consecutive (previous best was 5 in '77)... Played QB for four plays vs. Packers (12/9)... Threw two TD passes to Matt Suhey on halfback op-

MOOREHEAD'S PRO STATS

Year/Club	Gms/Sts	Receiving				Rushing			
		No.	Yds.	Avg.	TD	No.	Yds.	Avg.	TD
1984 Bears	16/9	29	497	17.1	1	1	-2	-2.0	0
1983 Bears	16/15	42	597	14.2	3	5	6	1.2	0
1982 Bears	9/9	30	363	12.1	5	2	3	1.5	0
1981 Bears	9/0	0	0	0.0	0	0	0	0.0	0
1980 Broncos	16/0	0	0	0.0	0	2	7	3.5	0
1979 Giants	13/4	9	62	6.9	0	36	95	2.6	0
1978 Giants	10/0	3	45	15.0	0	0	0	0.0	0
1977 Giants	13/7	12	143	11.9	1	1	5	5.0	0
Career	102/44	125	1,707	13.6	10	47	114	2.3	0

KOR 23 for 476 (20.7) in 1981; 1 for 18 in 1980; 1 for 16 in 1979. PTR: 2 for 52 (26.0) in 1978; 4 for 65 (16.3) in 1977.

tion . . . Went over 1,000 yard mark for 8th time in career tying an NFL record shared by Franco Harris . . . Broke Brown's record for most 100 yard games in career (58); now has 63 in 10 years . . . Rushed for 104 yards in playoff win over Redskins and had 75 yards to lead all rushers in Pro Bowl . . . Scored pair of TD's in wins over Tampa Bay (44-9) and L.A. Raiders (17-6) **Games Played:** 16. **Games Started:** 16.

PRO CAREER: Enters 11th pro season with 124 consecutive starts . . Has started in 140 of 146 games since joining team in '75 . . . Owns league single game rushing record of 275 yards vs. Vikings (11/20/77) . . . Now leads Brown by 997 yards on all-time rushing list and is shooting for 15,000 career rushing yards . . has 17,304 combined yards and leads Brown by 1,845 . . Now owns 16 of top 22 all-time Bear rushing days . . Owns 22 Bear records, 5 NFL records (rushing, combined yards, most 100 yard games, single game, rushing attempts) and shares another (8 1,000-yard games with Harris) . . Member of all-NFL squad of the '70's . . Has back-to-back 2,000+ yards combined during '83-'84 seasons . . Took unprecedented 5th consecutive NFC rushing Title in '80 with 1,460 . . Bears have won 41 times when he has gone over 100 yards in a game . . Youngest player to be voted NFL MVP at 23 years of age in '77 . . 1,852 yards rushing that year is 5th highest total in NFL history . . Won '75 kickoff return title with 31.7 . . Now owns Pro Bowl record for most rushing attempts in a career having surpassed O.J. Simpson's mark.

POST-SEASON HONORS: 1975—none (all-rookie runners Mike Thomas and Don Hardeman). **1976**—PFWA, AP all-Pro pick; Sporting News NFC Player of the Year; runner-up to Chuck Foreman NFL MVP by UPI; got 39 of possible 42 votes to UPI all NFC team . . Started Pro Bowl game for NFC . . Chicago Red Cloud Athlete-of-the-Year. **1977**—UPI Athlete-of-the-Year over baseball's Steve Carlton; NFL MVP by PFWA, NEA (Thorpe Trophy), Mutual Radio, AP FB Digest, Sport Magazine NFL Player-of-the-Year, AP NFL most valuable offensive player; UPI, Sporting News NFC Player-of-the-Year, AP NFL Pro Bowl squad; only unanimous choice to NFC Pro Bowl squad; leading vote getter to UPI all NFC team . . All-pro pick AP, UPI, NEA (top pick); Pro FB Weekly Offensive Player-of-the-Year; won Sea-

gram's "Oscar" award for football and $10,000 price; in '77 divisional playoff rushed 19 for 60, 3 rec for 33, 3 KORs for 57; MVP of Pro Bowl with 13 rushes for 77 yards and game winning TD. **1978**—All-Pro pick, NEA, PFWA; Pro Bowl starter; leading vote getter to UPI all NFC team. **1979**—Pro Bowl starter; AP all NFC; in wildcard playoff rushed 16 for 67, 3 rec for 52, 2 TDs, had 84-yard run called back by "motion" penalty. **1980**—Leading vote getter to NFC team for Pro Bowl. **1981**—None. **1982**—Wisconsin Pro Football Lombardi Dedication Award. **1983**—2nd Team UPI all NFC; 2nd team NEA all NFL, Pro Bowl backup; (11 carries for 40 yards; one incomplete pass; three receptions for 11 yards). **1984**—7th Pro Bowl appearance (11 carries, 76 yards, 1 TD, 3 receptions, 54 yards); 1st team TSN, PFW, Football Digest, AP, NEA, UPI, PFWA).

COLLEGIATE: Football Round-up College Player-of-the-Year . . . '74 . . Leading scorer in NCAA history with 464 points . . Led nation with 160 points in '73 . . First running back, 4th player selected in '75 draft (behind Steve Bartkowski, Randy White, Ken Huff) . . Scored 65 touchdowns, rushed for 3,563 (6.1) yards, kicked five field goals and 54 PAT, caught 27 passes for 474 yards, had 39.0 punting average, 43.0 kickoff return average, hit 14 of 19 passes for 4 TDs . . Played in College All-Star (Pittsburgh 21-14), East-West and Senior Bowl games.

PERSONAL: Was named the 1984 Black Athlete of the Year which was voted on by black media members nationwide . . Given name Walter Jerry Payton . . Nickname is Sweetness . . Married (Connie) . . One son (Jarrett) . . One daughter (Brittany) . . Resides in suburban Barrington, IL . . Part owner of Studebaker's Diner & Bar in suburban Schaumburg . . Active in many charities . . Served as the honorary chairman of the Ben Wilson memorial dinner in March ('84); Wilson was the former Simeon H.S. basketball player who was shot to death Nov. 20, 1984 . . Was honorary chairman for the '83 Heart Association Jump Rope for Heart . . Honorary chairman Illinois Mental Health Association '78-80 . . Also aids Boy Scouts, March of Dimes, Brian Piccolo Cancer Research Fund, United Way, Peace Corps . . Tremendous strength; 390 bench press, 600+ leg-press, 300 military . . Nominated NFL Man of the Year . . . Attended Columbia High but didn't start playing football until 11th grade . . . Father deceased, Mother (Alyne) resides in Columbia . . . Interests include drums, antique cars, privacy . . . Biography *Sweetness* published in '78 by Contemporary Books . . . Formed "Walter Payton Enterprises" (investments) in '79 . . . Received BA in special education at Jackson State in 3½ years.

PAYTON'S PRO STATS

Year	RUSHING Att.	Yds.	Avg.	TD	RECEIVING No.	Yds.	Avg.	TD	Games/Sts
1984	381	1684	4.4	11	45	368	8.2	0	16/16
1983	314	1421	4.5	6	53	607	11.5	2	16/16
1982	148	596	4.0	1	32	311	9.7	2	9/9
1981	339	1222	3.6	6	41	379	9.2	2	16/16
1980	317	1460	4.6	6	46	367	8.0	1	16/16
1979	369	1610	4.4	14	31	313	10.1	2	16/16
1978	333	1395	4.2	11	50	480	9.5	0	16/16
1977	339	1852	5.5	14	27	269	10.0	2	14/14
1976	311	1390	4.5	13	15	149	9.9	0	14/14
1975	196	679	3.5	7	33	213	6.5	0	13/7
Career	3047	13309	4.4	89	373	3455	9.3	9	146/140

Year	KICKOFF RETURNS No.	Yds.	Avg.	TD	PASSING Att.	Com.	Yds.	TD	Int.	PUNT RETURNS No.	Yds.	Avg.
1984	0	0	0.0	0	0	0	0	0	0	0	0	0.0
1983	0	0	0.0	0	6	3	95	3	2	0	0	0.0
1982	0	0	0.0	0	3	1	39	1	0	0	0	0.0
1981	0	0	0.0	0	2	0	0	0	0	0	0	0.0
1980	0	0	0.0	0	3	0	0	0	0	0	0	0.0
1979	0	0	0.0	0	1	1	54	1	0	0	0	0.0
1978	0	0	0.0	0	0	0	0	0	0	0	0	0.0
1977	2	95	47.5	0	0	0	0	0	0	0	0	0.0
1976	1	0	0.0	0	0	0	0	0	0	0	0	0.0
1975	14	444	31.7	0	1	0	0	0	1	39	39	39.0
Career	17	539	31.7	0	16	5	188	5	3	39	39	39.0

DAN RAINS 53

Linebacker   Cincinnati   4th Year
Ht: 6-1   Wt: 222   Born: 4/26/56
Rochester, PA

Acquisition: Signed as Free Agent May 14, 1982.
1984 SEASON: Valued special teams player who finished third in kamakaze tackles (6) . . . Also had 7 tackles (5 solos) in reserve role at linebacker . . . Had two stops vs. Denver (9/9) and Detroit (12/16). **Games Played:** 16 **Games Started:** 0.
PRO CAREER: Started 5 games in '83 and finished year with 25 tackles, 19 solos . . . Career best of 6 tackles vs. Detroit (10/30/83) . . . Discovered by Bears on a film of an '81 semi-pro game . . . Played in final two games of '82 after being placed on injured reserve for hernia (7/9/82) . . . Spent '80 season with Columbus Metros (semi-pro) . . . Moved up a level in '81 and was defensive MVP of West Virginia Rockets of American Football Association . . . Rockets beat Chicago Fire in championship game that year.
COLLEGIATE, PERSONAL: Honorable mention AP All-America at Cincinnati . . . Played in Japan Bowl . . . Four-year letterman and team MVP as senior . . . Redshirted in '75 . . . Native of Aliquippa, PA; same area as Mike Ditka, Jim Covert . . . Given name Daniel Paul Rains . . . Married (Debbie) . . . Prepped at Aliquippa (PA) Hopewell High . . . One of 10 children . . . BS degree in criminology . . . Involved in Sports Teams Organized for Prevention of Drug Abuse.

RAINS' PRO STATS

Year	Interceptions No.	Yds.	TD	Tkls Solo	Fum. Rec.	Pass Def.	Force Fum.	Blk Kick	Sack Yds	Gms Sts
1984	0	0	0	7/5	0	0	1	0	0/0	16/0
1983	0	0	0	25/19	1	0	1	0	0/0	15/5
1982	0	0	0	0/0	0	0	0	0	0/0	2/0
Career	0	0	0	32/24	1	0	2	0	0/0	33/5

RICHARDSON'S PRO STATS

| Year | Interceptions | | | Tkls/ Solos | Fum Rec. | Pass Def. | Force Fum. | Blk Kick | Sack/ Yds. | Gms/ Sts |
	No.	Yds.	TD							
1984	2	7	0	36/31	1	13	0	0	0/0	15/15
1983	5	9	0	68/57	1	20	0	1	0/0	16/14
Career	7	16	0	104/88	2	33	0	1	0/0	31/29

Also, 1 KOR for 21 yards in '83

RICHARDSON'S SINGLE GAME HIGHS

Long intercept: 7 vs. Minnesota 10/25/84. Most deflections: 3 (six times). Most Interceptions: 2 vs. Tampa Bay 11/20/83; vs. Green Bay 12/18/83. Most solos: 9 vs. Detroit 10/30/83. Most tackles: 9 vs. Detroit 10/30/83. Last interception: vs. Minnesota 10/28/84.

RON RIVERA   59

Linebacker   California   2nd Year
Ht: 6-3   Wt: 244   Born: 1/7/62
                                        Monterey, CA

Acquisition: Selected in the second round of the 1984 draft.
1984 SEASON: Employed primarily as special teams player . . . Played in final 15 games after sitting out season-opener with bruised shoulder . . . Suffered sciatic nerve injury in first practice which sidelined him much of preseason . . . Had 6 tackles as LB and three special teams tackles . . . Had two tackles in reserve action at Seattle (9/23) . . . 44th selection in '84 draft.

MIKE RICHARDSON   27

Cornerback   Arizona State   3rd Year
Ht: 6-0   Wt: 188   Born: 5/23/61,
                                        Compton, CA

Acquisition: Selected in the second round of the 1983 draft.
1984 SEASON: Started 15 games, missing St. Louis game (10/14) with broken wrist suffered previous week vs. New Orleans (10/7) . . . Had theft in final play of game in playoff win vs. Redskins . . . Also had one of team's six interceptions in season-opener vs. Bucs (9/2); also theft vs. Minnesota (10/28) . . . Season-high six tackles in finale at Detroit (12/16) . . . Led team in passes defended with 13 . . . Had 36 tackles, 31 solos. **Games Played:** 15 **Games Started:** 15.
PRO CAREER: Finished in second place tie (with Schmidt) on team with 5 interceptions in '83 . . . Also 5th on team in tackles as rookie with 68; 4th in solos with 57 . . . Had 20 passes defended to rank 2nd . . . Knocked down three passes pro debut vs. Falcons (9/4/83) . . . Awarded game ball vs. Philadelphia (9/23/83) after 5 tackles and 2 passes defended . . . 2 interceptions at Tampa Bay (11/20/83) and vs. Green Bay (12/18/83).
COLLEGIATE, PERSONAL: Four-year all-Pac 10 at ASU . . . Led secondary in tackles all four years . . . Two-year consensus All-America . . . Set school record with 18 career interceptions (2 shy of Pac-10 mark) . . . College stats: 326 tackles, 181 solos, 9 sacks, 7 fumble recoveries, 15 passes deflected, 18 interceptions, 2 TD's . . . Given name Michael Calvin Richardson . . . Has six sisters . . . All-America at Compton (GA) High . . . First defensive player to win California "Player of Year" Award . . . Captain as senior . . . Hobbies include swimming, Mexican food and ice cream . . . Business major.

COLLEGIATE, PERSONAL: Consensus first team All-America, Lombardi Award finalist and Pac 10 co-defensive player of the year as senior at Cal . . . Finished with 138 tackles (26 for losses) and 13 sacks as senior . . . Had double figure tackles in 9 of 11 games as senior . . . Also led team in tackles in '82 (99; 8 for losses) . . . 17 tackle performance as sophomore vs. defending national champ Georgia, 16 tackles vs. Texas A & M ('83) and Oregon State ('82) . . . Also returned interception 53 yards for TD vs. Beavers . . . Three-year letterman in football, baseball and basketball at Seaside (CA) High . . . 14 home runs in 20 games as junior . . . Given name Ron Rivera . . . Father career military man . . . Has lived in Germany, Panama, as well as Washington and Maryland before moving to Southern California . . . Sociology major.

RIVERA'S PRO STATS

Year	Interceptions			Tkls/ Solo	Fum. Rec.	Pass Def.	Force Fum.	Blk Kick	Sack	Sack Yds.	Gms/ Sts
	No.	Yds.	TD								
1984	0	0	0	6/5	0	0	0	0	0	0	15/0

MIKE SINGLETARY   50

Middle Linebacker   Baylor   5th Year
Ht: 6-0   Wt: 228   Born: 10/9/58
Houston, TX

Acquisition: Second round selection in the 1981 draft.
1984 SEASON: First-team all-NFL choice by Sporting News, PFW, Football Digest, AP, NEA, PFWA; UPI and all-NFC . . . Played in second straight Pro Bowl as starter . . . Led team in tackles for second consecutive year with 116, including 81 solos . . . Defensive captain and signal caller . . . Season-high 12 tackles at San Diego (12/3) . . . Game ball performance in season-opener vs. Tampa Bay (9/2) when he had only interception of season and five tackles . . . Tied a career-high with 3.5 sacks . . . Only linebacker to play in team's 46 pass defense . . . Second on team with three forced fumbles. Games Played: 16 Games Started: 16.
PRO CAREER: Made virtually every all-pro team in '83 when he was selected to first Pro Bowl . . . Led team in tackles (148), solos (118), assists (30) and fumble recoveries (4) in '83 . . . Earned game ball vs. Minnesota (12/11/83) after 11 tackles, 1 force fumble, 2 pass deflections and 1 sack . . . Tied for second on club with 71 tackles in '82 . . . Names PFWA, UPI, PFW and Football Digest all-rookie teams in '81 when he started last nine games . . . Game ball performance vs. Kansas City (11/8/81) included 10 tackles, 6 solos, and 1 forced fumble . . . Piccolo Award Winner . . . 38th player, 5th linebacker in draft . . . Bears received that choice from 49ers for a 5th round pick and exchange of 2nd round positions to skip past Vikings.
COLLEGIATE, PERSONAL: Consensus SWC "Player of Year" in '79 and '80 at Baylor . . . Only junior selected to all-SWC Team-of-the-70's . . . Consensus All-America . . . Averaged 15 tackles per game over career . . . Set school record with 232 tackles in '78 . . . Posted 20 tackles or more in 4 games; 30 or more 3 times . . . Never had less than 10 in a game . . . Finalist in '80 Lombardi Trophy voting . . . Tri-captain in '79, captain in '80 . . . Made career-high 33 stops vs. Arkansas . . . Played in Hula and Japan Bowls . . . College Stats: 5 interceptions, 21 yards, 662 tackles, 351 solos, 6 fumble recoveries, 18 passes defended . . . Given name Michael Singletary . . . Married (Kim) . . . Received first football uniform as sophomore at Houston Worthing High . . . Favorite book: "The Amazing Results of Positive Thinking" by Norman Vincent Peale . . . Has BA degree in management . . . Involved in Fellowship of Christian Athletes, Brian Piccolo Cancer Research Fund and Sports Teams Organized for Prevention of Drug Abuse . . . Recipient of Mayor Daley Award for Community Service at '85 Red Cloud Banquet.

SINGLETARY'S PRO STATS

Year	Interceptions No.	Interceptions Yds.	Tkls/ Solo	Fum. Rec.	Pass Def.	Force Fum.	Blk Kick	Sack/ Yds.	Gms/ Sts
1984	1	4	116/81	1	4	3	0	3.5/24	16/16
1983	1	0	*148/118*	4	7	1	0	3.5/23.5	16/16
1982	0	0	71/61	1	2	1	0	1/9	9/9
1981	1	-3	72/60	0	4	1	0	0/0	16/9
Career	3	1	407/320	6	17	6	0	8/56.5	57/50

*Led team.

SINGLETARY'S SINGLE GAME HIGHS

Most Tackles: 12, vs. 49ers 11/27/83; vs. Chargers 12/3/84. Most Solos: 10, at Rams 12/6/83.

*Team Leader

MATT SUHEY   26

Running Back	Penn State	6th Year
Ht: 5-11	Wt: 216	Born: 7/7/58
		State College, PA

Acquisition: Second round choice in 1980 draft.
1984 SEASON: Season-long starter at fullback . . . Second-leading rusher with 424 yards on 124 carries and 4 TD's . . . Also finished second in receptions (41) . . . Key 33-yd catch set up touchdown in playoff win over Redskins . . . Best outings were first two weeks of season rushing for 57 yards vs. Tampa Bay (9/2) and 59 vs. Denver (9/9) . . . Had 5 catches vs. St. Louis (10/14) and Green Bay (12/9) . . . Season-high of 45 yards on 3 catches vs. New Orleans . . . Caught two TD passes from Payton on half-back option. **Games Started:** 16. **Games Played:** 16.
PRO CAREER: Turned in best statistical season in '83 rushing for 681

yards on 141 attempts . . . Had first career 100 + yard game vs. Tampa Bay (11/20/83), rushing 19 times for 112 yards . . . Game ball performance vs. Minnesota (12/11/83) after rushing 17 times for 101 yards and passing 74 yards to Payton for TD . . . Became full-time starter in 1981 after starting one game as rookie (9/28/80) . . . 64-yard rushing, 1 TD effort vs. San Diego (10/25/81) earned him game ball . . . Had career-high 9 receptions for 87 yards vs. St. Louis (12/19/82) . . . Accounted for 180 combined yards at Pittsburgh—130 by KOR (9/28/80) . . . 7th running back selected in '80 draft, 46th player overall.
COLLEGIATE, PERSONAL: Penn State's third all-time rusher with 2,818 yards, trailing Curt Warner and Lydell Mitchell, but ahead of John Cappelletti and Franco Harris . . . Holds school record for rushing attempts in career (643) . . . 4th in school history in total offense (3,146), 4th in TD's (29) . . . Names to UPI's all-East team . . . Honorable mention all-America . . . Played in Hula Bowl . . . PSU's leading rusher in '77, '78, '79 . . . Also caught 39 passes for 328 yards and 2 TD's for Lions . . . Given name Matthew Jerome Suhey . . . Maternal grandfather Bob Higgins was a PSU All-America in 1919, played end for Canton Bulldogs against George Halas and Chicago Staleys in 1921 (Staleys won 10-0), and coached the Lions from 1930-48 . . . Father (Steve) was an All-America guard at PSU in 1947 and played with Jim Finks and Steelers in '49. He was inducted (1985) into the National Football Foundation's College Hall of Fame . . . Brothers Larry (RB) and Paul (LB) were on Lions' '76 team with Matt . . . Three-year all-state RB . . . Football captain, lettered in track and wrestling . . . Resides in Highland Park, IL . . . B.S. degree in Marketing . . . Pursuing MBA at Northwestern . . . Involved in Sports Teams Organized for Prevention of Drug Abuse, Chicago Boys Clubs and Lake Forest Chamber of Commerce.

SUHEY'S PRO STATS

Year	RUSHING No.	Yds.	Avg.	TD	RECEIVING No.	Yds.	Avg.	TD	Gms/Sts
1984	125	415	3.3	4	41	309	7.5	2	16/16

Year	No.	Yds.	Avg.	TD	No.	Yds.	Avg.	TD	Gms./Sts
1983	149	681	4.6	4	49	428	8.8	1	16/13
1982	70	206	2.9	3	36	333	9.3	0	9/9
1981	150	521	3.5	3	33	168	5.1	0	15/15
1980	22	45	2.0	0	7	60	8.6	0	16/1

SUHEY'S SINGLE GAME HIGHS

Most Rushes: 22 vs. Chargers, 10/25/81 (22-64). Most Yards Rush: 112 at Tampa Bay, 11/20/83 (19-112). Long Rush: 39 at Tampa Bay, 11/20/83. Most Rec.: 9 vs. Cardinals, 10/19/82 (9-87). Most Yards Rec.: 89 vs. Broncos, 10/2/83 (5-89). Long Catch: 52 vs. Broncos, 10/2/83. Combined Yards: 180 (twice) at Steelers 9/28/80 (130 by KOR, 50 by rushing); at Vikings 12/11/83 (101 rush, 5 rec, 74 pass). Most KOR: 6 vs. Vikings 9/21/80 (6-115) at Pittsburgh 9/28/80 (6-130). Most Yards KOR: 130 at Pittsburgh 9/28/80 (6-130). Long KOR: 31 vs. Bengals 12/14/80 (1-31).

CALVIN THOMAS   33

Running Back	Illinois	4th Year
Ht: 5-11	Wt: 245	Born: 1/7/60
		St. Louis, MO

Acquisition: Signed as Free Agent May 21, 1980.

1984 SEASON: Shared playing time with Matt Suhey at fullback the last half of season . . . Career-high 57 yards on 5 carries vs. Detroit (11/18) . . . 37-yard run vs. Lions was also career best . . . Scored first pro touchdown in season finale at Detroit (12/16) . . . Had 3 catches for 16 yards vs. San Diego (12/3) . . . Valued special teams performer who forced fumble in season opener vs. Tampa Bay (9/2) . . . Suffered shoulder separation in pre-season. **Games Played: 16 Games Started: 0.**

PRO CAREER: Played in final 13 games in '83 after recovering from shoulder separation suffered in final pre-season game . . . Primarily used on special teams in '82 and '83 . . . Had 25 yards on 8 carries, 2 catches for 13 yards in '83 . . . Played in 6 of last 7 games in '82 . . . 9 carries, 59 yards and TD in 27-21 win over Raiders in '83 preseason.

COLLEGIATE, PERSONAL: Four-year letterman at Illinois . . . Illinois stats: 325 carried, 1,194 yards, (3.7 avg.), 8 TD's, 42 catches, 328 yards (7.8 avg.), 0 TD's . . . Played in Blue-Gray Game . . . Given name Calvin Lewis Thomas . . . All-state at St. Louis McKinley High . . . Hobbies include basketball, music . . . Four-year letterman in track . . . Sociology and history major . . . Involved in Red Cloud Athletic Fund.

THOMAS' PRO STATS

	Rushing				Receiving				
Year	No.	Yds.	Avg.	TD	No.	Yds.	Avg.	TD	Gms./Sts
1984	40	186	4.7	1	9	39	4.3	0	16/0
1983	8	25	3.1	0	2	13	6.5	0	13/0
1982	5	4	0.8	0	0	0	0	0	6/0
Career	53	215	4.1	1	11	52	4.7	0	35/0

THOMAS' SINGLE GAME HIGHS

Most Rushes: 6 vs. Detroit 12/16/84 (6-4). Most Yards Rush: 52 vs. Detroit 11/18/84 (5-52). Long Rush: 37 vs. Detroit 11/18/84. Most. Rec.: 3, vs. San Diego, 12/3/84 (3-16). Most Yards Rec.: 16 vs. San Diego, 12/3/84 (3-16). Long Rec.: 9 (twice) vs. Rams (11/11/84) and vs. San Diego (12/3/84).

KEITH VAN HORNE   78

Tackle	USC	5th Year
Ht: 6-7	Wt: 276	Born: 11/6/57
		Mt. Lebanon, PA

Acquisition: First round draft choice in 1981.

1984 SEASON: Best season of career, fulfilling potential shown when drafted . . . Started 14 games, missing New Orleans (10/7) and St. Louis (10/14) games with pulled hamstring. **Games Played: 14 Games Started: 14**

PRO CAREER: Started 10 games in '83 before suffering ankle injury vs. Rams (11/6) that limited his playing time for remainder of season . . . Started all 9 games in '82 . . . PFWA, UPI, Football Digest all-rookie choice in '81 when he started last 12 games . . . Played LT in '81 preseason . . . 11th player selected (1st lineman) in '81 draft.

COLLEGIATE, PERSONAL: 1980 Outland Trophy runner-up to Pitt's Mark May . . . Consensus All-America as senior . . . Academic All-Pac 10 final two years . . . Redshirted as freshman in '76 after foot injury . . . Played in Hula Bowl with fellow Bear draftees Mike Singletary and Ken Margerum . . . Trojans were 39-7-2 during his four years . . . Given name is Keith Van Horne . . . Two-year all-conference TD/DL at Fullerton (CA) High (former President Nixon's school) . . . 59' shot put . . . Arrived at USC as 230-pound tight end . . . Brother Peter was signed by Cubs in '77 as CF, 1B . . . Avid weight-lifter in off-season . . . Parents live in Clarendon Hills (IL) . . . Has BA degree in broadcast journalism . . . Involved in Red Cloud Athletic Fund, Chicago Sports Medicine and Dane Injury Center.

VAN HORNE'S PRO STATS

Total Games: 51: Bears 1981 (14), 1982 (9), 1983 (14), 1984 (14). Total Starts: 45: Bears 1981 (12), 1982 (9), 1983 (10), 1984 (14). 1982: Recovered fumble and made 1 tackle.

HENRY WAECHTER

Defensive Tackle	Nebraska	70	4th Year
Ht: 6-5	Wt: 270		Born: 2/13/59
			Dubuque, IA

Acquisition: Signed as Free Agent, 12/5/84

1984 SEASON: Solid late-season replacement for injured Mike Hartenstine at defensive end . . . Started final two games of season and played extensively in playoffs . . . Had two sacks in season finale vs. Detroit (12/16) . . . Also sacked Joe Theismann in playoff win over Redskins . . . Played first four games with Colts before being waived. Games Played: 2 Games Started: 2.

PRO CAREER: Bears 7th round draft choice in '82 . . . Started for injured Al Harris at right end vs. Saints (9/19/82) and vs. Cardinals (12/19/82) . . . Played in all nine games in '82 . . . Waived prior to '83 season . . . Played final 12 games of '83 season with Colts . . . Waived by Colts following fourth game of '84.

COLLEGIATE, PERSONAL: Two-year starter at Nebraska after transferring from Woldord (IA) Junior College . . . Had 119 tackles, 77 solos as Cornhusker . . . Coaches' defensive player of game in 31-7 win over Iowa State with 5 solos and interception which set up TD . . . Redshirted in '79 . . . All-America at Waldorf J.C. . . . Given name Henry Carl Waechter . . . All-conference DT-TE at Western Dubuque (IA) High . . . Earned business degree from Nebraska in off-season.

WAECHTER'S PRO STATS

	Tkls/Solo	Fum. Rec.	Sack/Yrds	Gms/Sts
1984 Colts/Bears	10/8	0	2/7	*6/2
1983 Colts	14/9	0	1.5/13	11/0
1982 Bears	15/10	0	0/0	9/2
Career	39/27	0	3.5/20	

*4 games with Colts

WAECHTER'S SINGLE GAME HIGHS

Most Tackles: 7 vs. Saints 9/19/82. Most Solos: 6 vs. Saints 9/19/82. Most Sacks: 2 vs. Detroit (12/16/84).

OTIS WILSON

Linebacker	Louisville	55	6th Year
Ht: 6-2	Wt: 231		Born: 9/15/57
			New York, NY

WILSON'S PRO STATS

Year	Interceptions			Fum. Rec.	Tkds/ Solos	Pass Def.	Force Fum.	Blk Kick	Sack/ Yds	Games/ Starts
	No.	Yds.	TD							
1984	0	0	0	0	61/47	3	1	0	7.5/75	15/15
1983	0	6	0	0	100/84	7	2	0	3/30	16/16
1982	2	39	1	0	40/31	1	0	0	2/9	9/9
1981	0	0	0	3	81/65	3	2	1	0/0	15/12
1980	2	4	0	0	15/13	1	0	0	2/18	16/1
Career	5	49	1	3	297/240	15	5	1	14.5/132	71/53

WILSON'S SINGLE GAME HIGHS

Most Tackles: 10 (5 times), last vs. Rams (11/11/84). Most Solos: 10, vs. 49ers (11/27/83). Long Fum Return: 31, vs. Rams (9/28/81).

Acquisition: Bears' number one selection in 1980 draft.

1984 SEASON: Enjoyed best season in pro career, finishing fifth on team in tackles (61) and fourth in sacks (7.5) . . . Consistent played earned him game ball vs. Green Bay (9/23) and New Orleans (10/7) . . . Had season-highs of 10 tackles vs. Rams (11/11) and two sacks vs. Detroit (12/16) . . . Nine-tackle, 1.5 sack performance vs. Raiders (11/4) . . . Pulled groin vs. Seattle (9/23) and missed following game vs. Dallas (10/30). **Games Played: 15 Games Started: 15.**

PRO CAREER: Team's second leading tackler in '83 (100); third leading tackler in '83 (100) . . . Had 39-yard interception return for TD vs. Tampa Bay (1/2/83) . . . Made first pro start in finale of rookie season vs. Tampa Bay in place of injured Jerry Muckensturm and responded with 7 solos and an interception . . . First career theft came against Archie Manning (9/14/80), first sack on Gary Danielson (10/19/80) . . . First linebacker, 19th player selected in '80 draft.

COLLEGIATE, PERSONAL: NEA, Sporting News All-America at Louisville . . . Made 175 tackles as senior enroute to breaking two of Doug Buffone's tackling records . . . Ranks second to Buffone in career tackles (495-485) . . . Also had 10 interceptions and 8 fumble recoveries for Cardinals . . . Defensive MVP in '77 Independence Bowl . . . Played in East-West, Senior Bowl games . . . Given name Otis Ray Wilson . . . Nickname: Big O . . . One son (Quincy), one daughter (Chyla) . . . Prepped at Brooklyn Thomas Jefferson High . . . Grew up in Brownsville neighborhood which produced John Brockington, basketball pro Lloyd B. Free and WBA champ Eddie Gregory . . . Hobbies include hunting, basketball . . . Is involved in Red Cloud Athletic Fund and Lake Forest Chamber of Commerce.

1985 BEAR ROOKIE BIOGRAPHIES

WILLIAM PERRY 72

Defensive Tackle
Ht: 6-2

Clemson
Wt: 318

Born: 12/16/62, Aiken, SC

Acquisition: First round selection in 1985 draft (22nd player).

SENIOR SEASON: Outland and Lombardi Trophy finalist . . . Finished first among Division I players in tackles for loss with 2.45 average (27 in 11 games) . . . Led Tigers in tackles with 100 and became first player in history to lead team in tackles as down lineman . . . Finished year with 10 sacks and became all-time Clemson leader with 25 . . . Had 16 tackles against Maryland, the third highest total of a down lineman in Clemson history . . . Had more tackles than any other down lineman in the conference in 1984 . . . Named first-team all-America by the Walter Camp Foundation in 1983 and 1984 . . . Only the second unanimous All-America in Clemson history . . . 1984 preseason All-America by TSN and Street & Smith . . . Had 36-yard punt return off a blocked punt against Wake Forest, longest punt return for Tiger player in four years.

COLLEGIATE, PERSONAL: Nicknamed "the Refrigerator" . . . All-time Clemson leader in fumble involvement (caused fumbles and recovered fumbles) in a career with 15 . . . Led team in tackles in '83 for loss with 15 and for negative yardage in tackles . . . Had seven tackles, including three for losses and QB sack against Georgia . . . Despite weight, he runs 40 in 5.1 and has been clocked at 5.05 . . . One of the all-time legends in weight lifting at Clemson . . . Bench pressed 465 pounds . . . Also has the all-time Clemson record for overall strength category, he lifted 1,638 in '84 spring to lead the team . . . Was Tigers' first All-America sophomore in history . . . Also made honorable mentioned teams chosen by UPI and Football News . . . Had at least one tackle for loss in each of 11 games in

'82 . . . Most highly touted player to sign with Clemson for '81 season . . . Prep All-America according to Parade and Addidas . . . Three-sport letterman in high school . . . Married (Sherry) with one daughter (Latavia).

PERRY'S COLLEGE STATS

Year/School	Tackles/ Solos	Fumble Rec.	Forced Fumble	Sacks/ Yards	TL/ Yds.	Games/ Starts
1981 Clemson	48/33	2	1	4/44	9/50	12/4
1982 Clemson	52/30	1	3	5/38	9/66	11/7
1983 Clemson	61/38	1	2	6/40	15/67	11/4
1984 Clemson	100/69	3	2	10/68	27/111	11/11
TOTALS	261/170	7	8	25/190	60/294	45/36

REGGIE PHILLIPS 36

Cornerback
Ht: 5-10

Southern Methodist
Wt: 168

Born: 12/20/60, Houston, TX

Acquisition: Third round selection in 1985 draft (49th player).

SENIOR SEASON: Second-team all-SWC by AP, UPI and Dallas Times-Herald . . . Led secondary in tackles with 52 . . . Had 3 interceptions including TD on 100-yard return vs. Louisville . . . AP Southwest Player of Week following Louisville game . . . Recovered three fumbles and made two tackles for losses (−9).

COLLEGIATE, PERSONAL: Lone returnee in secondary as senior . . . Made 32 tackles in 1983 plus five in Sun Bowl . . . Broke up 5 passes as junior . . . 4.45 speed in 40 . . . Played behind All-American Russell Carter in 1982 but played in all 11 games . . . Missed fall semester of 1981 after playing behind All-American John Simmons in 1980 . . . Prepped at Houston Yates H.S. where he was selected on Houston Top Sixty List . . . Averaged 6.1 yards rushing as senior . . . Communications major.

PHILLIPS' COLLEGIATE STATS

Year/School	Games	Tackles	Sacks	Int.	FR
1980 SMU	11	14	0	0	0
1982 SMU	11	10	0	1	0
1983 SMU	11	32	0	0	3
1984 SMU	11	52	0	3	0
TOTAL	44	108	0	4	3

91

JAMES MANESS

Wide Receiver — Texas Christian — Born: 5/1/63, Decatur, TX
Ht: 6-1   Wt: 174

Acquisition: Third round selection in 1985 draft (78th player).

SENIOR SEASON: Set school record with 871 yards receiving in senior year . . . Also set SWC record and tied NCAA mark with 99-yard TD catch vs. Rice . . . Set school record with 22.4 yard average per catch.

COLLEGIATE: 97 Career catches ranks fourth in TCU charts and his 2,171 career yards is third best in school history and seventh best on the SWC list . . . Two-time NCAA Track and Field All-American sprinter . . . Recorded 11 100-plus yard games for Horn Frogs . . . Also respectable open field blocker and fierce competitor . . . Two greatest track moments came when he anchored TCU's 800-meter relay team to world's fourth fastest time ever (1:20.84 in '83) and his scintillating opening leg on Frogs' indoor mile-relay combo which set a world's best (indoor) of 3:04.82.

PERSONAL: Attended Decatur H.S. (Decatur, TX) . . . All-district as safety and WR . . . Made All-State as WR . . . Ran 100 meters in 10.3 and 200 meters in 21.2 . . . Set Decatur record for most catches in one season with 27.

MANESS' CAREER STATS

Year/School	Receiving			
	No.	Yards	Avg.	TD's
1981 TCU	1	56	56.0	1
1982 TCU	19	554	29.2	5
1983 TCU	37	694	18.6	1
1984 TCU	40	871	21.8	4
TOTALS	97	2,175	22.4	11

6

KEVIN BUTLER

Placekicker — Georgia — Born: 7/24/62, Savannah, GA
Ht: 6-1   Wt: 190

Acquisition: Fourth round selection in 1985 draft (105th player).

SENIOR SEASON: Consensus All-America including Kodak, Football Writers, Walter Camp, Football News . . . Finished season with 23 FG's in 28 . . . Set numerous NCAA and SEC records including: NCAA: most games kicking two or more field goals (27); SEC: most career points (353); most career points scored by a kicker (353); most field goal attempts (98); most field goals (77); longest field goal (60-yards vs. Clemson, 1984) . . . UPI Southeastern Offensive Player of Week and WTBS TV SEC Player of Week performance against Clemson—14 points including 60-yard field goal with 11 seconds left to win game, 26-23.

COLLEGIATE, PERSONAL: Three-time all-SEC; All-America mention last two years . . . In his career, converted 25 of 31 FG's (81%) and 10 of 10 PAT's to tie a game or give Georgia the lead . . . One of only five kickers in NCAA history to kick over 50 FG's and have an accuracy mark of 75 percent or better (77 of 98 = 79%) . . . Only 50 of 184 kickoffs at Georgia were returnable . . . Special teams captain as junior and senior . . . 59-yard field goal vs. Ole Miss as sophomore to set new school record . . . Banner freshman year included tying NCAA record for most FG's in season for frosh with 19 . . . 19 FG's set Georgia and SEC record

1 TD and had long run of 33 yards . . . Durable runner who excels at breaking tackles.

COLLEGIATE, PERSONAL: Became full-time starter last year after recovering from injury which sidelined him for 1983 season . . . Enjoyed fine sophomore season which included 344 yards and 3 TD's . . . Best game as underclassman came vs. TCU when he gained 72 yards on 18 rushes ('81) . . . Team's 5th leading rusher as junior despite playing in just 5 games . . . All-district, all-state and all-America at Giddings (TX) High School . . . Industrial education major.

SANDERS' COLLEGE STATS

Year/School	Att.	Yds.	Avg.	TD	Long
		Rushing			
1980 Texas A&M	52	201	3.9	1	13
1981 Texas A&M	94	344	3.7	3	16
1982 Texas A&M	18	96	5.3	1	16
1984 Texas A&M	167	738	4.4	1	33
TOTALS	331	1,379	4.2	6	33

1985 BEAR FREE AGENTS BIOGRAPHIES

MAURY BUFORD   8

Punter   Texas Tech   4th Year
Ht: 6-0   Wt: 191   Born: 2/18/60
Mount Pleasant, TX

Acquisition: Trade from San Diego (8/20/85) for conditional draft choice in 1986.

---

for most points scored by kicking in season with 94 . . . Converted 37 of 38 PAT's as freshman and 19 of 26 FG's . . . All-state kicker at Redan High (GA) . . . Kicked six FG's over 50 yards as prep . . . Also played soccer and defensive back in football.

BUTLER'S COLLEGIATE STATS

Year	PAT	FG	LG	TP
1981	37/38	19/26	52	94
1982	34/36	17/21	59	85
1983	28/28	18/23	53	82
1984	23/23	23/28	60	92
TOTALS	122/125	77/98	60	353

KICK FOR KICK

	10-19	20-29	30-39	40-49	50-59	60-69
			Yards			
1981	2/2	5/7	4/5	6/7	2/4	0/1
1982	0/0	7/7	6/6	2/4	2/4	0/0
1983	0/0	8/8	6/7	2/3	2/4	0/1
1984	0/0	4/5	8/9	6/7	4/5	1/2
TOTALS	2/2	24/27	24/27	16/21	10/17	1/4

THOMAS SANDERS   31

Running Back   Texas A & M   Born: 1/4/62
Ht: 5-11   Wt: 203   Giddings, TX

Acquisition: Ninth round selection in 1985 draft (246th player).
SENIOR SEASON: Led Aggies in rushing with 738 yards on 167 carries even though he wasn't expected to play after surgery for herniated disc after 1982 season . . . Surprised coaches when he arrived at practice last August with doctor's release to play . . . Averaged 65.1 yards per game, scored

BACKGROUND: Chargers' punter last three seasons . . . Best season was 1983 when he averaged 43.9 yards, third best in NFL . . . Chargers' all-time leading punter with 42.7 yard average . . . Longest punt of his career was 71 yards against Denver in 1982 . . . Chargers' wighth round choice in 1982 draft.

KEN TAYLOR 31

Cornerback   Oregon State   Rookie
Ht: 6-1   Wt: 186   Born: 9/2/63
San Jose, CA

Acquisition: Fa 5/23/85

BACKGROUND: Finished college career with 8 interceptions (8th in school history) and 8 blocked kicks . . . Led team with four thefts as a senior . . . Broke up nine passes and had three tackles for loss in 1984 . . . All-Pac 10 as senior.

TOM THAYER 57

Guard/center   Notre Dame   Rookie
Ht: 6-4   Wt: 261   Born: 7/16/59
Joliet, IL

Acquisition: FA: 7/7/85

BACKGROUND: Fourth round Bears draft choice in 1983 but signed with United States Football League, playing last three seasons with Chicago Blitz and Arizona Wranglers . . . Three-year starter at Notre Dame . . . Prepped at Joliet Catholic High School.

CLIFF THRIFT 52

Linebacker   E. Central Okla.   7th Year
Ht: 6-1   Wt: 237   Born: 5/3/56
Dallas, TX

Acquisition: FA: 7/9/85

BACKGROUND: Has been backup in 1983 and 1984 after being San Diego Chargers' starting middle linebacker in 1982 . . . Chargers' third round draft choice in 1979.

MIKE TOMCZAK 18

Quarterback   Ohio State   Rookie
Ht: 6-1   Wt: 195   Born: 10/23/62
Calumet City, IL

Acquisition: FA 5/9/85

BACKGROUND: Three-year starter who led Buckeyes to three 9-3 seasons . . . Broke leg (5/5/84) but returned third week of season to lead OSU to Big Ten title and Rose Bowl . . . Second leading passer in Buckeye history in yards (5,569), attempts (675), completions (376 and total offense (6,015) . . . Completed 145 of 244 for 1,952 yards as senior . . . Prepped at Thornton Fractional North in Calumet City, Ill.

TIM WRIGHTMAN 80

Tight End   UCLA   Rookie
Ht: 6-3   Wt: 237   Born: 3/27/60
Harbor City, CA

Acquisition: FA 3/28/85

BACKGROUND: Originally drafted by Bears in third round of 1982 draft, when Ditka vowed to make him another Mike Ditka. But shunned Bears and signed with George Allen's Chicago Blitz to become first player to sign in United States Football League . . . Only six catches in injury-riddled USFL stint . . . All-American at UCLA where he caught 73 passes and 10 TDs in career . . . Only fifth player in Bruin history to receive unanimous All-American honors . . . All-Pac 10 as junior and senior.

SECTION 3

Bears Photo Section

Coaches

Mike Ditka

Jim Dooley

Dale Haupt

Ed Hughes

Steve Kazor

Jim LaRue

Ted Plumb

Johnny Roland

Buddy Ryan

Dick Stanfel

Players

Brad Anderson

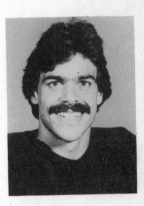

Brian Baschnagel

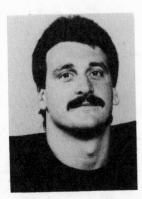

Kurt Becker

Todd Bell

Mark Bortz

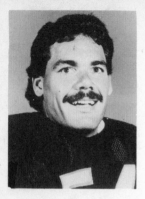

Brian Cabral

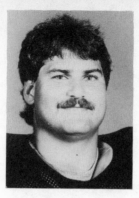

Jim Covert

Richard Dent

Dave Duerson

Pat Dunsmore

Gary Fencik

Jeff Fisher

Leslie Frazier

Andy Frederick

Steve Fuller

Willie Gault

Shaun Gayle

Dennis Gentry

Dan Hampton

Al Harris

Mike Hartenstine

Jay Hilgenberg

Stefan Humphries

Tyrone Keys

Mitch Krenk

Ken Margerum

Wilber Marshall

Dennis McKinnon

Jim McMahon

Steve McMichael

Emery Moorehead

Walter Payton

Dan Rains

Mike Richardson

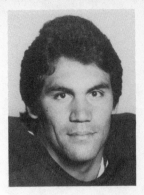

Ron Rivera

Mike Singletary

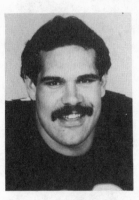

Matt Suhey

Calvin Thomas

Keith Van Horne

Henry Waechter

Otis Wilson

Rookies

Kevin Butler

James Maness

James Morrissey

Reggie Phillips

Thomas Sanders

William "The Refrigerator" Perry

1985 BEARS TEAM ROSTER

No.	Player	Pos.	Hgt.	Wgt.	Birthdate	NFL Exp.	College	Gms '84
4	Fuller, Steve	QB	6-4	195	01/05/57	7	Clemson	6
6	Butler, Kevin	K	6-1	204	07/24/62	R	Georgia	0
8	Buford, Maury	P	6-0	191	02/18/60	4	Texas Tech	16
9	McMahon, Jim	QB	6-1	190	08/21/59	4	BYU	9
18	Tomczak, Mike	QB	6-1	195	10/23/62	R	Ohio State	0
20	Sanders, Thomas	RB	5-11	203	01/04/62	R	Texas A & M	0
21	Frazier, Leslie	CB	6-0	187	04/03/59	5	Alcorn St.	11
22	Duerson, Dave	S	6-1	203	11/28/60	3	Notre Dame	16
23	Gayle, Shaun	CB	5-11	193	03/08/62	2	Ohio St.	16
24	Fisher, Jeff	DB	5-10	195	02/25/58	5	USC	16
25	Bell, Todd	S	6-1	205	11/28/58	5	Ohio St.	16
26	Suhey, Matt	FB	5-11	216	07/07/58	6	Penn State	16
27	Richardson, Mike	CB	6-0	188	05/23/61	3	Arizona St.	15
29	Gentry, Dennis	RB	5-8	181	02/10/59	4	Baylor	16
31	Taylor, Ken	CB	6-1	185	09/02/63	R	Oregon State	0
33	Thomas, Calvin	FB	5-11	245	01/07/60	4	Illinois	16
34	Payton, Walter	RB	5-10	202	07/25/54	11	Jackson St.	16
45	Fencik, Gary	S	6-1	196	06/11/54	10	Yale	16
48	Phillips, Reggie	DB	5-10	170	12/12/60	R	S. Methodist	0
50	Singletary, Mike	LB	6-0	228	10/09/58	5	Baylor	16
52	Thrift, Cliff	LB	6-1	237	05/03/56	7	E. Ctrl. Oklahoma	16
53	Rains, Dan	LB	6-1	229	04/26/56	3	Cincinnati	15
54	Cabral, Brian	LB	6-1	226	06/23/56	7	Colorado	16
55	Wilson, Otis	LB	6-2	232	09/15/57	6	Louisville	15
57	Thayer, Tom	G/C	6-4	261	07/16/59	R	Notre Dame	0
58	Marshall, Wilber	LB	6-1	225	04/18/62	2	Florida	15
59	Rivera, Ron	LB	6-3	239	01/07/62	2	California	15
60	Andrews, Tom	C	6-4	267	01/21/61	2	Louisville	7
62	Bortz, Mark	G	6-6	269	02/12/61	3	Iowa	15
63	Hilgenberg, Jay	C	6-3	258	03/21/59	5	Iowa	16
70	Waechter, Henry	DT	6-5	275	02/13/59	4	Nebraska	2
71	Frederick, Andy	T	6-6	265	07/25/54	9	New Mexico	16
72	Perry, William	DT	6-2	325	12/16/62	R	Clemson	0
73	Hartenstine, Mike	DE	6-3	254	07/27/53	11	Penn State	16
74	Covert, Jim	T	6-4	271	03/22/60	3	Pittsburgh	16
75	Humphries, Stefan	G	6-3	263	01/20/62	2	Michigan	10
76	McMichael, Steve	DT	6-2	260	10/17/57	6	Texas	16
78	Van Horne, Keith	T	6-6	280	11/06/57	5	USC	14
79	Becker, Kurt	G	6-5	267	12/22/58	4	Michigan	16
80	Wrightman, Tim	TE	6-3	237	03/27/60	R	UCLA	0
81	Maness, James	WR	6-1	174	06/01/63	R	Texas Christian	0
82	Margerum, Ken	WR	6-0	180	10/05/58	4	Stanford	0
83	Gault, Willie	WR	6-0	178	09/05/60	3	Tennessee	16
84	Baschnagel, Brian	WR	5-11	193	01/08/54	10	Ohio State	16
85	McKinnon, Dennis	WR	6-1	185	08/22/61	3	Florida St	12
86	Anderson, Brad	WR	6-2	198	01/21/61	2	Arizona	13
87	Moorehead, Emery	TE	6-2	220	03/22/54	9	Colorado	16
88	Dunsmore, Pat	TE	6-3	237	10/02/59	3	Drake	11
89	Krenk, Mitch	TE	6-2	233	11/19/59	2	Nebraska	8
90	Harris, Al	LB	6-5	253	12/31/56	7	Arizona St.	16
95	Dent, Richard	DE	6-5	263	12/13/60	3	Tenn State	16
98	Keys, Tyrone	DE	6-7	267	10/24/59	3	Miss. State	14
99	Hampton, Dan	DT	6-5	267	09/19/57	7	Arkansas	15

SECTION 4

The NFL
1984 & 1985

1984 FINAL NFL STANDINGS

NATIONAL CONFERENCE

Central Division

	W	L	T	Pct.	Pts.	Opp.
BEARS	10	6	0	.625	325	248
Green Bay	8	8	0	.500	390	309
Tampa Bay	6	10	0	.375	335	380
Detroit	4	11	1	.281	283	408
Minnesota	3	13	0	.188	276	484

Eastern Division

	W	L	T	Pct.	Pts.	Opp.
Washington	11	5	0	.688	426	310
N.Y. Giants	9	7	0	.563	299	301
St. Louis	9	7	0	.563	423	345
Dallas	9	7	0	.563	308	308
Philadelphia	6	9	1	.406	278	320

Western Division

	W	L	T	Pct.	Pts.	Opp.
San Francisco	15	1	0	.938	475	227
L.A. Rams	10	6	0	.625	346	316
New Orleans	7	9	0	.438	298	361
Atlanta	4	12	0	.250	281	382

N.Y. Giants clinched wild card based on 3-1 record vs. St. Louis 2-2 and Cowboys 1-3. St. Louis finished ahead of Dallas based on better division record 5-3 to 3-5.

AMERICAN CONFERENCE

Eastern Division

	W	L	T	Pct.	Pts.	Opp.
Miami	14	2	0	.875	513	298
New England	9	7	0	.563	362	352
N.Y. Jets	7	9	0	.438	332	364
Indianpolis	4	12	0	.250	239	414
Buffalo	2	14	0	.125	250	454

Central Division

	W	L	T	Pct.	Pts.	Opp.
Pittsburgh	9	7	0	.563	387	310
Cincinnati	8	8	0	.500	339	339
Cleveland	5	11	0	.313	250	297
Houston	3	13	0	.188	240	437

Western Division

	W	L	T	Pct.	Pts.	Opp.
Denver	13	3	0	.813	353	241
Seattle	12	4	0	.750	418	282
L.A. Raiders	11	5	0	.688	368	278
Kansas City	8	8	0	.500	314	324
San Diego	7	9	0	.438	394	413

AFC, NFC, AND NFL SUMMARY

	AFC Offense Total	AFC Offense Average	AFC Defense Total	AFC Defense Average	NFC Offense Total	NFC Offense Average	NFC Defense Total	NFC Defense Average	NFL Total	NFL Average
First Downs	4305	307.5	4426	316.1	4352	310.9	4231	302.2	8657	309.2
Rushing	1508	107.7	1603	114.5	1715	122.5	1620	115.7	3223	115.1
Passing	2464	176.0	2497	178.4	2344	167.4	2311	165.1	4808	171.7
Penalty	333	23.8	326	23.3	293	20.9	300	21.4	626	22.4
Rushes	6797	485.5	6971	497.9	7014	501.0	6840	488.6	13,811	493.3
Net Yds. Gained	26,305	1878.9	27,613	1972.4	29,198	2085.6	27,890	1992.1	55,503	1982.3
Avg. Gain	—	3.9	—	4.0	—	4.2	—	4.1	—	4.0
Avg. Yds. per Game	—	117.4	—	123.3	—	130.3	—	124.5	—	123.9
Passes Attempted	7198	514.1	7299	521.4	7127	509.1	7026	501.9	14,325	511.6
Completed	4054	289.6	4156	296.9	4022	287.3	3920	280.0	8076	288.4
% Completed	—	56.3	—	56.9	—	56.4	—	55.8	—	56.4
Total Yds. Gained	51,627	3687.6	52,167	3726.2	50,606	3614.7	50,066	3576.1	102,233	3651.2
Times Sacked	634	45.3	630	45.0	679	48.5	683	48.8	1313	46.9
Yds. Lost	4861	347.2	4896	349.7	5134	366.7	5099	364.2	9995	357.0
Net Yds. Gained	46,766	3340.4	47,271	3376.5	45,472	3248.0	44,967	3211.9	92,238	3294.2
Avg. Yds. per Game	—	208.8	—	211.0	—	203.0	—	200.7	—	205.9
Net Yds. per Pass Play	—	5.97	—	5.96	—	5.83	—	5.83	—	5.90
Yds. Gained per Comp.	—	12.73	—	12.55	—	12.58	—	12.77	—	12.66
Combined Net Yds. Gained	73,071	5219.4	74,884	5348.9	74,670	5333.6	72,857	5204.1	147,741	5276.5
% Total Yds. Rushing	—	36.00	—	36.87	—	39.10	—	38.28	—	37.57
% Total Yds. Passing	—	64.00	—	63.13	—	60.90	—	61.72	—	62.43
Avg. Yds. per Game	—	326.2	—	334.3	—	333.3	—	325.3	—	329.8
Ball Control Plays	14,629	1044.9	14,900	1064.3	14,820	1058.6	14,549	1039.2	29,449	1051.8
Avg. Yds. per Play	—	5.0	—	5.0	—	5.0	—	5.0	—	5.0
Third Down Efficiency	—	38.6	—	38.8	—	38.7	—	38.5	—	38.7

Interceptions	304	21.7	317	22.6	280	20.0	267	19.1	584	20.9
Yds. Returned	4812	343.7	4949	353.5	3704	264.6	3567	254.8	8516	304.1
Returned for TD	30	2.1	30	2.1	21	1.5	21	1.5	51	1.8
Punts	1153	82.4	1128	80.6	1107	79.1	1132	80.9	2260	80.7
Yds. Punted	48,005	3428.9	46,575	3326.8	44,716	3194.0	46,146	3296.1	92,721	3311.5
Avg. Yds. per Punt	—	41.6	—	41.3	—	40.4	—	40.8	—	41.0
Punt Returns	585	41.8	604	43.1	622	44.4	603	43.1	1207	43.1
Yds. Returned	5364	383.1	5532	395.1	5053	360.9	4885	348.9	10,417	372.0
Avg. Yds. per Return	—	9.2	—	9.2	—	8.1	—	8.1	—	8.6
Returned for TD	5	0.4	3	0.2	3	0.2	5	0.4	8	0.3
Kickoff Returns	836	59.7	825	58.9	908	64.9	919	65.6	1744	62.3
Yds. Returned	16,486	1177.6	16,658	1189.9	18,058	1289.9	17,886	1277.6	34,544	1233.7
Avg. Yds. per Return	—	19.7	—	20.2	—	19.9	—	19.5	—	19.8
Returned for TD	2	0.1	2	0.1	3	0.2	3	0.2	5	0.2
Penalties	1431	102.2	1417	101.2	1434	102.4	1448	103.4	2865	102.3
Yds. Penalized	12,005	857.5	11,835	845.4	12,051	860.8	12,221	872.9	24,056	859.1
Fumbles	457	32.6	441	31.5	417	29.8	433	30.9	874	31.2
Lost	215	15.4	216	15.4	214	15.3	213	15.2	429	15.3
Out of Bounds	32	2.3	29	2.1	17	1.2	20	1.4	49	1.8
Own Rec. for TD	—	0.1	1	0.1	1	0.1	2	0.1	3	0.1
Opp. Rec.	214	15.3	213	15.2	210	15.0	211	15.1	424	15.1
Opp. Rec. for TD	14	1.0	11	0.8	9	0.6	12	0.9	23	0.8
Total Points Scored	4759	339.9	4803	343.1	4743	338.8	4699	335.6	9502	339.4
Total TDs	568	40.6	567	40.5	550	39.3	551	39.4	1118	39.9
TDs Rushing	197	14.1	214	15.3	213	15.2	196	14.0	410	14.6
TDs Passing	317	22.6	305	21.8	298	21.3	310	22.1	615	22.0
TDs on Ret. and Rec.	54	3.9	48	3.4	39	2.8	45	3.2	93	3.3
Extra Points	548	39.1	545	38.9	527	37.6	530	37.9	1075	38.4
Safeties	7	0.6	8	0.6	8	0.6	7	0.5	15	0.5
Field Goals Made	263	18.8	280	20.0	300	21.4	283	20.2	563	20.1
Field Goals Attempted	373	26.6	382	27.3	412	29.4	403	28.8	785	28.0
% Successful	—	70.5	—	73.3	—	72.8	—	70.2	—	71.7

NATIONAL CONFERENCE OFFENSE

	Atl.	Chi.	Dall.	Det.	G.B.	Rams	Minn.	N.O.	N.Y.G.	Phil.	St.L.	S.F.	T.B.	Wash.
First Downs	292	297	323	306	315	258	289	298	310	280	345	356	344	339
Rushing	123	164	93	118	120	140	111	131	97	83	129	138	114	154
Passing	151	115	202	170	168	100	150	137	198	176	200	204	209	164
Penalty	18	18	28	18	27	18	28	30	15	21	16	14	21	21
Rushes	489	674	469	446	461	541	444	523	493	381	488	534	483	588
Net Yds. Gained	1994	2974	1714	2017	2019	2864	1844	2171	1660	1338	2088	2465	1776	2274
Avg. Gain	4.1	4.4	3.7	4.5	4.4	5.3	4.2	4.2	3.4	3.5	4.3	4.6	3.7	3.9
Avg. Yds. per Game	124.6	185.9	107.1	126.1	126.2	179.0	115.3	135.7	103.8	83.6	130.5	154.1	111.0	142.1
Passes Attempted	478	390	604	531	506	358	533	476	535	606	566	496	563	485
Completed	294	226	322	298	281	176	281	246	288	331	347	312	334	286
% Completed	61.5	57.9	53.3	56.1	55.5	49.2	52.7	51.7	53.8	54.6	61.3	62.9	59.3	59.0
Total Yds. Gained	3546	2695	3995	3787	3740	2382	3337	3198	4066	3823	4634	4079	3907	3417
Times Sacked	67	36	48	61	42	32	64	45	55	60	49	27	45	48
Yds. Lost	496	232	389	486	310	240	465	361	434	463	377	178	362	341
Net Yds. Gained	3050	2463	3606	3301	3430	2142	2872	2837	3632	3360	4257	3901	3545	3076
Avg. Yds. per Game	190.6	153.9	225.4	206.3	214.4	133.9	179.5	177.3	227.0	210.0	266.1	243.8	221.6	192.3
Net Yds. per Pass Play	5.60	5.78	5.53	5.58	6.26	5.49	4.81	5.45	6.16	5.05	6.92	7.46	5.83	5.77
Yds. Gained per Comp.	12.06	11.92	12.41	12.71	13.31	13.53	11.88	13.00	14.12	11.55	13.35	13.07	11.70	11.95
Combined Net Yds. Gained	5044	5437	5320	5318	5449	5006	4716	5008	5292	4698	6345	6366	5321	5350
% Total Yds. Rushing	39.5	54.7	32.2	37.9	37.1	57.2	39.1	43.4	31.4	28.5	32.9	38.7	33.4	42.5
% Total Yds. Passing	60.5	45.3	67.8	62.1	62.9	42.8	60.9	56.6	68.6	71.5	67.1	61.3	66.6	57.5
Avg. Yds. per Game	315.3	339.8	332.5	332.4	340.6	312.9	294.8	313.0	330.8	293.6	396.6	397.9	332.6	334.4
Ball Control Plays	1034	1100	1121	1038	1009	931	1041	1044	1083	1047	1103	1057	1091	1121
Avg. Yds. per Play	4.9	4.9	4.7	5.1	5.4	5.4	4.5	4.8	4.9	4.5	5.8	6.0	4.9	4.8
Avg. Time of Poss.	30:14	35:08	29:00	29:43	26:48	28:22	28:14	30:13	30:44	29:30	32:43	30:26	31:17	32:49
Third Down Efficiency	35.3	41.2	34.9	39.1	36.6	33.3	34.7	39.7	36.6	33.2	41.4	46.4	42.9	45.3
Had Intercepted	20	15	26	22	30	17	25	28	18	17	16	10	23	13
Yds. Opp. Returned	304	241	372	251	317	240	344	420	222	211	219	155	249	159
Ret. by Opp. for TD	2	3	4	1	2	2	2	3	1	1	0	0	0	0

Punts	70	85	108	76	85	74	82	70	94	92	68	62	68	73
Yds. Punted	2855	3328	4123	3164	3596	2866	3473	3020	3598	3880	2594	2536	2849	2834
Avg. Yds. per Punt	40.8	39.2	38.2	41.6	42.3	38.7	42.4	43.1	38.3	42.2	38.1	40.9	41.9	38.8
Punt Returns	41	63	54	36	48	40	31	33	55	40	47	45	34	55
Yds. Returned	264	558	446	241	351	489	217	268	368	250	399	521	207	474
Avg. Yds. per Return	6.4	8.9	8.3	6.7	7.3	12.2	7.0	8.1	6.7	6.3	8.5	11.6	6.1	8.6
Returned for TD	0	0	0	0	0	2	0	0	0	0	0	1	0	0
Kickoff Returns	70	49	63	74	67	58	86	72	61	59	74	47	68	60
Yds. Returned	1367	896	1199	1347	1362	1244	1775	1465	1117	1156	1563	1039	1354	1174
Avg. Yds. per Return	19.5	18.3	19.0	18.2	20.3	21.4	20.6	20.3	18.3	19.6	21.1	22.1	19.9	19.6
Returned for TD	0	0	0	0	1	1	0	0	0	1	0	0	0	0
Penalties	125	114	100	138	110	93	90	101	79	77	109	100	118	80
Yds. Penalized	1011	851	947	1165	915	830	762	849	703	632	904	884	875	723
Fumbles	39	31	35	36	17	31	39	22	17	23	32	26	36	33
Lost	21	16	17	14	7	18	16	13	9	16	20	12	20	15
Out of Bounds	0	4	4	1	0	2	1	0	0	0	2	1	0	2
Own Rec. for TD	0	0	0	0	0	0	0	0	0	0	0	0	0	1
Opp. Rec. by	20	13	16	11	15	22	17	10	16	11	12	12	14	21
Opp. Rec. for TD	0	0	1	0	0	0	2	1	1	0	1	1	0	2
Total Points Scored	281	325	308	283	390	346	276	298	299	278	423	475	335	426
Total TDs	31	37	34	32	51	38	31	34	36	27	51	57	40	51
TDs Rushing	16	22	12	13	18	16	10	9	12	6	21	21	17	20
TDs Passing	14	14	19	19	30	16	18	21	22	19	28	32	22	24
TDs on Ret. and Rec.	1	1	3	0	3	6	3	4	2	2	4	4	1	7
Extra Points	31	35	33	31	48	37	30	34	32	26	48	56	38	48
Safeties	2	1	1	0	0	3	0	0	0	0	0	1	0	0
Field Goals Made	20	22	23	20	12	25	20	20	17	30	23	25	19	24
Field Goals Attempted	27	28	29	27	21	33	23	27	33	37	35	35	26	31
% Successful	74.1	78.6	79.3	74.1	57.1	75.8	87.0	74.1	51.5	81.1	65.7	71.4	73.1	77.4

AMERICAN CONFERENCE OFFENSE

	Buff.	Cin.	Clev.	Den.	Hou.	Ind.	K.C.	Raid.	Mia.	N.E.	N.Y.J.	Pitt.	S.D.	Sea.
First Downs	263	339	295	299	284	254	295	301	387	315	310	302	374	287
Rushing	98	135	89	121	95	114	88	114	115	104	118	117	106	94
Passing	149	179	180	152	164	117	178	162	243	186	176	167	240	171
Penalty	16	25	26	26	25	23	29	25	29	25	16	18	28	22
Rushes	398	540	489	508	433	510	408	516	484	482	504	574	456	495
Net Yds. Gained	1643	2179	1696	2076	1656	2025	1527	1886	1918	2032	2189	2179	1654	1645
Avg. Gain	4.1	4.0	3.5	4.1	3.8	4.0	3.7	3.7	4.0	4.2	4.3	3.8	3.6	3.3
Avg. Yds. per Game	102.7	136.2	106.0	129.8	103.5	126.6	95.4	117.9	119.9	127.0	136.8	136.2	103.4	102.8
Passes Attempted	588	496	495	475	487	411	593	491	572	500	488	443	662	497
Completed	298	306	273	263	282	206	305	266	367	292	272	240	401	283
% Completed	50.7	61.7	55.2	55.4	57.9	50.1	51.4	54.2	64.2	58.4	55.7	54.2	60.6	56.9
Total Yds. Gained	3252	3659	3490	3116	3610	2543	3869	3718	5146	3685	3341	3519	4928	3751
Times Sacked	60	45	55	35	49	58	33	54	14	66	52	35	36	42
Yds. Lost	554	358	358	257	382	436	301	360	128	454	382	278	285	328
Net Yds. Gained	2698	3301	3132	2859	3228	2107	3568	3358	5018	3231	2959	3241	4643	3423
Avg. Yds. per Game	168.6	206.3	195.8	178.7	201.8	131.7	223.0	209.9	313.6	201.9	184.9	202.6	290.2	213.9
Net Yds. per Pass Play	4.16	6.10	5.69	5.61	6.02	4.49	5.70	6.16	8.56	5.71	5.48	6.78	6.65	6.35
Yds. Gained per Comp.	10.91	11.96	12.78	11.85	12.80	12.34	12.69	13.98	14.02	12.62	12.28	14.66	12.29	13.25
Combined Net Yds. Gained	4341	5480	4828	4935	4884	4132	5095	5244	6936	5263	5148	5420	6297	5068
% Total Yds. Rushing	37.8	39.8	35.1	42.1	33.9	49.0	30.0	36.0	27.7	38.6	42.5	40.2	26.3	32.5
% Total Yds. Passing	62.2	60.2	64.9	57.9	66.1	51.0	70.0	64.0	72.3	61.4	57.5	59.8	73.7	67.5
Avg. Yds. per Game	271.3	342.5	301.8	308.4	305.3	258.3	318.4	327.8	433.5	328.9	321.8	338.8	393.6	316.8
Ball Control Plays	1046	1081	1039	1018	969	979	1034	1061	1070	1048	1044	1052	1154	1034
Avg. Yds. per Play	4.2	5.1	4.6	4.8	5.0	4.2	4.9	4.9	6.5	5.0	4.9	5.2	5.5	4.9
Avg. Time of Poss.	28:43	30:50	30:53	28:56	28:02	27:24	27:25	29:26	30:18	29:51	30:02	30:33	31:43	30:46
Third Down Efficiency	35.4	44.1	39.0	32.5	33.2	29.9	32.7	35.9	51.5	39.6	41.5	40.3	47.1	37.8
Had Intercepted	30	22	23	17	15	22	22	28	18	14	21	25	21	26
Yds. Opp. Returned	416	364	518	189	214	423	683	300	377	237	207	371	180	333
Ret. by Opp. for TD	4	2	3	0	2	2	7	2	1	3	0	1	0	3

Punts														
Yds. Punted	95	66	70	75	92	51	91	98	98	88	96	76	67	90
	3567	2773	2883	2935	3904	2281	3809	4397	4383	3482	3850	3213	2832	3696
Avg. Yds. per Punt	37.5	42.0	41.2	39.1	42.4	44.7	41.9	44.9	44.7	39.6	40.1	42.3	42.3	41.1
Punt Returns														
Yds. Returned	44	33	61	35	48	39	67	42	38	26	41	40	38	33
	484	212	696	324	430	365	667	346	278	152	318	322	473	297
Avg. Yds. per Return	11.0	6.4	11.4	9.3	9.0	9.4	10.0	8.2	7.3	5.8	7.8	8.1	12.4	9.0
Returned for TD	1	1	1	0	0	1	1	1	1	0	0	1	0	0
Kickoff Returns														
Yds. Returned	54	63	54	65	63	44	56	56	69	69	45	61	61	76
	1007	1319	1026	1498	1246	799	1216	1061	1331	1352	897	1157	1155	1422
Avg. Yds. per Return	18.6	20.9	19.0	23.0	19.8	18.2	21.7	18.9	19.3	19.6	19.9	19.0	18.9	18.7
Returned for TD	0	0	0	1	0	0	0	0	1	0	0	0	0	0
Penalties														
Yds. Penalized	128	112	112	96	86	67	143	98	95	99	78	111	85	121
	1179	1023	948	779	674	527	1209	801	798	813	636	928	693	997
Fumbles	24	35	40	26	29	26	42	34	35	36	36	31	32	31
Lost	13	17	15	13	15	10	20	15	17	16	17	16	17	14
Out of Bounds					2		2	3				1	2	6
Own Rec. for TD	3			1	1									0
Opp. Rec. by	25	17		18	8	12	14	11	13	11	24	15	15	21
Opp. Rec. for TD	1	0	2	2	0	1	1	0	0	1	4	0	0	2
Total Points Scored	418	394	387	332	362	513	368	314	239	240	353	250	339	250
Total TDs	51	48	45	40	42	70	44	35	28	28	42	25	39	31
TDs Rushing	10	18	13	17	15	18	19	12	13	13	12	10	18	9
TDs Passing	32	25	25	20	26	49	21	21	13	14	22	14	17	18
TDs on Ret. and Rec.	9	5	7	3	1	3	4	2	2	1	8	1	4	4
Extra Points	50	46	45	39	42	66	40	35	27	27	38	25	37	31
Safeties	1	0	0	1	1	0	2	0	1	0	0	0	1	0
Field Goals Made	20	20	24	17	22	9	20	23	14	15	21	25	22	11
Field Goals Attempted	24	29	32	24	28	19	27	33	23	19	28	35	31	21
% Successful	83.3	69.0	75.0	70.8	78.6	47.4	74.1	69.7	60.9	78.9	75.0	71.4	71.0	52.4

NATIONAL CONFERENCE DEFENSE

	Atl.	Chi.	Dall.	Det.	G.B.	Rams	Minn.	N.O.	N.Y.G.	Phil.	St.L.	S.F.	T.B.	Wash.
First Downs	317	216	283	328	323	309	342	298	296	307	292	302	311	307
Rushing	131	72	106	120	136	108	144	134	107	123	108	101	139	91
Passing	162	122	155	177	166	179	182	142	174	171	157	173	157	194
Penalty	24	22	22	31	21	22	16	22	15	13	27	28	15	22
Rushes	538	378	510	519	545	449	547	549	474	556	442	432	511	390
Net Yds. Gained	2153	1377	2226	1808	2145	1600	2573	2461	1818	2189	1923	1795	2233	1589
Avg. Gain	4.0	3.6	4.4	3.5	3.9	3.6	4.7	4.5	3.8	3.9	4.4	4.2	4.4	4.1
Avg. Yds. per Game	134.6	86.1	139.1	113.0	134.1	100.0	160.8	153.8	113.6	136.8	120.2	112.2	139.6	99.3
Passes Attempted	443	435	527	466	551	566	490	422	529	492	494	546	490	575
Completed	262	198	250	288	315	346	319	239	288	262	251	298	286	318
% Completed	59.1	45.5	47.4	61.8	57.2	61.1	65.1	56.6	54.4	53.3	50.8	54.6	58.4	55.3
Total Yds. Gained	3413	3069	3200	3782	3470	3964	3954	2873	3736	3506	3574	3744	3480	4301
Times Sacked	38	72	57	37	44	43	25	55	48	60	55	51	32	66
Yds. Lost	287	583	390	271	324	298	175	420	361	456	403	363	239	529
Net Yds. Gained	3126	2486	2810	3511	3146	3666	3779	2453	3375	3050	3171	3381	3241	3772
Avg. Yds. per Game	195.4	155.4	175.6	219.4	196.6	229.1	236.2	153.3	210.9	190.6	198.2	211.3	202.6	235.8
Net Yds. per Pass Play	6.50	4.90	4.81	6.98	5.29	6.02	7.34	5.14	5.85	5.53	5.78	5.66	6.21	5.88
Yds. Gained per Comp.	13.03	15.50	12.80	13.13	11.02	11.46	12.39	12.02	12.97	13.38	14.24	12.56	12.17	13.53
Combined Net Yds. Gained	5279	3863	5036	5319	5291	5266	6352	4914	5193	5239	5094	5176	5474	5361
% Total Yds. Rushing	40.8	35.6	44.2	34.0	40.5	30.4	40.5	50.1	35.0	41.8	37.8	34.7	40.8	29.6
% Total Yds. Passing	59.2	64.4	55.8	66.0	59.5	69.6	59.5	49.9	65.0	58.2	62.2	65.3	59.2	70.4
Avg. Yds. per Game	329.9	241.4	314.8	332.4	330.7	329.1	397.0	307.1	324.6	327.4	318.4	323.5	342.1	335.1
Ball Control Plays	1019	885	1094	1022	1140	1058	1062	1026	1051	1108	991	1029	1033	1031
Avg. Yds. per Play	5.2	4.4	4.6	5.2	4.6	5.0	6.0	4.8	4.9	4.7	5.1	5.0	5.3	5.2
Third Down Efficiency	44.3	26.4	33.6	45.4	36.6	39.1	45.5	37.7	37.5	41.7	34.8	35.2	43.9	37.4
Intercepted by	12	21	28	14	27	17	11	13	19	20	21	25	18	21
Yds. Returned by	147	290	297	87	338	399	120	213	182	287	163	345	308	391
Returned for TD	1	1	2	0	2	3	1	3	0	0	1	2	1	4

Punts														
Yds. Punted	78	68	80	81	89	92	84	68	71	89	73	99	100	60
	3114	2787	3239	3157	3497	3677	3492	2777	2949	3643	2921	4236	4160	2497
Avg. Yds. per Punt	39.9	41.0	40.5	39.0	39.3	40.0	41.6	40.8	41.5	40.9	40.0	42.8	41.6	41.6
Punt Returns	38	36	30	27	58	50	47	49	35	46	49	55	41	42
Yds. Returned	187	310	190	239	486	479	550	435	196	368	516	230	249	450
Avg. Yds. per Return	4.9	8.6	6.3	8.9	8.4	9.6	11.7	8.9	5.6	8.0	10.5	4.2	6.1	10.7
Returned for TD	0	0	0	0	0	2	1	0	0	0	1	0	0	1
Kickoff Returns	73	67	78	85	69	55	45	59	74	73	60	65	68	48
Yds. Returned	1404	1336	1499	1549	1298	1088	916	1281	1288	1171	1250	1310	1443	1053
Avg. Yds. per Return	19.2	19.9	19.2	18.2	18.8	19.8	20.4	21.7	17.4	16.0	20.8	20.2	21.2	21.9
Returned for TD	1	0	0	1	0	0	0	0	0	0	0	0	1	0
Penalties	84	136	91	75	96	93	119	113	115	145	107	95	86	93
Yds. Penalized	803	1078	723	578	904	699	1025	1047	871	1129	978	868	698	820
Fumbles	32	27	28	20	32	24	28	35	42	33	28	35	33	36
Lost	22	14	13	12	11	16	10	18	22	15	11	16	13	20
Out of Bounds	1	0	1	0	6	0	1	2	3	2	0	2	2	0
Own Rec. for TD	0	0	0	0	1	0	0	1	0	0	0	0	0	0
Opp. Rec. by	15	20	12	20	16	9	13	15	17	7	13	17	16	21
Opp. Rec. for TD	0	0	0	1	0	1	1	1	0	2	2	1	1	2
Total Points Scored	310	380	227	345	320	301	361	484	316	309	408	308	248	382
Total TDs	39	47	24	39	36	35	41	59	36	34	48	36	29	48
TDs Rushing	13	27	10	11	12	10	13	20	15	14	17	8	10	16
TDs Passing	25	20	14	26	22	20	23	35	18	16	27	23	14	27
TDs on Ret. and Rec.	1	0	0	2	2	5	5	4	3	4	4	5	5	5
Extra Points	37	44	24	36	36	34	41	58	32	33	48	35	26	46
Safeties	0	0	1	0	1	3	1	0	1	0	0	0	0	0
Field Goals Made	13	18	19	25	22	17	24	24	22	24	24	19	16	16
Field Goals Attempted	20	27	25	38	35	26	33	28	31	31	29	28	22	30
% Successful	65.0	66.7	76.0	65.8	62.9	65.4	72.7	85.7	71.0	77.4	82.8	67.9	72.7	53.3

AMERICAN CONFERENCE DEFENSE

	Buff.	Cin.	Clev.	Den.	Hou.	Ind.	K.C.	Raid.	Mia.	N.E.	N.Y.J.	Pitt.	S.D.	Sea.
First Downs	345	322	270	311	345	343	335	297	314	311	341	282	322	288
Rushing	134	115	103	90	158	124	121	107	130	109	117	87	109	99
Passing	186	191	145	206	168	194	192	147	172	182	198	167	189	160
Penalty	25	16	22	15	19	25	22	43	12	20	26	28	24	29
Rushes	531	477	494	435	596	559	523	517	458	498	497	454	457	475
Net Yds. Gained	2106	1868	1945	1664	2789	2007	1980	1892	2155	1886	2064	1617	1851	1789
Avg. Gain	4.0	3.9	3.9	3.8	4.7	3.6	3.8	3.7	4.7	3.8	4.2	3.6	4.1	3.8
Avg. Yds. per Game	131.6	116.8	121.6	104.0	174.3	125.4	123.8	118.3	134.7	117.9	129.0	101.1	115.7	111.8
Passes Attempted	495	517	458	631	447	515	586	508	551	513	511	515	531	521
Completed	300	302	261	346	271	298	332	254	310	283	312	299	323	265
% Completed	60.6	58.4	57.0	54.8	60.6	57.9	56.7	50.0	56.3	55.2	61.1	58.1	60.8	50.9
Total Yds. Gained	3667	3689	3049	4453	3446	3890	4009	3268	3604	3666	3862	3689	4303	3572
Times Sacked	26	40	43	57	32	42	50	64	42	55	44	47	33	55
Yds. Lost	191	298	353	430	267	320	364	516	339	452	360	390	218	398
Net Yds. Gained	3476	3391	2696	4023	3179	3570	3645	2752	3265	3214	3502	3299	4085	3174
Avg. Yds. per Game	217.3	211.9	168.5	251.4	198.7	223.1	227.8	172.0	204.1	200.9	218.9	206.2	255.3	198.4
Net Yds. per Pass Play	6.67	6.09	5.38	5.85	6.64	6.41	5.73	4.81	5.51	5.66	6.31	5.87	7.24	5.51
Yds. Gained per Comp.	12.22	12.22	11.68	12.87	12.72	13.05	12.08	12.87	11.63	12.95	12.38	12.34	13.32	13.48
Combined Net Yds. Gained	5582	5259	4641	5687	5968	5577	5625	4644	5420	5100	5566	4916	5936	4963
% Total Yds. Rushing	37.7	35.5	41.9	29.3	46.7	36.0	35.2	40.7	39.8	37.0	37.1	32.9	31.2	36.0
% Total Yds. Passing	62.3	64.5	58.1	70.7	53.3	64.0	64.8	59.3	60.2	63.0	62.9	67.1	68.8	64.0
Avg. Yds. per Game	348.9	328.7	290.1	355.4	373.0	348.6	351.6	290.3	338.8	318.8	347.9	307.3	371.0	310.2
Ball Control Plays	1052	1034	995	1123	1075	1116	1159	1089	1051	1066	1052	1016	1021	1051
Avg. Yds. per Play	5.3	5.1	4.7	5.1	5.6	5.0	4.9	4.3	5.2	4.8	5.3	4.8	5.8	4.7
Third Down Efficiency	42.9	40.6	39.6	35.4	47.7	42.6	36.6	30.1	41.1	39.7	39.7	32.9	42.1	34.0
Intercepted by	16	25	20	31	13	18	30	20	24	17	15	31	19	38
Yds. Returned by	233	368	236	510	139	190	465	339	478	210	152	433	499	697
Returned for TD	0	4	0	4	0	1	2	2	2	0	0	4	4	7

	1	2	3	4	5	6	7	8	9	10	11	12	13	14
Punts	72	67	77	81	64	80	91	117	83	83	67	90	73	83
Yds. Punted	2812	2771	3123	3361	2702	3363	3642	5071	3476	3347	2854	3818	2890	3345
Avg. Yds. per Punt	39.1	41.4	40.6	41.5	42.2	42.0	40.0	43.3	41.9	40.3	42.6	42.4	39.6	40.3
Punt Returns	52	38	43	44	60	62	60	34	17	45	37	37	43	32
Yds. Returned	597	310	489	335	618	600	461	345	138	442	242	351	399	205
Avg. Yds. per Return	11.5	8.2	11.4	7.6	10.3	9.7	7.7	10.1	8.1	9.8	6.5	9.5	9.3	6.4
Returned for TD	0	0	0	0	0	0	0	0	0	1	0	1	0	1
Kickoff Returns	44	69	52	55	51	42	64	61	66	73	48	61	72	67
Yds. Returned	958	1446	1159	1181	986	849	1354	1063	1368	1373	1030	1338	1437	1116
Avg. Yds. per Return	21.8	21.0	22.3	21.5	19.3	20.2	21.2	17.4	20.7	18.8	21.5	21.9	20.0	16.7
Returned for TD	0	1	0	0	0	0	0	0	0	0	0	1	0	0
Penalties	87	90	108	104	105	98	108	121	93	87	87	107	108	114
Yds. Penalized	734	743	765	891	876	813	951	1061	772	773	723	945	905	883
Fumbles	36	27	34	44	24	29	18	28	23	33	34	30	34	47
Lost	21	15	15	24	11	13	11	14	12	8	19	11	17	25
Out of Bounds	1	2	0	3	0	2	1	5	1	4	1	2	3	3
Own Rec. for TD	1	0	0	0	0	0	0	0	0	0	0	0	0	0
Opp. Rec. by	14	16	16	17	16	16	15	20	10	15	13	15	17	13
Opp. Rec. for TD	0	0	2	0	1	1	2	0	0	2	0	1	1	1
Total Points Scored	454	339	297	241	437	414	324	278	298	352	364	310	413	282
Total TDs	56	39	30	26	53	50	38	33	39	42	41	35	51	34
TDs Rushing	19	21	10	10	27	16	10	12	16	11	16	12	23	11
TDs Passing	32	15	15	16	23	31	19	19	22	25	24	19	27	18
TDs on Ret. and Rec.	5	3	5	0	3	3	9	2	1	6	1	4	1	5
Extra Points	56	37	30	26	51	47	37	29	37	37	40	34	50	34
Safeties	1	1	0	1	1	2	1	0	0	0	0	0	0	1
Field Goals Made	20	22	29	19	22	21	19	17	9	21	26	22	19	14
Field Goals Attempted	28	27	33	33	30	23	27	21	17	31	37	28	25	22
% Successful	71.4	81.5	87.9	57.6	73.3	91.3	70.4	81.0	52.9	67.7	70.3	78.6	76.0	63.6

CLUB LEADERS & CLUB RANKINGS BY YARDS

CLUB LEADERS

	Offense	Defense
First Downs		
Rushing	Mia. 387	Chi. 216
Passing	Chi. 164	Chi. 72
Penalty	Mia. 243	Chi. 122
	N.O. 30	Mia. 12
Rushes	Chi. 674	Chi. 378
Net Yds. Gained	Chi. 2974	Chi. 1377
Avg. Gain	Rams 5.3	Det. 3.5
Passes Attempted	S.D. 662	N.O. 422
Completed	S.D. 401	Chi. 198
% Completed	Mia. 64.2	Chi. 45.5
Total Yds. Gained	Mia. 5146	N.O. 2873
Times Sacked	Mia. 14	Chi. 72
Yds. Lost	Mia. 128	Chi. 583
Net Yds. Gained	Mia. 5018	N.O. 2453
Net Yds. per Pass Play	Mia. 8.56	Raid. & Dal. 4.81
Yds. Gained per Comp.	Pitt. 14.66	G.B. 11.02
Combined Net Yds. Gained	Mia. 6936	Chi. 3863
% Total Yds. Rushing	Rams 57.2	Den. 29.3
% Total Yds. Passing	S.D. 73.7	N.O. 49.9
Ball Control Plays	S.D. 1154	Chi. 885
Avg. Yds. per Play	Mia. 6.5	Raiders 4.3
Avg. Time of Poss.	Chi. 35:08	—
Third Down Efficiency	Mia. 51.5	Chi. 26.4
Interceptions		Sea. 38
Yds. Returned	—	Sea. 697
Returned for TD	—	Sea. 7
Punts	Dall. 108	—
Yds. Punted	K.C. 4397	—
Avg. Yds. per Punt	K.C. 44.9	—
Punt Returns	Raiders 67	Mia. 17
Yds. Returned	Pitt. 696	Mia. 138
Avg. Yds. per Return	Cin. 12.4	Dall. 4.2
Returned for TD	Rams 2	—
Kickoff Returns	Minn. 86	Ind. 42
Yds. Returned	Minn. 1775	Ind. 849
Avg. Yds. per Return	N.Y.J. 23.0	G.B. 16.0
Returned for TD	Five with 1	—

Total Points Scored		
Total Points Scored	Mia. 513	S.F. 227
Total TDs	Mia. 70	S.F. 24
TDs Rushing	Chi. 22	Dall. 8
TDs Passing	Mia. 49	Chi. & S.F. 14
TDs on Ret. and Rec.	Sea. 9	Three with 0
Extra Points	Mia. 66	S.F. 24
Safeties	Rams. 3	
Field Goals Made	Phil. 30	Mia. 9
Field Goals Attempted	Phil. 37	Mia. 17
% Successful	Minn. 87.0	Mia. 52.9

CLUB RANKINGS BY YARDS

Team	Offense			Defense		
	Total	Rush	Pass	Total	Rush	Pass
Atlanta	19	15	20	15	21	7
Buffalo	27	26	25	23	19	19
Chicago	7	1	26	1	1	2
Cincinnati	5	6t	13t	13	11	18
Cleveland	24	21	18	2	15	3
Dallas	11	20	6	7	24	5
Denver	22	10	23	25	5	27
Detroit	12	14	13t	17	8	21
Green Bay	6	13	9	16	20	8
Houston	23	23	17	27	28	11
Indianapolis	28	12	28	22	17	22
Kansas City	17	27	7	24	16	23
Los Angeles Raiders	15	17	12	3	13	4
Los Angeles Rams	21	2	27	14	13	24
Miami	25	18	1	19	22	14
Minnesota	14	16	22	28	27	26
New England	20	11	16	9	12	12
New Orleans	13	8	24	4	26	1
New York Giants	16	22	5	11	9	16
New York Jets	26	5	21	21	18	20
Philadelphia	8	28	11	12	23	6
Pittsburgh	8	6t	15	5	9	9
St. Louis	3	9	3	8	24	15
San Diego	4	24	4	26	10	17
San Francisco	2	3	10	10	7	17
Seattle	18	25	8	6	6	10
Tampa Bay	10	4	19	20	25	13
Washington	9	19	25	18	2	25

NFC QUARTERBACK RATINGS

	Att	Comp	Pct Comp	Yds	Avg Gain	TD	Pct TD	Long	Int	Pct Int	Rating Points
Montana, Joe, S.F.	432	279	64.6	3630	8.40	28	6.5	t80	10	2.3	102.9
Lomax, Neil, St.L.	560	345	61.6	4614	8.24	28	5.0	t83	16	2.9	92.5
Bartkowski, Steve, At.	269	181	67.3	2158	8.02	11	4.1	61	10	3.7	89.7
Theismann, Joe, Wash.	477	283	59.3	3391	7.11	24	5.0	t80	13	2.7	86.6
Dickey, Lynn, G.B.	401	237	59.1	3195	7.97	25	6.2	t79	19	4.7	85.6
Danielson, Gary, Det.	410	252	61.5	3076	7.50	17	4.1	t77	15	3.7	83.1
DeBerg, Steve, T.B.	509	308	60.5	3554	6.98	19	3.7	55	18	3.5	79.3
Kemp, Jeff, Rams	284	143	50.4	2021	7.12	13	4.6	t63	7	2.5	78.7
Simms, Phil, Giants	533	286	53.7	4044	7.59	22	4.1	t65	18	3.4	78.1
Jaworski, Ron, Phil.	427	234	54.8	2754	6.45	16	3.7	t90	14	3.3	73.5
White, Danny, Dall.	233	126	54.1	1580	6.78	11	4.7	t66	11	4.7	71.5
Kramer, Tommy, Minn.	236	124	52.5	1678	7.11	9	3.8	t70	10	4.2	70.6
Hogeboom, Gary, Dall.	367	195	53.1	2366	6.45	7	1.9	t68	14	3.8	63.7
Todd, Richard, N.O.	312	161	51.6	2178	6.98	11	3.5	74	19	6.1	60.6

Bears quarterbacks did not have enough passing attempts to qualify for NFC ratings. Their stats are below.

	Att	Comp	Pct Comp	Yds	Avg Gain	TD	Pct TD	Long	Int	Pct Int	Rating Points
Fuller, Steve, Chi.	78	53	67.9	595	7.63	3	3.8	31	0	0.0	103.3
McMahon, Jim, Chi.	143	85	59.4	1146	8.01	8	5.6	t61	2	1.4	97.8

AFC QUARTERBACK RATINGS

	Att	Comp	Pct Comp	Yds	Avg Gain	TD	Pct TD	Long	Int	Pct Int	Rating Points
Marino, Dan, Mia.	564	362	64.2	5084	9.01	48	8.5	t80	17	3.0	108.9
Eason, Tony, N.E.	431	259	60.1	3228	7.49	23	5.3	t76	8	1.9	93.4
Fouts, Dan, S.D.	507	317	62.5	3740	7.38	19	3.7	t61	17	3.4	83.4
Krieg, Dave, Sea.	480	276	57.5	3671	7.65	32	6.7	t80	24	5.0	83.3
Anderson, Ken, Cin.	275	175	63.6	2107	7.66	10	3.6	t80	12	4.4	81.0
Kenney, Bill, K.C.	282	151	53.5	2098	7.44	15	5.3	t65	10	3.5	80.7
Moon, Warren, Hou.	450	259	57.6	3338	7.42	12	2.7	76	14	3.1	76.9
Elway, John, Den.	380	214	56.3	2598	6.84	18	4.7	73	15	3.9	76.8
Malone, Mark, Pitt.	272	147	54.0	2137	7.86	16	5.9	t61	17	6.3	73.4
Ryan, Pat, Jets	285	156	54.7	1939	6.80	14	4.9	t44	14	4.9	72.0
Wilson, Marc, Raiders	282	153	54.3	2151	7.63	15	5.3	92	17	6.0	71.7
McDonald, Paul, Clev.	493	271	55.0	3472	7.04	14	2.8	64	23	4.7	67.3
Ferguson, Joe, Buff.	344	191	55.5	1991	5.79	12	3.5	t68	17	4.9	63.5
Blackledge, Todd, K.C.	294	147	50.0	1707	5.81	6	2.0	t46	11	3.7	59.2

TOP 25 RUSHERS & RECEIVERS

NFC—TOP 25 INDIVIDUAL RUSHERS

	Att	Yards	Avg	Long	TD
Dickerson, Eric, Rams	379	2105	5.6	66	14
Payton, Walter, Chi.	381	1684	4.4	t72	11
Wilder, James, T.B.	407	1544	3.8	37	13
Riggs, Gerald, Atl.	353	1486	4.2	57	13
Tyler, Wendell, S.F.	246	1262	5.1	40	7
Riggins, John, Wash.	327	1239	3.8	24	14
Dorsett, Tony, Dall.	302	1189	3.9	t31	6
Anderson, Ottis, St.L.	289	1174	4.1	24	6
Rogers, George, N.O.	239	914	3.8	28	2
Carpenter, Rob, Giants	250	795	3.2	22	7
Montgomery, Wilbert, Phil.	201	789	3.9	27	2
Anderson, Alfred, Minn.	201	773	3.8	23	2
Sims, Billy, Det.	130	687	5.3	81	5
Craig, Roger, S.F.	155	649	4.2	28	7
Gajan, Hokie, N.O.	102	615	6.0	t62	5
Ellis, Gerry, G.B.	123	581	4.7	50	4
Ivery, Eddie Lee, G.B.	99	552	5.6	49	6
Jones, James, Det.	137	532	3.9	34	3
Morris, Joe, Giants	133	510	3.8	28	4
Campbell, Earl, Hou.–N.O.	146	468	3.2	22	4
Brown, Ted, Minn.	98	442	4.5	19	3
Mitchell, Stump, St.L.	81	434	5.4	39	9
Suhey, Matt, Chi.	124	424	3.4	21	4
Griffin, Keith, Wash.	97	408	4.2	31	0
Nelson, Darrin, Minn.	80	406	5.1	39	3

NFC—TOP 25 RECEIVERS BY YARDS

	Yards	No	Avg	Long	TD
Green, Roy, St.L.	1555	78	19.9	t83	12
Monk, Art, Wash.	1372	106	12.9	72	7
Lofton, James, G.B.	1361	62	22.0	t79	7
Bailey, Stacey, At.	1138	67	17.0	61	6
Quick, Mike, Phil.	1052	61	17.2	t90	9
House, Kevin, T.B.	1005	76	13.2	55	5
Clark, Dwight, S.F.	880	52	16.9	t80	6
Hill, Tony, Dall.	864	58	14.9	t66	5
Lewis, Leo, Minn.	830	47	17.7	56	4
Carter, Gerald, T.B.	816	60	13.6	t74	5
Johnson, Bob, Giants	795	48	16.6	45	7
Cosbie, Doug, Dall.	789	60	13.2	36	4
Thompson, Leonard, Det.	773	50	15.5	t66	6
Tilley, Pat, St.L.	758	52	14.6	42	5
Nichols, Mark, Det.	744	34	21.9	t77	1
Solomon, Freddie, S.F.	737	40	18.4	t64	10
Jackson, Alfred, Atl.	731	52	14.1	t50	2
Muhammad, Calvin, Wash.	729	42	17.4	t80	4
Spagnola, John, Phil.	701	65	10.8	34	1
Mowatt, Zeke, Giants	698	48	14.5	34	6
Wilder, James, T.B.	685	85	8.1	50	0
Craig, Roger, S.F.	675	71	9.5	t64	3
Jones, James, Det.	662	77	8.6	39	5
Ellard, Henry, Rams	622	34	18.3	t63	6
Manuel, Lionel, Giants	619	33	18.8	53	4

AFC—TOP 25 INDIVIDUAL RUSHERS

	Att	Yards	Avg	Long	TD
Jackson, Earnest, S.D.	296	1179	4.0	t32	8
Allen, Marcus, Raiders	275	1168	4.2	t52	13
Winder, Sammy, Den.	296	1153	3.9	24	4
Bell, Greg, Buff.	262	1100	4.2	t85	7
McNeil, Freeman, Jets	229	1070	4.7	53	5
Pollard, Frank, Pitt.	213	851	4.0	52	6
James, Craig, N.E.	160	790	4.9	73	1
Moriarty, Larry, Hou.	189	785	4.2	t51	6
McMillan, Randy, Ind.	163	705	4.3	t31	5
Heard, Herman, K.C.	165	684	4.1	t69	4
Green, Boyce, Clev.	202	673	3.3	29	0
Kinnebrew, Larry, Cin.	154	623	4.0	23	9
Abercrombie, Walter, Pitt.	145	610	4.2	31	1
Bennett, Woody, Mia.	144	606	4.2	23	7
Nathan, Tony, Mia.	118	558	4.7	22	1
Tatupu, Mosi, N.E.	133	533	4.2	t20	4
Collins, Anthony, N.E.	138	550	4.0	21	5
Hector, Johnny, Jets	124	531	4.3	64	1
Dickey, Curtis, Ind.	131	523	4.0	30	3
Pruitt, Mike, Clev.	163	506	3.1	14	6
Carter, Joe, Mia.	100	495	5.0	35	1
Alexander, Charles, Cin.	132	479	3.6	22	2
Byner, Earnest, Clev.	72	426	5.9	54	2
Erenberg, Rich, Pitt.	115	405	3.5	t31	2
Brooks, James, Cin.	103	396	3.8	33	2

AFC—TOP 25 RECEIVERS BY YARDS

	Yards	No	Avg	Long	TD
Stallworth, John, Pitt.	1395	80	17.4	51	11
Clayton, Mark, Mia.	1389	73	19.0	t65	18
Duper, Mark, Mia.	1306	71	18.4	t80	8
Watson, Steve, Den.	1170	69	17.0	73	7
Largent, Steve, Sea.	1164	74	15.7	65	12
Smith, Tim, Hou.	1141	69	16.5	t75	4
Carson, Carlos, K.C.	1078	57	18.9	57	4
Christensen, Todd, Raiders	1007	80	12.6	38	7
Newsome, Ozzie, Clev.	1001	89	11.2	52	5
Collinsworth, Cris, Cin.	989	64	15.5	t57	6
Marshall, Henry, K.C.	912	62	14.7	37	4
Franklin, Byron, Buff.	862	69	12.5	t64	4
Lipps, Louis, Pitt.	860	45	19.1	t80	9
Barnwell, Malcolm, Raiders	851	45	18.9	t51	2
Joiner, Charlie, S.D.	793	61	13.0	41	6
Ramsey, Derrick, N.E.	792	66	12.0	34	7
Shuler, Mickey, Jets	782	68	11.5	49	6
Harris, M.L., Cin.	759	48	15.8	t80	2
Allen, Marcus, Raiders	758	64	11.8	92	5
Holohan, Pete, S.D.	734	56	13.1	51	1
Duckworth, Bobby, S.D.	715	25	28.6	t88	4
Turner, Daryl, Sea.	715	35	20.4	t80	10
Morgan, Stanley, N.E.	709	38	18.7	t76	5
Chandler, Wes, S.D.	708	52	13.6	t63	6
Butler, Raymond, Ind.	664	43	15.4	t74	6

1984 NFL "TOP TEN"

RUSHERS

	Att	Yards	Avg	Long	TD
Dickerson, Eric, Rams	379	2105	5.6	66	14
Payton, Walter, Chi.	381	1684	4.4	t72	11
Wilder, James, T.B.	407	1544	3.8	37	13
Riggs, Gerald, Atl.	353	1486	4.2	57	13
Tyler, Wendell, S.F.	246	1262	5.1	40	7
Riggins, John, Wash.	327	1239	3.8	24	14
Dorsett, Tony, Dall.	302	1189	3.9	t31	6
Jackson, Earnest, S.D.	296	1179	4.0	t32	8
Anderson, Ottis, St.L.	289	1174	4.1	24	6
Allen, Marcus, Raiders	275	1168	4.2	t52	13

SCORERS—NON-KICKERS

	TD	TDR	TDP	TDM	PTS
Allen, Marcus, Raiders	18	13	5	0	108
Clayton, Mark, Mia.	18	0	18	0	108
Dickerson, Eric, Rams	14	14	0	0	94
Riggins, John, Wash.	14	14	0	0	84
Riggs, Gerald, Atl.	13	13	0	0	78
Wilder, James, T.B.	13	13	0	0	78
Green, Roy, St.L.	12	0	12	0	72
Johnson, Pete, S.D.-Mia.	12	12	0	0	72
Largent, Steve, Sea.	12	0	12	0	72
Five players tied with	11				66

PUNT RETURNERS

	No	FC	Yards	Avg	Long	TD
Martin, Mike, Cin.	24	5	376	15.7	55	0
Ellard, Henry, Rams	30	3	403	13.4	t83	2
Lipps, Louis, Pitt.	53	2	656	12.4	t76	1
McLemore, Dana, S.F.	45	11	521	11.6	t79	1
Willhite, Gerald, Den.	20	9	200	10.0	35	0
Fryar, Irving, N.E.	36	10	347	9.6	55	0
Wilson, Don, Buff.	33	8	297	9.0	t65	1
Pruitt, Greg, Raiders	53	16	473	8.9	38	0
Springs, Kirk, Jets	28	10	247	8.8	33	0
Mitchell, Stump, St.L.	38	3	333	8.8	39	0

SCORERS—KICKERS

	XP	XPA	FG	FGA	PTS
Wersching, Ray, S.F.	56	56	25	35	131
Moseley, Mark, Wash.	48	51	24	31	120
Anderson, Gary, Pitt.	45	45	24	32	117
O'Donoghue, Neil, St.L.	48	51	23	35	117
McFadden, Paul, Phil.	26	27	30	37	116
Lansford, Mike, Rams	37	38	25	33	112
Johnson, Norm, Sea.	50	51	20	24	110
Franklin, Tony, N.E.	42	42	22	28	108
Lowery, Nick, K.C.	35	35	23	33	104
Breech, Jim, Cin.	37	37	22	31	103

INTERCEPTORS

	No	Yards	Avg	Long	TD
Easley, Ken, Sea.	10	126	12.6	t58	2
Flynn, Tom, G.B.	9	106	11.8	31	0
Brown, Dave, Sea.	8	179	22.4	t90	2
Lewis, Tim, G.B.	7	151	21.6	t99	1
Downs, Mike, Dall.	7	126	18.0	t27	1
Ellis, Ray, Phil.	7	119	17.0	31	0
Dean, Vernon, Wash.	7	114	16.3	t36	2
Haynes, Mark, Giants	7	90	12.9	22	0
Cherry, Deron, K.C.	7	140	20.0	67	0
Shell, Donnie, Pitt.	7	61	8.7	t52	1

PASS RECEIVERS

	No	Yards	Avg	Long	TD
Monk, Art, Wash.	106	1372	12.9	72	7
Newsome, Ozzie, Clev.	89	1001	11.2	52	5
Wilder, James, T.B.	85	685	8.1	50	0
Stallworth, John, Pitt.	80	1395	17.4	51	11
Christensen, Todd, Raiders	80	1007	12.6	38	7
Green, Roy, St.L.	78	1555	19.9	t83	12
Jones, James, Det.	77	662	8.6	39	5
House, Kevin, T.B.	76	1005	13.2	55	5
Largent, Steve, Sea.	74	1164	15.7	65	12
Clayton, Mark, Mia.	73	1389	19.0	t65	18

KICKOFF RETURNERS

	No	Yards	Avg	Long	TD
Humphery, Bobby, Jets	22	675	30.7	t97	1
Williams, Dokie, Raiders	24	621	25.9	62	0
Anderson, Larry, Ind.	22	525	23.9	69	0
Redden, Barry, Rams	23	530	23.0	40	0
Mitchell, Stump, St.L.	35	804	23.0	56	0
Nelson, Darrin, Minn.	39	891	22.8	47	0
Springs, Kirk, Jets	23	521	22.7	73	0
Roaches, Carl, Hou.	30	679	22.6	49	0
James, Lionel, S.D.	43	959	22.3	55	0
Antony, Tyrone, N.O.	22	490	22.3	64	0

PASS RECEIVERS BY YARDS

	Yards	No	Avg	Long	TD
Green, Roy, St.L.	1555	78	19.9	t83	12
Stallworth, John, Pitt.	1395	80	17.4	51	11
Clayton, Mark, Mia.	1389	73	19.0	t65	18
Monk, Art, Wash.	1372	106	12.9	72	7
Lofton, James, G.B.	1361	62	22.0	t79	7
Duper, Mark, Mia.	1306	71	18.4	t80	8
Watson, Steve, Den.	1170	69	17.0	73	7
Largent, Steve, Sea.	1164	74	15.7	65	12
Smith, Tim, Hou.	1141	69	16.5	t75	4
Bailey, Stacey, Atl.	1138	67	17.0	61	6

"TOP TEN" CONT'D.

INDIVIDUAL PASSING QUALIFIERS

	Att	Comp	Pct Comp	Yds	Avg Gain	TD	Pct TD	Long	Int	Pct Int	Rating Points
Marino, Dan, Mia.	564	362	64.2	5084	9.01	48	8.5	t80	17	3.0	108.9
Montana, Joe, S.F.	432	279	64.6	3630	8.40	28	6.5	t80	10	2.3	102.9
Eason, Tony, N.E.	431	259	60.1	3228	7.49	23	5.3	t76	8	1.9	83.4
Lomax, Neil, St.L.	560	345	61.6	4614	8.24	28	5.0	t83	16	2.9	92.5
Bartkowski, Steve, Atl.	269	181	67.3	2158	8.02	11	4.1	61	10	3.7	89.7
Theismann, Joe, Wash.	477	283	59.3	3391	7.11	24	5.0	t80	13	2.7	86.6
Dickey, Lynn, G.B.	401	237	59.1	3195	7.97	25	6.2	t79	19	4.7	85.6
Fouts, Dan, S.D.	507	317	62.5	3740	7.38	19	3.7	t61	17	3.4	83.4
Krieg, Dave, Sea.	480	276	57.5	3671	7.65	32	6.7	t80	24	5.0	83.3
Danielson, Gary, Det.	410	252	61.5	3076	7.50	17	4.1	t77	15	3.7	83.1

INDIVIDUAL PUNTERS

	No	Yards	Long	Avg	Total Punts	TB	Blk	Opp Ret	Ret Yds	In 20	Net Avg
Arnold, Jim, K.C.	98	4397	63	44.9	98	13	0	60	461	22	37.5
Roby, Reggie, Mia.	51	2281	69	44.7	51	10	0	17	138	15	38.1
Stark, Rohn, Ind.	98	4383	72	44.7	98	7	0	62	600	21	37.2
Hansen, Brian, N.O.	69	3020	66	43.8	70	7	1	47	550	9	33.3
Cox, Steve, Clev.	74	3213	69	43.4	76	8	2	43	489	16	33.7
Prestridge, Luke, N.E.	44	1884	89	42.8	44	5	0	21	228	8	35.4
Coleman, Greg, Minn.	82	3473	62	42.4	82	2	0	49	435	16	36.6
Scribner, Bucky, G.B.	85	3596	61	42.3	85	12	0	46	368	18	35.2
McInally, Pat, Cin.	67	2832	61	42.3	67	8	0	38	310	19	35.3
Horan, Mike, Phil.	92	3880	69	42.2	92	6	0	58	486	21	35.6

Guards Kurt Becker (79) and Mark Bortz (62) lead the blocking on the sweep.

NFL Weekly Schedule

Sunday, Sept. 8

Detroit at Atlanta
Green Bay at New England
Indianapolis at Pittsburgh
Kansas City at New Orleans
Miami at Houston
Philadelphia at New York Giants
St. Louis at Cleveland
San Francisco at Minnesota
Seattle at Cincinnati
Tampa Bay at Chicago
San Diego at Buffalo
Denver at Los Angeles Rams
New York Jets at Los Angeles
 Raiders

Monday, Sept. 9

Washington at Dallas

Thursday, Sept. 12

Los Angeles Raiders at Kansas
 City

Sunday, Sept. 15

Buffalo at New York Jets
Cincinnati at St. Louis
Dallas at Detroit
Houston at Washington
Los Angeles Rams at
 Philadelphia
New England at Chicago
Minnesota at Tampa Bay
Indianapolis at Miami
New Orleans at Denver
New York Giants at Green Bay
Atlanta at San Francisco

Monday, Sept. 16

Pittsburgh at Cleveland

Thursday, Sept. 19

Chicago at Minnesota

Sunday, Sept. 22

Cleveland at Dallas
Denver at Atlanta
Detroit at Indianapolis
Houston at Pittsburgh
New England at Buffalo
Philadelphia at Washington
Tampa Bay at New Orleans
St. Louis at New York Giants
San Diego at Cincinnati
Kansas City at Miami
New York Jets vs. Green Bay
 (Mil.)
San Francisco at Los Angeles
 Raiders

Monday, Sept. 23

Los Angeles Rams at Seattle

Sunday, Sept. 29

Dallas at Houston
Green Bay at St. Louis
Los Angeles Raiders at New
 England
Minnesota at Buffalo
New York Giants at Philadelphia
Seattle at Kansas City
Tampa Bay at Detroit
Washington at Chicago
New Orleans at San Francisco
Miami at Denver
Indianapolis at New York Jets
Atlanta at Los Angeles Rams
Cleveland at San Diego

Monday, Sept. 30

Cincinnati at Pittsburgh

Sunday, Oct. 6

Buffalo at Indianapolis
Chicago at Tampa Bay
Detroit at Green Bay
New England at Cleveland
Philadelphia at New Orleans
San Francisco at Atlanta
Pittsburgh at Miami
Houston at Denver
New York Jets at Cincinnati
Kansas City at Los Angeles
 Raiders
Minnesota at Los Angeles Rams
San Diego at Seattle
Dallas at New York Giants

Monday, Oct. 7

St. Louis at Washington

Sunday, Oct. 13

Buffalo at New England
Cleveland at Houston
Denver at Indianapolis
Detroit at Washington
Los Angeles Rams at Tampa Bay
Minnesota vs. Green Bay (Mil.)
New York Giants at Cincinnati
Philadelphia at St. Louis
Pittsburgh at Dallas
New Orleans at Los Angeles
 Raiders
Kansas City at San Diego
Chicago at San Francisco
Atlanta at Seattle

Monday, Oct. 14

Miami at New York Jets

Sunday, Oct. 20

Cincinnati at Houston
Dallas at Philadelphia
Indianapolis at Buffalo
Los Angeles Raiders at Cleveland
Los Angeles Rams at Kansas City
New Orleans at Atlanta
Washington at New York Giants
St. Louis at Pittsburgh
San Diego at Minnesota
San Francisco at Detroit
New York Jets at New England
Seattle at Denver
Tampa Bay at Miami

Monday, Oct. 21

Green Bay at Chicago

Sunday, Oct. 27

Atlanta at Dallas
Buffalo at Philadelphia
Denver at Kansas City
Green Bay at Indianapolis
Houston at St. Louis
Miami at Detroit
Minnesota at Chicago
New England at Tampa Bay
Seattle at New York Jets
Washington at Cleveland
Pittsburgh at Cincinnati
New York Giants at New Orleans
San Francisco at Los Angeles
 Rams

Monday, Oct. 28

San Diego at Los Angeles
 Raiders

Sunday, Nov. 3

Chicago at Green Bay
Cincinnati at Buffalo
Cleveland at Pittsburgh
Detroit at Minnesota
Kansas City at Houston
Miami at New England
Tampa Bay at New York Giants
Washington at Atlanta
Los Angeles Raiders at Seattle
New Orleans at Los Angeles
 Rams
New York Jets at Indianapolis
Philadelphia at San Francisco
Denver at San Diego

Monday, Nov. 4

Dallas at St. Louis

Sunday, Nov. 10

Atlanta at Philadelphia
Cleveland at Cincinnati
Detroit at Chicago
Green Bay at Minnesota
Houston at Buffalo
Indianapolis at New England
Los Angeles Rams at New York
  Giants
Pittsburgh at Kansas City
St. Louis at Tampa Bay
Seattle at New Orleans
Los Angeles Raiders at San
  Diego
New York Jets at Miami
Dallas at Washington

Monday, Nov. 11

San Francisco at Denver

Sunday, Nov. 17

Buffalo at Cleveland
Chicago at Dallas
Tampa Bay at New York Jets
Los Angeles Rams at Atlanta
Miami at Indianapolis
New Orleans vs. Green Bay (Mil.)
Pittsburgh at Houston
St. Louis at Philadelphia
San Diego at Denver
Minnesota at Detroit
New England at Seattle
Cincinnati at Los Angeles Raiders
Kansas City at San Francisco

Monday, Nov. 18

New York Giants at Washington

Sunday, Nov. 24

Atlanta at Chicago
Cincinnati at Cleveland
Detroit at Tampa Bay
San Diego at Houston
Washington at Pittsburgh
Miami at Buffalo
New England at New York Jets
New Orleans at Minnesota
New York Giants at St. Louis
Philadelphia at Dallas
Green Bay at Los Angeles Rams
Indianapolis at Kansas City
Denver at Los Angeles Raiders

Monday, Nov. 25

Seattle at San Francisco

Thursday, Nov. 28

New York Jets at Detroit
St. Louis at Dallas

Sunday, Dec. 1

Cleveland at New York Giants
Denver at Pittsburgh
Houston at Cincinnati
Tampa Bay at Green Bay
Los Angeles Rams at New
  Orleans
Minnesota at Philadelphia
New England at Indianapolis
Los Angeles Raiders at Atlanta
Kansas City at Seattle
San Francisco at Washington
Buffalo at San Diego

Monday, Dec. 2

Chicago at Miami

Thursday, Dec. 5

Pittsburgh at San Diego

Sunday, Dec. 8

Atlanta at Kansas City
Washington at Philadelphia
Dallas at Cincinnati
Detroit at New England
Indianapolis at Chicago
Miami at Green Bay
New Orleans at St. Louis
New York Jets at Buffalo
Los Angeles Raiders at Denver
New York Giants at Houston
Tampa Bay at Minnesota
Cleveland at Seattle

Monday, Dec. 9

Los Angeles Rams at San
  Francisco

Saturday, Dec. 14

Chicago at New York Jets
Kansas City at Denver

Sunday, Dec. 15

Buffalo at Pittsburgh
Cincinnati at Washington
Green Bay at Detroit
Houston at Cleveland
Indianapolis at Tampa Bay
Minnesota at Atlanta
New York Giants at Dallas
San Francisco at New Orleans
Philadelphia at San Diego
St. Louis at Los Angeles Rams
Seattle at Los Angeles Raiders

Monday, Dec. 16

New England at Miami

Friday, Dec. 20

Denver at Seattle

Saturday, Dec. 21

Pittsburgh at New York Giants
Washington at St. Louis

Sunday, Dec. 22

Atlanta at New Orleans
Buffalo at Miami
Chicago at Detroit
Cincinnati at New England
Cleveland at New York Jets
Green Bay at Tampa Bay
Philadelphia at Minnesota
San Diego at Kansas City
Houston at Indianapolis
Dallas at San Francisco

Monday, Dec. 23

Los Angeles Raiders at Los
  Angeles Rams

POSTSEASON

SUNDAY, Dec. 29 AFC and NFC
  first-round playoffs
SATURDAY, Jan. 4 AFC and
  NFC divisional playoffs
SUNDAY, Jan. 5 AFC and NFC
  divisional playoffs
SUNDAY, Jan. 12 AFC and NFC
  championship games
SUNDAY, Jan. 26 Super Bowl XX
  at Louisiana Superdome,
  New Orleans
SUNDAY, Feb. 2 AFC-NFC Pro
  Bowl, Honolulu

1985 Team Schedules
NATIONAL CONFERENCE

ATLANTA

Sept. 8-Detroit
Sept. 15-at San Francisco
Sept. 22-Denver
Sept. 29-at LA Rams
Oct. 6-San Francisco
Oct. 13-at Seattle
Oct. 20-New Orleans
Oct. 27-at Dallas
Nov. 3-Washington
Nov. 10-at Philadelphia
Nov. 17-LA Rams
Nov. 24-at Chicago
Dec. 1-LA Raiders
Dec. 8-at Kansas City
Dec. 15-Minnesota
Dec. 22-at New Orleans

CHICAGO

Sept. 8-Tampa Bay
Sept. 15-New England
Sept. 19-at Minnesota [Thurs.]
Sept. 29-Washington
Oct. 6-at Tampa Bay
Oct. 13-at San Francisco
Oct. 21-Green Bay [Mon.]
Oct. 27-Minnesota
Nov. 3-at Green Bay
Nov. 10-Detroit
Nov. 17-at Dallas
Nov. 24-Atlanta
Dec. 2-at Miami [Mon.]
Dec. 8-Indianapolis
Dec. 14-at NY Jets [Sat.]
Dec. 22-at Detroit

DALLAS

Sept. 9-Washington [Mon.]
Sept. 15-at Detroit
Sept. 22-Cleveland
Sept. 29-at Houston
Oct. 6-at NY Giants [night]
Oct. 13-Pittsburgh
Oct. 20-at Philadelphia
Oct. 27-Atlanta
Nov. 4-at St. Louis
Nov. 10-at Washington
Nov. 17-Chicago
Nov. 24-Philadelphia
Nov. 28-St. Louis [Thanks.]
Dec. 8-at Cincinnati
Dec. 15-NY Giants
Dec. 22-at San Francisco

DETROIT

Sept. 8-at Atlanta
Sept. 15-Dallas
Sept. 22-at Indianapolis
Sept. 29-Tampa Bay
Oct. 6-at Green Bay
Oct. 13-at Washington
Oct. 20-San Francisco

Oct. 27-Miami
Nov. 3-at Minnesota
Nov. 10-at Chicago
Nov. 17-Minnesota
Nov. 24-at Tampa Bay
Nov. 28-NY Jets [Thanks.]
Dec. 8-at New England
Dec. 15-Green Bay
Dec. 22-Chicago

GREEN BAY

Sept. 8-at New England
Sept. 15-NY Giants
Sept. 22-NY Jets (Mil.)
Sept. 29-at St. Louis
Oct. 6-Detroit
Oct. 13-Minnesota (Mil.)
Oct. 21-at Chicago [Mon.]
Oct. 27-at Indianapolis
Nov. 3-Chicago
Nov. 10-at Minnesota
Nov. 17-New Orleans (Mil.)
Nov. 24-at LA Rams
Dec. 1-Tampa Bay
Dec. 8-Miami
Dec. 15-at Detroit
Dec. 22-at Tampa Bay

LOS ANGELES RAMS

Sept. 8-Denver
Sept. 15-at Philadelphia
Sept. 23-at Seattle [Mon.]
Sept. 29-Atlanta
Oct. 6-Minnesota
Oct. 13-at Tampa Bay
Oct. 20-at Kansas City
Oct. 27-San Francisco
Nov. 3-New Orleans
Nov. 10-at NY Giants
Dec. 2-at San Francisco [Mon.]
Dec. 15-St. Louis
Dec. 23-LA Raiders [Mon.]

MINNESOTA

Sept. 8-San Francisco
Sept. 15-at Tampa Bay
Sept. 19-Chicago [Thurs.]
Sept. 29-at Buffalo
Oct. 6-at LA Rams
Oct. 13-Green Bay (Mil.)
Oct. 20-San Diego
Oct. 27-at Chicago
Nov. 3-Detroit
Nov. 10-Green Bay
Nov. 17-at Detroit
Nov. 24-New Orleans
Dec. 1-at Philadelphia
Dec. 8-Tampa Bay
Dec. 15-at Atlanta
Dec. 22-Philadelphia

NEW ORLEANS

Sept. 8-Kansas City
Sept. 15-at Denver
Sept. 22-Tampa Bay
Sept. 29-at San Francisco
Oct. 6-Philadelphia
Oct. 13-at LA Raiders
Oct. 20-at Atlanta
Oct. 27-NY Giants
Nov. 3-at LA Rams
Nov. 10-Seattle
Nov. 17-Green Bay (Mil.)
Nov. 24-at Minnesota
Dec. 1-LA Rams
Dec. 8-at St. Louis
Dec. 15-San Francisco
Dec. 22-Atlanta

NEW YORK GIANTS

Sept. 8-Philadelphia
Sept. 15-at Green Bay
Sept. 22-St. Louis
Sept. 29-at Philadelphia
Oct. 6-Dallas
Oct. 13-at Cincinnati
Oct. 20-Washington
Oct. 27-at New Orleans
Nov. 3-Tampa Bay
Nov. 10-LA Rams
Nov. 18-at Washington [Mon.]
Nov. 24-at St. Louis
Dec. 1-Cleveland
Dec. 8-at Houston
Dec. 15-at Dallas
Dec. 21-Pittsburgh [Sat.]

PHILADELPHIA

Sept. 8-at NY Giants
Sept. 15-LA Rams
Sept. 22-at Washington
Sept. 29-NY Giants
Oct. 6-at New Orleans
Oct. 13-at St. Louis
Oct. 20-Dallas
Oct. 27-Buffalo
Nov. 3-at San Francisco
Nov. 10-Atlanta
Nov. 24-at Dallas
Dec. 1-Minnesota
Dec. 9-LA Rams [Mon.]
Dec. 15-at New Orleans
Dec. 22-Dallas

172

ST. LOUIS

Sept. 8-at Cleveland
Sept. 15-Cincinnati
Sept. 22-at New York Giants
Sept. 29-Green Bay
Oct. 7-at Washington
Oct. 13-Philadelphia
Oct. 20-at Pittsburgh
Oct. 27-Houston
Nov. 4-Dallas
Nov. 10-at Tampa Bay
Nov. 17-at Philadelphia
Nov. 24-N.Y. Giants
Nov. 28-at Dallas
Dec. 8-New Orleans
Dec. 15-at L.S. Rams
Dec. 21-Washington,

SAN FRANCISCO

Sept. 8-at Minnesota
Sept. 15-Atlanta
Sept. 22-at L.A. Raiders
Sept. 29-New Orleans
Oct. 6-at Atlanta
Oct. 13-Chicago
Oct. 20-at Detroit
Oct. 27-at L.A. Rams
Nov. 3-Philadelphia
Nov. 11-at Denver
Nov. 17-Kansas City
Nov. 25-Seattle
Dec. 1-at Washington
Dec. 9-L.A. Rams
Dec. 15-at New Orleans
Dec. 22-Dallas

TAMPA BAY

Sept. 8-at Chicago
Sept. 15-Minnesota
Sept. 22-at New Orleans
Sept. 29-at Detroit
Oct. 6-Chicago
Oct. 13-L.A. Rams
Oct. 20-at Miami
Oct. 27-New England
Nov. 3-at N.Y. Giants
Nov. 10-St. Louis
Nov. 17-at NY Jets
Nov. 24-Detroit
Dec. 1-at Green Bay
Dec. 8-at Minnesota
Dec. 15-Indianapolis
Dec. 22-Green Bay

WASHINGTON

Sept. 9-at Dallas
Sept. 15-Houston
Sept. 22-Philadelphia
Sept. 29-at Chicago
Oct. 7-St. Louis
Oct. 13-Detroit

Oct. 20-at NY Giants
Oct. 27-at Cleveland
Nov. 3-at Atlanta
Nov. 10-Dallas
Nov. 18-NY Giants

Nov. 24- at Pittsburgh
Dec. 1-San Francisco
Dec. 8-At Philadelphia
Dec. 15-Cincinnati
Dec. 21-at St. Louis

AMERICAN CONFERENCE

BUFFALO

Sept. 8-San Diego
Sept. 15-at NY Jets
Sept. 22-New England
Sept. 19-Minnesota
Oct. 6-at Indianapolis
Oct. 13-at New England
Oct. 20-Indianapolis
Oct. 27-at Philadelphia
Nov. 3-Cincinnati
Nov. 10-Houston
Nov. 17-at Cleveland
Nov. 23-Miami
Dec. 1-at San Diego
Dec. 8-NY Jets
Dec. 15-at Pittsburgh
Dec. 22-at Miami

CLEVELAND

Sept. 8-St. Louis
Sept. 16-Pittsburgh [Mon.]
Sept. 22-at Dallas
Sept. 29-at San Diego
Oct. 6-New England
Oct. 13-at Houston
Oct. 20-LA Raiders
Oct. 27-at Washington
Nov. 3-at Pittsburgh
Nov. 10-at Cincinnati
Nov. 17-Buffalo
Nov. 24-Cincinnati
Dec. 1-at NY Giants
Dec. 8-at.Seattle
Dec. 15-Houston
Dec. 22-at NY Jets

HOUSTON

Sept. 8-Miami
Sept. 15-at Washington
Sept. 22-at Pittsburgh
Sept. 29-Dallas
Oct. 6-at Denver
Oct. 13-Cleveland
Oct. 20-Cincinnati
Oct. 27-at St. Louis
Nov. 3-Kansas City
Nov. 10-at Buffalo
Nov. 17-Pittsburgh
Nov. 24-San Diego
Dec. 1-at Cincinnati
Dec. 8-NY Giants
Dec. 15-Cleveland
Dec. 22-at Indianapolis

CINCINNATI

Sept. 8-Seattle
Sept. 15-at St. Louis
Sept. 22-San Diego
Sept. 30-at Pittsburgh [Mon.]
Oct. 6-NY Jets
Oct. 13-NY Giants
Oct. 20-at Houston
Oct. 27-Pittsburgh
Nov. 3-at Buffalo
Nov. 10-Cleveland
Nov. 17-at LA Raiders
Nov. 24-at Cleveland
Dec. 1-Houston
Dec. 8-Dallas
Dec. 15-at Washington
Dec. 22-at New England

DENVER

Sept. 8-at LA Rams
Sept. 15-New Orleans
Sept. 22-at Atlanta
Sept. 29-Miami
Oct. 6-Houston
Oct. 13-at Indianapolis
Oct. 20-Seattle
Oct. 27-at Kansas City
Nov. 3-at San Diego
Nov. 11-San Francisco [Mon.]
Nov. 17-San Diego
Nov. 24-at LA Raiders
Dec. 1-at Pittsburgh
Dec. 8-LA Raiders
Dec. 14-Kansas City [Sat.]
Dec. 20-at Seattle [Fri.]

INDIANAPOLIS

Sept. 8-at Pittsburgh
Sept. 15-at Miami
Sept. 22-Detroit
Sept. 29-at NY Jets
Oct. 6-Buffalo
Oct. 13-Denver
Oct. 20-at Buffalo
Oct. 27-Green Bay
Nov. 3-NY Jets
Nov. 10-at New England
Nov. 17-Miami
Nov. 24-at Kansas City
Dec. 1-New England
Dec. 8-at Chicago
Dec. 15-at Tampa Bay
Dec. 22-Houston

KANSAS CITY

Sept. 8-at New Orleans
Sept. 12-LA Raiders (Thurs.]
Sept. 22-at Miami
Sept. 29-Seattle
Oct. 6-at LA Raiders
Oct. 13-at San Diego
Oct. 20-LA Rams
Oct. 27-Denver
Nov. 3-at Houston
Nov. 10-Pittsburgh
Nov. 17-at San Francisco
Nov. 24-Indianapolis
Dec. 1-at Seattle
Dec. 8-Atlanta
Dec. 14-at Denver [Sat.]
Dec. 22-San Diego

NEW ENGLAND

Sept. 8-Green Bay
Sept. 15-at Chicago
Sept. 22-at Buffalo
Sept. 29-LA Raiders
Oct. 6-at Cleveland
Oct. 13-Buffalo
Oct. 20-NY Jets
Oct. 27-at Tampa Bay
Nov. 3-Miami
Nov. 10-Indianapolis
Nov. 17-at Seattle
Nov. 24-at NY Jets
Dec. 1-Indianapolis
Dec. 8-Detroit
Dec. 16-at Miami [Mon.]
Dec. 22-Cincinnati

SAN DIEGO

Sept. 8-at Buffalo
Sept. 15-Seattle
Sept. 22-at Cincinnati
Sept. 29-Cleveland
Oct. 6-at Seattle
Oct. 13-Kansas City
Oct. 20-at Minnesota
Oct. 28-at LA Raiders [Mon.]
Nov. 3-Denver
Nov. 10-LA Raiders
Nov. 17-at Denver
Nov. 24-at Houston
Dec. 1-Buffalo
Dec. 5-Pittsburgh [Thurs.]
Dec. 15-Philadelphia
Dec. 22-at Kansas City

LOS ANGELES RAIDERS

Sept. 8-NY Jets
Sept. 12-at Kansas City [Thurs.]
Sept. 12-San Francisco
Sept. 29-at New England
Oct. 6-Kansas City
Oct. 13-New Orleans
Oct. 20-at Cleveland
Oct. 28-San Diego [Mon.]
Nov. 3-at Seattle
Nov. 10-at San Diego
Nov. 17-at Cincinnati
Nov. 24-Denver
Dec. 1-at Atlanta
Dec. 8-at Denver
Dec. 15-Seattle
Dec. 23-at LA Rams [Mon.]

NEW YORK JETS

Sept. 8-at LA Raiders
Sept. 13-Buffalo
Sept. 22-at Green Bay
Sept. 29-Indianapolis
Oct. 6-at Cincinnati
Oct. 14-Miami [Mon.]
Oct. 20-at New England
Oct. 27-Seattle
Nov. 3-at Indianapolis
Nov. 10-at Miami
Nov. 17-Tampa Bay
Nov. 24-New England
Nov. 28-at Detroit [Thurs.]
Dec. 8-at Buffalo
Dec. 14-Chicago [Sat.]
Dec. 22-Cleveland

SEATTLE

Sept. 8-at Cincinnati
Sept. 15-at San Diego
Sept. 23-LA Rams [Mon.]
Sept. 29-at Kansas City
Oct. 6-San Diego
Oct. 13-Atlanta
Oct. 20-at Denver
Oct. 27-at NY Jets
Nov. 3-LA Raiders
Nov. 10-at New Orleans
Nov. 17-New England
Nov. 25-at San Francisco [Mon.]
Dec. 1-Kansas City
Dec. 8-Cleveland
Dec. 15-at LA Raiders
Dec. 20-Denver [Fri.]

MIAMI

Sept. 8-at Houston
Sept. 15-Indianapolis
Sept. 22-Kansas City
Sept. 29-at Denver
Oct. 6-Pittsburgh
Oct. 14-at NY Jets [Mon.]
Oct. 20-Tampa Bay
Oct. 27-at Detroit
Nov. 3-at New England
Nov. 10-NY Jets
Nov. 17-at Indianapolis
Nov. 24-at Buffalo
Dec. 2-Chicago [Mon.]
Dec. 8-at Green Bay
Dec. 16-New England [Mon.]
Dec. 22-Buffalo

PITTSBURGH

Sept. 8-Indianapolis
Sept. 16-at Cleveland [Mon.]
Sept. 22-Houston
Sept. 30-Cincinnati [Mon.]
Oct. 6-at Miami
Oct. 13-at Dallas
Oct. 20-St. Louis
Oct. 27-at Cincinnati
Nov. 3-Cleveland
Nov. 10-at Kansas City
Nov. 17-at Houston
Nov. 24-Washington
Dec. 1-Denver
Dec. 5-at San Diego [Thurs.]
Dec. 15-Buffalo
Dec. 21-at NY Giants [Sat.]

SECTION 5

The Super Bowl

SUPER BOWLS AT-A-GLANCE

YEAR	DATE	WINNER	LOSER	SITE	ATTENDANCE
1967	Jan. 15	Green Bay (NFL) 35	Kansas City (AFL) 10	Los Angeles	61,949
1968	Jan. 14	Green Bay (NFL) 33	Oakland (AFL) 14	Miami	75,546
1969	Jan. 12	New York (AFL) 16	Baltimore (NFL) 7	Miami	75,389
1970	Jan. 11	Kansas City (AFL) 23	Minnesota (NFL) 7	New Orleans	80,562
1971	Jan. 17	Baltimore (AFC) 16	Dallas (NFC) 13	Miami	79,204
1972	Jan. 16	Dallas (NFC) 24	Miami (AFC) 3	New Orleans	80,591
1973	Jan. 14	Miami (AFC) 14	Washington (NFC) 7	Los Angeles	90,182
1974	Jan. 13	Miami (AFC) 24	Minnesota (NFC) 7	Houston	71,882
1975	Jan. 12	Pittsburgh (AFC) 16	Minnesota (NFC) 6	New Orleans	80,997
1976	Jan. 18	Pittsburgh (AFC) 21	Dallas (NFC) 17	Miami	80,187
1977	Jan. 9	Oakland (AFC) 32	Minnesota (NFC) 14	Pasadena	100,421
1978	Jan. 15	Dallas (NFC) 27	Denver (AFC) 10	New Orleans	76,400
1979	Jan. 21	Pittsburgh (AFC) 35	Dallas (NFC) 31	Miami	79,484
1980	Jan. 20	Pittsburgh (AFC) 31	Los Angeles (NFC) 19	Pasadena	103,985
1981	Jan. 25	Oakland (AFC) 27	Philadelphia (NFC) 10	New Orleans	76,135
1982	Jan. 24	San Francisco (NFC) 26	Cincinnati (AFC) 21	Pontiac	81,270
1983	Jan. 30	Washington (NFC) 27	Miami (AFC) 17	Pasadena	103,667
1984	Jan. 22	Los Angeles (AFC) 38	Washington (NFC) 9	Tampa	72,920
1985	Jan. 20	San Francisco (NFC) 38	Miami (AFC) 16	Palo Alto	84,059

SUPER BOWL I

After years of anticipation, the big event finally arrived. And Coach Vince Lombardi's Green Bay Packers, carrying the prestige of the old-line National Football League against the upstart American Football League, were magnificent. The Packers won the first Super Bowl 35-10 over Kansas City behind the passing of Bart Starr, the receiving of Max McGee, and a key interception by Willie Wood. The Packers, who started slowly, broke the game open with three second-half touchdowns as Starr began picking on the Chiefs' young cornermen, highlighted by McGee's one-handed, behind-the-back catch of a Starr pass. McGee, filling in for ailing Boyd Dowler after having caught only three passes all season, caught seven for 138 yards and two touchdowns. Elijah Pitts ran for two other scores. Starr completed 16 of 23 passes for 250 yards and two touchdowns. He was chosen most valuable player. Paul Hornung, the Packers' Golden Boy, sat out the game because of a pinched neck nerve. The Packers collected $15,000 per man and the Chiefs $7,500—largest single-game shares ever paid in any team sport.

Kansas City (AFL)	0	10	0	0—10
Green Bay (NFL)	7	7	14	7—35

Green Bay—McGee, 37-yard pass from Starr (Chandler kick).
Kansas City—McClinton, 7-yard pass from Dawson (Mercer kick).
Green Bay—Taylor, 14-yard run (Chandler kick).
Kansas City—Mercer, 31-yard field goal.
Green Bay—Pitts, 5-yard run (Chandler kick).
Green Bay—McGee, 13-yard pass from Starr (Chandler kick).
Green Bay—Pitts, 1-yard run (Chandler kick).

SUPER BOWL II

Bart Starr again was the hero as the Packers, after winning their third consecutive NFL championship, won the Super Bowl for the second straight year 33-14 over the AFL champion Oakland Raiders. With Miami's Orange Bowl as the setting, the game drew the first $3 million gate in football history. Starr, again named MVP, clicked on 13 of 24 aerial bullets for 202 yards and one TD while directing a Green Bay attack which built a 16-7 halftime lead and stayed in control all the way. Four field goals by Don Chandler and a 60-yard interception return by Herb Adderley off Daryle Lamonica spiced the Packer victory, the last with Vince Lombardi at the helm. Lombardi turned over the reins to Phil Bengtson after a nine-year reign in Green Bay in which he won six Western Conference titles, five NFL crowns, and two Super Bowls.

Green Bay (NFL)	3	13	10	7—33
Oakland (AFL)	0	7	0	7—14

Green Bay—Chandler, 39-yard field goal.
Green Bay—Chandler, 20-yard field goal.
Green Bay—Dowler, 62-yard pass from Starr (Chandler kick).
Oakland—Miller, 23-yard pass from Lamonica (Blanda kick).
Green Bay—Chandler, 43-yard field goal.
Green Bay—Anderson, 2-yard run (Chandler kick).
Green Bay—Chandler, 31-yard field goal.
Green Bay—Adderley, 60-yard interception return (Chandler kick).
Oakland—Miller, 23-yard pass from Lamonica (Blanda kick).

SUPER BOWL III

Jan. 12, 1969, Orange Bowl Stadium, Miami
NEW YORK JETS 16, BALTIMORE 7

"We will beat the Colts. I'll guarantee it," quarterback Joe Namath declared at a banquet in Miami a few evenings before Super Bowl III. Namath made good on his promise, and the American Football League came of age as the New York Jets won 16-7 over a Baltimore Colt team which had lost only once in 16 games during the season. Namath, hitting on 17 of 28 passes for 206 yards, was virtually flawless in directing the Jet attack. Broadway Joe was named the game's most valuable player as the Jets pierced the Colt defense for 337 yards, including 121 yards rushing by Matt Snell. Jim Turner chipped in three field goals. The New York defense intercepted Earl Morrall three times in the first half. Ailing Johnny Unitas came off the bench to lead the Colts to their only TD in the fourth quarter, but it was too late.

New York (AFL)	0	7	6	3—16
Baltimore (NFL)	0	0	0	7— 7

New York—Snell, 4-yard run (Turner kick).
New York—Turner, 32-yard field goal.
New York—Turner, 30-yard field goal.
New York—Turner, 9-yard field goal.
Baltimore—Hill, 1-yard run (Michaels kick).

SUPER BOWL IV

Jan. 11, 1970, Tulane Stadium, New Orleans
KANSAS CITY 23, MINNESOTA 7

Picking up where Namath and the Jets had left off the previous year, the Kansas City Chiefs whipped the Minnesota Vikings 23-7 to enable the AFL to square the Super Bowl series with the NFL at two games apiece. Len Dawson, physically ill because of totally unconfirmed television reports linking him with gamblers, led the Chiefs to a 16-0 halftime lead and became the fourth consecutive quarterback to be chosen for MVP honors in the Super Bowl. Dawson completed 12 of 17 passes and hit Otis Taylor on a 46-yard play for the final KC touchdown. The Chiefs' defense recovered two fumbles, made three interceptions and held the Vikings' running game to 67 yards.

Minnesota (NFL)	0	0	7	0— 7
Kansas City (AFL)	3	13	7	0—23

Kansas City—Stenerud, 48-yard field goal.
Kansas City—Stenerud, 32-yard field goal.
Kansas City—Stenerud, 25-yard field goal.
Kansas City—Garrett, 5-yard run (Stenerud kick).
Minnesota—Osborn, 4-yard run (Cox kick).
Kansas City—Taylor, 46-yard pass from Dawson (Stenerud kick).

SUPER BOWL V

Jan. 17, 1971, Orange Bowl Stadium, Miami
BALTIMORE 16, DALLAS 13

This first Super Bowl after the official amalgamation of the National and American Football Leagues was one of the zaniest games ever played. Each team had three interceptions and there were 11 turnovers in an error-filled carnival of freaky plays. A 32-yard field goal by rookie kicker Jim O'Brien with five seconds remaining brought an end to the bizarre contest and gave the Baltimore Colts, now representing the American Football Conference, a 16-13 victory over the Dallas Cowboys of the National Conference. Dallas led 13-6 at the half, but interceptions by Rick Volk and Mike Curtis set up a Baltimore touchdown and O'Brien's climactic kick. John Unitas, who was relieved by Earl Morrall in the first half, completed the Colts' only scoring pass in one of the game's goofy plays. The long pass by Unitas caromed off receiver Eddie Hinton's finger tips, off Dallas defensive back Mel Renfro, and finally into the hands of John Mackey, who rambled 45 yards to score on a 75-yard cardiac special. Dallas linebacker Chuck Howley was MVP.

Baltimore (AFC)	0	6	0	10	—16
Dallas (NFC)	3	10	0	0	—13

Dallas—Clark, 13-yard field goal.
Dallas—Clark, 30-yard field goal.
Baltimore—Mackey, 75-yard pass from Unitas (kick blocked).
Dallas—Thomas, 7-yard pass from Morton (Clark kick).
Baltimore—Nowatzke, 2-yard run (O'Brien kick).
Baltimore—O'Brien, 32-yard field goal.

SUPER BOWL VI
Jan. 16, 1972, Tulane Stadium, New Orleans
DALLAS 24, MIAMI 3

The Dallas Cowboys rebounded from their defeat in Super Bowl V to defeat the Miami Dolphins 24-3. The victory was to be the last for at least five years in the Super Bowl by an established NFL power over the new guard coming into the league from the old American League. The Cowboys rushed for a record 252 yards and their defense limited the Dolphins to a low of 185 yards while not yielding a touchdown for the first time in Super Bowl history. Dallas converted Chuck Howley's recovery of Larry Csonka's first fumble of the season into a 3-0 advantage and led at halftime 10-3. After the Cowboys received the second half kickoff, Duane Thomas led a 71-yard march in eight plays for a 17-3 margin. Howley intercepted a Bob Griese pass at the 50 and returned it to the Miami 9 early in the fourth period, and three plays later Roger Staubach passed 7 yards to Mike Ditka for the final touchdown. Staubach won the MVP award.

Dallas (NFC)	3	7	7	7	—24
Miami (AFC)	0	3	0	0	— 3

Dallas—Clark, 9-yard field goal.
Dallas—Alworth, 7-yard pass from Staubach (Clark kick).
Miami—Yepremian, 31-yard field goal.
Dallas—Thomas, 3-yard run (Clark kick).
Dallas—Ditka, 7-yard pass from Staubach (Clark kick).

SUPER BOWL VII
Jan. 14, 1973, Los Angeles Coliseum
MIAMI 14, WASHINGTON 7

Miami's 14-7 triumph over the Washington Redskins was a low-scoring affair, but it was significant on two counts. First, it established Coach Don Shula's Dolphins as the finest team since Lombardi's Packers of the sixties. Miami finished 16-0, the only perfect season in NFL history. Secondly, the Miami victory underlined the shifting in the balance of power in the NFL, igniting a string of victories by teams from the American Football Conference. The Dolphins played virtually perfect football in the first half. Defensive back Jake Scott was MVP. The Dolphin defense allowed the Redskins to cross midfield only once. Miami's first scoring drive, starting from its 37-yard line, was highlighted by Bob Griese's 18-yard pass to Paul Warfield and capped by a 28-yard TD fling from Griese to Howard Twilley. After Washington moved from its 17 to the Miami 48 with two minutes remaining in the first half, Nick Buoniconti intercepted a Bill Kilmer pass at the Dolphin 41 and returned it to the Redskin 27 to set up Jim Kiick's 1-yard scoring plunge.

Miami (AFC) 7   7   0   0—14
Washington (NFC) 0   0   0   7— 7

Miami—Twilley, 28-yard pass from Griese (Yepremian kick).
Miami—Kiick, 1-yard plunge (Yepremian kick).
Washington—Bass, 49-yard run with interception (Knight kick).

SUPER BOWL VIII

Jan. 13, 1974, Rice Stadium, Houston
MIAMI 24, MINNESOTA 7

Representing the AFC for the third straight year, the Miami Dolphins scored the first two times they had possession to romp over the Minnesota Vikings 24-7 and take their place among pro football's legendary teams. The Dolphins generated marches of 62 and 56 yards in the first quarter while the Miami defense held the Vikings to only seven plays. Larry Csonka capped the initial 10-play drive with a 5-yard touchdown run through right guard. Four plays later, Miami initiated another scoring march of 10 plays, ending with Jim Kiick's 1-yard smash over guard. Garo Yepremian's 28-yard field goal midway in the second period built a 17-0 Dolphin halftime lead. MVP Csonka set a Super Bowl record by rushing for 145 yards.

Minnesota (NFC) 0   0   3   7— 7
Miami (AFC) 14   3   0   7—24

Miami—Csonka, 5-yard run (Yepremian kick).
Miami—Kiick, 1-yard run (Yepremian kick).
Miami—Yepremian, 28-yard field goal.
Miami—Csonka, 2-yard run
Minnesota—Tarkenton, 4-yard run (Cox kick).

SUPER BOWL IX

Jan. 12, 1975, Tulane Stadium, New Orleans
PITTSBURGH 16, MINNESOTA 6

Pittsburgh's Steelers had been a favorite of fans all season as they won their first championship in history for venerable owner Arthur Rooney. Now champions of the AFC and making their initial Super Bowl appearance against the NFC Vikings, the Steelers had to work hard to defeat the veteran Minnesota contender 16-6. The teams struggled through a first half in which the only score was produced by the Pitt defense when Dwight White downed Fran Tarkenton in the end zone for a safety. The Steelers boosted their edge to 9-0 by forcing another break on the second half kickoff when Minnesota's Bill Brown fumbled and Marv Kellum recovered for Pitt on the Vike 30. MVP Franco Harris' 9-yard TD sprint followed. The Vikings rallied in the final period when Terry Brown recovered in the end zone for a touchdown after Matt Blair blocked Bobby Walden's punt. But the Steelers traveled 66 yards in 11 plays with the ensuing kickoff to the clincher on Terry Bradshaw's 4-yard scoring pass to Larry Brown with 3:31 remaining.

Pittsburgh (AFC) 0   2   7   7—16
Minnesota (NFC) 0   0   0   6— 6

Pittsburgh—White tackled Tarkenton in end zone for safety.
Pittsburgh—Harris, 9-yard run (Gerela kick).
Minnesota—T. Brown, recovered blocked kick in end zone (kick failed).
Pittsburgh—L. Brown, 4-yard pass from Bradshaw (Gerela kick).

SUPER BOWL X

Jan. 18, 1976, Orange Bowl Stadium, Miami
PITTSBURGH 21, DALLAS 17

The football world began talking about a Steeler dynasty after Chuck Noll's Pittsburgh club edged the Dallas Cowboys 21-17 for the Steelers' second Super Bowl victory in a row. Pitt won it on Terry Bradshaw's 64-yard fourth quarter touchdown pass to Lynn Swann and a vigorous defense that stifled a late Cowboy rally with an end zone interception on the final play of the game. Roger Staubach, bringing the Dallas offense onto the field after Pittsburgh had run on fourth down and given up the ball on the Cowboy 39 with 1:22 to play, ran and passed for two first downs. But Staubach's final desperation fling was plucked off by Pitt's Glen Edwards. Swann, the Steelers' superlative receiver, set a Super Bowl record by gaining 161 yards on four catches and was MVP. Randy Grossman also was on the receiving end of a 7-yard TD pass from Bradshaw, and Roy Gerela contributed two field goals. Dallas' scoring came on two Staubach passes, to Drew Pearson for 29 yards and to Percy Howard for 34.

Dallas (NFC)	7	3	0	7—17
Pittsburgh (AFC)	7	0	0	14—21

Dallas—Pearson, 29-yard pass from Staubach (Fritsch kick).
Pittsburgh—Grossman, 7-yard pass from Bradshaw (Gerela kick).
Dallas—Fritsch, 36-yard field goal.
Pittsburgh—Harrison blocked Hoopes' punt through end zone, safety.
Pittsburgh—Gerela, 36-yard field goal.
Pittsburgh—Gerela, 18-yard field goal.
Pittsburgh—Swann, 64-yard pass from Bradshaw (kick failed).
Dallas—P. Howard, 34-yard pass from Staubach (Fritsch kick).

SUPER BOWL XI

Jan. 9, 1977, Rose Bowl Stadium, Pasadena
OAKLAND 32, MINNESOTA 14

The Oakland Raiders, the team that historically couldn't win the big one,

finally did it by defeating the Minnesota Vikings 32-14: The Vikes' fourth Super Bowl embarrassment came in front of a record Super Bowl throng of 100,421 plus 81 million television viewers, largest TV audience ever to watch a sporting event. The Raiders gained a record-breaking 429 yards including 139 yards rushing by Clarence Davis. Wide receiver Fred Biletnikoff caught four key passes to become most valuable player of the game. The Vikings had an early chance, but failed to cash in on a blocked punt recovery at Oakland's 3-yard line. From that point, the Raiders marched 97 yards to score on Errol Mann's 24-yard field goal early in the second quarter. Oakland traveled 64 yards on its next possession to score as Kenny Stabler tossed a 1-yard pass to Dave Casper for a 10-0 lead. By halftime it was 16-0 and, for all intents and purposes, all over when Neal Colzie returned a punt 25 yards to the Viking 35 and Pete Banaszak ran 1 yard for a TD five plays later to finish the first-half scoring.

Oakland (AFC)	0	16	3	13—32
Minnesota (NFC)	0	0	7	7—14

Oakland—Mann, 24-yard field goal.
Oakland—Casper, 1-yard pass from Stabler (Mann kick).
Oakland—Banaszak, 1-yard run (kick failed).
Oakland—Mann, 40-yard field goal.
Minnesota—S. White, 8-yard pass from Tarkenton (Cox kick).
Oakland—Banaszak, 2-yard run (Mann kick).
Oakland—Brown, 75-yard interception return (kick failed).
Minnesota—Voigt, 13-yard pass from Lee (Cox kick).

SUPER BOWL XII

Jan. 15, 1978, Louisiana Superdome, New Orleans
DALLAS 27, DENVER 10

And here came the computerized Cowboys, back in the Super Bowl after a two-year absence and ready once again to spread the gospel of Tom Landry. The Cowboys made believers out of Red Miller and the Denver Broncos, not to mention 90 million television viewers, the largest audience ever to watch a sporting event, as Dallas evened its Super Bowl record at 2-2. Craig Morton always had wanted to pass the Cowboys to a Super Bowl title and he finally did it. Morton, the quarterback of the Broncos who once had lost out to Roger Staubach in a bid for the starting job on the Cowboys, was yanked by Miller after yielding a Super Bowl record four interceptions. Dallas converted two pass interceptions by safety Randy Hughes and cornerback Aaron Kyle into 10 points and Efren Herrera added a 35-yard field goal to give the Cowboys a 13-0 halftime edge. The Broncos, who had lost three fumbles and been intercepted twice on their last five possessions of the first half, rallied at the outset of the third period, as Jim Turner booted a 47-yard field goal. Then Dallas' Butch Johnson made a diving catch in the end zone to complete a 45-yard TD pass from Staubach. The Cowboys led 20-3 and the rout was on. Harvey Martin and Randy White were named co-MVPs as the Cowboy defense recovered four fumbles and intercepted four passes.

Dallas (NFC)	10	3	7	7—27
Denver (AFC)	0	0	10	0—10

Dallas—Dorsett, 3-yard run (Herrera kick).
Dallas—Herrera, 35-yard field goal.
Dallas—Herrera, 43-yard field goal.
Denver—Turner, 47-yard field goal.
Dallas—Johnson, 45-yard pass from Staubach (Herrera kick).
Denver—Lytle, 1-yard run (Turner kick).
Dallas—Richards, 29-yard pass from Newhouse (Herrera kick).

SUPER BOWL XIII

Jan. 21, 1979, Orange Bowl Stadium, Miami
PITTSBURGH 35, DALLAS 31

Many fans feel this was the greatest Super Bowl game ever played. Terry Bradshaw, who was never more spectacular, threw a record four touchdown passes to lead the Steelers to victory in the highest-scoring Super Bowl game in history. Bradshaw, the game's most valuable player, completed 17 of 30 passes for 318 yards to help Pittsburgh become the first team to win three Super Bowls. Bradshaw had three touchdown passes in the first half—two to John Stallworth—and the third, with 26 seconds remaining in the second period, to Rocky Bleier. The Cowboys scored twice before intermission on Roger Staubach's 39-yard pass to Tony Hill and a 37-yard run by linebacker Mike Hegman, who stole the ball from Bradshaw. The Steelers broke open the game with two touchdowns in a span of 19 seconds midway through the final period. Franco Harris rambled 22 yards up the middle to give Pittsburgh a 28-17 lead with 7:10 left. Pittsburgh got the ball right back when Randy White fumbled the kickoff and Dennis Winston recovered. On first down, Bradshaw hit Lynn Swann with an 18-yard scoring pass to boost the Steeler lead to 35-17 with 6:51 left. The Cowboys refused to give up, as Staubach connected with Billy Joe DuPree on an eight-yard scoring pass with 2:23 left. After Dallas recovered an onside kick, Staubach passed four yards to Butch Johnson for a TD with 22 seconds remaining. Bleier's recovery of an onside kick sealed the Steeler win.

Pittsburgh (AFC)	7	14	0	14—35
Dallas (NFC)	7	7	3	14—31

Pittsburgh—Stallworth, 28-yard pass from Bradshaw (Gerela kick).
Dallas—Hill, 39-yard pass from Staubach (Septien kick).
Dallas—Hegman, 37-yard fumble recovery return (Septien kick).
Pittsburgh—Stallworth, 75-yard pass from Bradshaw (Gerela kick).
Pittsburgh—Bleier, 7-yard pass from Bradshaw (Gerela kick).
Dallas—Septien, 27-yard field goal.
Pittsburgh—Harris, 22-yard run (Gerela kick).
Pittsburgh—Swann, 18-yard pass from Bradshaw (Gerela kick).
Dallas—DuPree, 7-yard pass from Staubach (Septien kick).
Dallas—B. Johnson, 4-yard pass from Staubach (Septien kick).

SUPER BOWL XIV

Jan. 20, 1980, Rose Bowl Stadium, Pasadena
PITTSBURGH 31, LOS ANGELES RAMS 19

It was another big day for Bradshaw, although the balding quarterback endured a frightening second half. Bradshaw completed 14 of 21 passes for 309 yards and set two passing records as the Steelers became the first team to win four Super Bowls. Despite three interceptions by the Rams, Bradshaw kept his cool and brought the Steelers from behind twice in the second half. Trailing 13-10 at halftime, Pittsburgh went ahead 17-13 when Bradshaw hit Lynn Swann with a 47-yard touchdown pass after 2:48 of the third quarter. On the Rams' next possession, Vince Ferragamo, who completed 15 of 25 passes for 212 yards, responded with a 50-yard pass to Billy Waddy that moved Los Angeles from its own 26 to the Steeler 24. On the following play, Lawrence McCutcheon connected with Ron Smith on a halfback option pass that gave the Rams a 19-17 lead. On Pittsburgh's initial possession of the final period, Bradshaw lofted a 73-yard scoring pass to John Stallworth to put the Steelers in front to stay, 24-19. Franco Harris scored on a one-yard run later in the quarter to seal the win. A 45-yard pass from Bradshaw to Stallworth was the key play in the drive to Harris' score. Bradshaw, the game's most valuable player for the second straight year, set career Super Bowl records for most TD passes (9) and most passing yards (932). Larry Anderson gave the Steelers superb field position with five kickoff returns for 162 yards.

Lost Angeles Rams (NFC)	7	6	6	0	19
Pittsburgh (AFC)	3	7	7	14	31

Pittsburgh—Bahr, 41-yard field goal.
Los Angeles—Bryant, 1-yard run (Corral kick).
Pittsburgh—Harris, 1-yard run (Bahr kick).
Los Angeles—Corral, 31-yard field goal.
Los Angeles—Corral, 45-yard field goal.
Pittsburgh—Swann, 47-yard pass from Bradshaw (Bahr kick).
Los Angeles—Smith, 24-yard pass from McCutcheon (kick failed).
Pittsburgh—Stallworth, 73-yard pass from Bradshaw (Bahr kick).
Pittsburgh—Harris, 1-yard run (Bahr kick).

SUPER BOWL XV

Jan. 25, 1981, Louisiana Superdome, New Orleans
OAKLAND 27, PHILADELPHIA 10

Could they do it? The much hated, much feared, much admired Oakland Raiders were, after all, just a wild card team. And no team with merely wild card credentials had ever before ascended to the pro football pinnacle. Surly, salty Al Davis ruling over Pete Rozelle's sacred, glossy empire? Ridiculous. But it happened. Jim Plunkett, who had been forsaken as a lost cause by two previous National Football League employers, threw three touchdown passes to win most valuable player honors on the greatest day of his life. Plunkett, who was there at quarterback for the Raiders only because Davis believed in him, hurled an 80-yard TD pass to Kenny King and connected twice to Cliff Branch (for 3 and 29 yards) for the scores that made Oakland the NFL's first wild card champion. Chris Bahr added field goals of 46 and 35 yards. Afterwards, Rozelle and Davis, two long-time enemies and soon to be courtroom adversaries when the Raiders moved to Los Angeles, posed for the cameras and appeared on television together, grinning like two long-lost brothers. A crowd of 76,135 watched the Raider defense shut the Eagles out of the end zone until the fourth quarter.

Oakland (AFC)	14	0	10	3	27
Philadelphia (NFC)	0	3	0	7	10

Oakland—Branch, 2-yard pass from Plunkett (Bahr kick).
Oakland—King, 80-yard pass from Plunkett (Bahr kick).
Philadelphia—Franklin, 30-yard field goal.
Oakland—Branch, 29-yard pass from Plunkett (Bahr kick).
Oakland—Bahr, 46-yard field goal.
Philadelphia—Krepfle, 8-yard pass from Jaworski (Franklin kick).
Oakland—Bahr, 35-yard field goal.

SUPER BOWL XVI

Jan. 24, 1982, Pontiac Silverdome, Pontiac, Mich.
SAN FRANCISCO 26, CINCINNATI 21

A great goal line stand against a giant fullback sparked the 49ers to their first world title after 36 years in the National Football League. No team had been in the NFL longer than the 49ers when coach Bill Walsch's club finally scaled the pinnacle. The key to the victory came late in the third quarter when Bengal fullback Pete Johnson tried to score from the 49ers' 1-yard line and failed. Cincinnati, trailing 20-7 but apparently building momentum, failed on three successive tries from the 49er 1-yard line. Ray Wersching's Super Bowl record-tying four field goals and Joe Montana's controlled passing sparked the San Francisco attack. Montana won the MVP award. The 49ers built a 20-0 halftime lead via Montana's one-yard TD run, fullback Earl Cooper's 11-yard scoring pass from Montana, and Wersching's 22 and 26-yard kicks. The Bengals closed the gap to 20-14 in the second half on Ken Anderson's five-yard run and Dan Ross's four-yard catch from Anderson. Ross set a Super Bowl record with 11 receptions for 104 yards. Cincinnati compiled 356 yards to San Francisco's 275, which marked the first time in Super Bowl history that the team that gained the most yards from scrimmage lost the game.

San Francisco (NFC)	7	13	0	6	26
Cincinnati (AFC)	0	0	7	14	21

San Francisco—Montana, 1-yard run (Wersching kick).
San Francisco—Cooper, 11-yard pass from Montana (Wersching kick).
San Francisco—Wersching, 22-yard field goal.
San Francisco—Wersching, 26-yard field goal.
Cincinnati—Anderson, 5-yard run (Breech kick).
Cincinnati—Ross, 4-yard pass from Anderson (Breech kick).
San Francisco—Wersching, 40-yard field goal.
San Francisco—Wersching, 23-yard field goal.
Cincinnati—Ross, 3-yard pass from Anderson (Breech kick).

SUPER BOWL XVII

Jan. 30, 1983, Rose Bowl Stadium, Pasadena
WASHINGTON 27, MIAMI 17

This Super Bowl capped the season which will forever be referred to as "the 1982 strike-abbreviated season." Following the near-disastrous 57-day players' strike, an expanded playoff format was designed for the postseason with eight teams from the AFC and eight teams from the NFC qualifying for the Super Bowl Tournament. Frankly, it was boring, but it got the league through a critical time. And it got the Redskins a Super Bowl victory. In front of a huge crowd of 103,667 in the Rose Bowl, fullback John Riggins, the game's most valuable player, rushed 166 yards on 38 carries (both Super Bowl records). The Redskins accounted for 400 total yards (including a record 276 rushing), exceeded only by the 429 total yards posted by Oakland in Super Bowl XI. The Dolphins built a 17-10 halftime lead on a 76-yard pass from David Woodley to James Cefalo, a 20-yard field goal by Uwe von Schamann and a Super Bowl record 98-yard kickoff return by Fulton Walker. The second half was all Washington. After a third period 20-yard field goal by Mark Moseley, the Redskins tied a Super Bowl record of 14 points in the fourth quarter with Riggins' 43-yard TD run and a 6-yard pass from Joe Theismann to Charlie Brown.

Miami (AFC) 7   10   0   0—17
Washington (NFC) 0   10   3   14—27

Miami—Cefalo, 76-yard pass from Woodley (von Schamann kick).
Washington—Moseley, 31-yard field goal.
Miami—von Schamann, 20-yard field goal.
Washington—Garrett, 4-yard pass from Theismann (Mosley kick).
Miami—Walker, 98-yard kickoff return (von Schamann kick).
Washington—Moseley, 20-yard field goal.
Washington—Riggins, 43-yard run (Moseley kick).
Washington—Brown, 6-yard pass from Theismann (Moseley kick).

SUPER BOWL XVIII

Jan. 22, 1984, Tampa Stadium, Tampa, Fla.
LOS ANGELES RAIDERS 38, WASHINGTON 9

All the experts predicted this was one Super Bowl that couldn't miss. A showdown between two overwhelming powerhouses that would not be denied. Guaranteed, signed, Pete Rozelle. But the promotional dream became a competitive nightmare when the Raiders achieved the most lopsided (29 points) victory in Super Bowl history. Marcus Allen, who set game records for yards (191) and longest rush from scrimmage (74 yards, touchdown), was most valuable player. The Raiders scored on a blocked punt recovery in the end zone by Derrick Jensen and a 12-yard pass from Jim Plunkett to Cliff Branch. Mark Moseley's 24-yard field goal for the Redskins was followed by Jack Squirek's five-yard TD interception to give the Raiders a 21-3 halftime lead. John Riggins closed out Washington's scoring with a one-yard TD run before Allen's two TD runs of 5 and 74 yards in the third quarter and Chris Bahr's 21-yard fourth period field goal set a record for most points by a Super Bowl team.

Washington (NFC) 0   3   6   0— 9
L.A. Raiders (AFC) 7   14   14   3—38

Los Angeles—Jensen recovered block punt in end zone (Bahr kick).
Los Angeles—Branch, 12-yard pass from Plunkett (Bahr kick).
Washington—Moseley, 24-yard field goal.
Los Angeles—Squirek, 5-yard interception return (Bahr kick).
Washington—Riggins, 1-yard run (kick blocked).
Los Angeles—Allen, 5-yard run (Bahr kick).
Los Angeles—Allen, 74-yard run (Bahr kick).
Los Angeles—Bahr, 21-yard field goal.

SUPER BOWL XIX

Jan. 20, 1985, Stanford Stadium, Palo Alto, Cal.
SAN FRANCISCO 38, MIAMI 16

This highly ballyhooed, long-awaited showdown between two of pro football's hottest teams proved to be a letdown when the Dolphins, to all intents and purposes, failed to show up. The powerful, poised 49ers captured their second Super Bowl title with a dominating offense and a defense which tamed Miami's heretofore explosive passing attack. The Dolphins held a 10-7 lead at the end of the first period, which represented the most points scored by two teams in an opening quarter of a Super Bowl. However, the 49ers used excellent field position in the second period to build a 28-16 halftime lead. San Francisco scored touchdowns during the second quarter on a four-play, 47-yard drive; a six-play, 55-yard march, and a nine-play, 52-yard drive. RB Roger Craig set a Super Bowl record by scoring three TDs on pass receptions of 8 and 16 yards and a run of 2 yards. San Francisco QB Joe Montana was MVP, joining Green Bay's Bart Starr and Pittsburgh's Terry Bradshaw as the only two-time MVP winners. Montana completed 24 of 35 passes for a Super Bowl record 331 yards and three touchdowns, and rushed five times for 59 yards, including a 6-yard TD. Craig finished with 15 rushes for 58 yards and 7 catches for 77 yards. RB Wendell Tyler rushed 13 for 65 yards and caught 4 for 70 yards. WR Dwight Clark caught 6 for 77 yards, while TE Russ Francis and 5 catches for 60 yards. San Francisco's 537 total net yards bettered the previous Super Bowl record of 429 yards by Oakland in 1977. The 49ers held a time of possession advantage over the Dolphins of 37:11 to 22:49. On defense, the 49ers had four sacks of Miami QB Dan Marino, who was sacked only 13 times during the regular season. The 49ers' 38 points tied the Super Bowl record set the previous year by the Raiders.

Miami (AFC)	10	6	0	0—16
San Francisco	7	21	10	0—38

Miami—von Schamann, 37-yard field goal.
San Francisco—Monroe, 33-yard pass from Montana (Wersching kick).

Miami—D. Johnson, 2-yard pass from Marino (von Schamann kick).
San Francisco—Craig, 8-yard pass from Montana (Wersching kick).
San Francisco—Montana, 6-yard run (Wersching kick).
San Francisco—Craig, 2-yard run (Wersching kick).
Miami—von Schamann, 31-yard field goal.
Miami—von Schamann, 30-yard field goal.
San Francisco—Wersching, 27-yard field goal.
San Francisco—Craig, 16-yard pass from Montana (Wersching kick).

SECTION 6

Briefs

THE BEARS RADIO/TV BROADCAST TEAMS

Bear football widows should be ecstatic this season. They get their husbands back on *four* Sunday afternoons because of Bear football assignments on other days of the week!

The 1985 Bears will play two Monday night games and a Thursday night prime time game before announcer Frank Gifford and the ABC cameras. They also have a Saturday date on December 14 with the New York Jets, with CBS footing the TV bill. NBC gets the Bears twice on Sundays during the 16-game regular season.

It's impossible to pinpoint the specific announcing crews for many of the telecasts, since the decisions in some cases won't be made until later in the season by the network brass. But it's safe to say that Gifford will be the play-by-play man for ABC, Johnny Morris will have a heavy role in CBS's 10-game Bears package, with occasional help from John Madden, Pat Summerall and Dan Jiggetts; and Merlin Olsen is a good bet to be tabbed by NBC for Chicago duty.

Twenty-seven regular season NFL games will be televised nationally by the three networks. NBC again will concentrate on AFC games, including eight Sunday double headers, the AFC playoffs, the AFC title game and Super Bowl XX. CBS again will originate NFC games, including eight Sunday doubleheaders, the NFC playoffs and the NFC championship game. ABC has the 21-game prime time package, plus the AFC-NFC Pro Bowl.

For the first time, the NBC Radio Network will broadcast 37 games nationally, including all Monday night games, five specials, the traditional Thanksgiving Day doubleheader, late-season Saturday games, and all postseason games, including the Super Bowl and Pro Bowl.

WGN takes over the Bears radio coverage and plans an ambitious eight-hour schedule on game days. The station has hired ex-Bear stàr Dick Butkus and former Cardinal quarterback Jim Hart, a native Chicagoan, as color men to supplement new play-by-play announcer Wayne Larrivee, who left the Kansas City Chiefs to take the Bears job. The new WGN team replaces the WBBM tandem of Joe McConnell and Brad Palmer, who were with the club for eight years.

WGN will throw its heavy artillery into an attempt to create a new "family atmosphere and family image," says sports director Chuck Swirsky, who will host a pregame tailgate party that will include such personalities as announcer Jack Brickhouse, oddsmaker Danny Sheridan and former official George Rennix.

"I'm going to have to go to school again to learn what they're doing on defense," Butkus said when he agreed to take the WGN mike.

BEARS TELEVISION SCHEDULE

The majority of games (11) will be aired on CBS, or WBBM-TV (Channel 2) in Chicago, pending the lifting of local blackouts when home games are sold out 72 hours in advance. Three night games also will be broadcast by ABC (WLS-TV, Channel 7) and two games by NBC (WMAQ-TV, Channel 5).

Here is the tentative schedule:

Sept. 8—Tampa Bay, noon, WBBM.
Sept. 15—New England, noon, WMAQ.
Sept. 19—at Minnesota, 7 p.m., WLS.
Sept. 29—Washington, noon, WBBM.
Oct. 6—at Tampa Bay, noon, WBBM.
Oct. 13—at San Francisco, 3 p.m., WBBM.
Oct. 21—Green Bay, 8 p.m., WLS.
Oct. 27—Minnesota, noon, WBBM.
Nov. 3—at Green Bay, noon, WBBM.
Nov. 10—Detroit, noon, WBBM.
Nov. 17—at Dallas, noon, WBBM.
Nov. 24—Atlanta, noon, WBBM.
Dec. 2—at Miami, 8 p.m., WLS.
Dec. 8—Indianapolis, noon, WMAQ.
Dec. 14—at New York Jets, 11:30 a.m., WBBM.
Dec. 22—at Detroit, noon, WBBM.

ABC-TV NFL SCHEDULE

(Chicago Times)

Monday, Sept. 9

Washington at Dallas, 8 p.m.

Thursday, Sept. 12

Los Angeles Raiders at Kansas City, 7 p.m.

Monday, Sept. 16

Pittsburgh at Cleveland, 8 p.m.

Thursday, Sept. 19

Chicago at Minnesota, 7 p.m.

Monday, Sept. 23

Los Angeles Rams at Seattle, 8 p.m.

Monday, Sept. 30

Cincinnati at Pittsburgh, 8 p.m.

Sunday, Oct. 6

Dallas at New York Giants, 7 p.m.

Monday, Oct. 7

St. Louis at Washington, 8 p.m.

Monday, Oct. 14

Miami at New York Jets, 8 p.m.

Monday, Oct. 21

Green Bay at Chicago, 8 p.m.

Monday, Oct. 28

San Diego at Los Angeles Raiders, 8 p.m.

Monday, Nov. 4

Dallas at St. Louis, 8 p.m.

Monday, Nov. 11

San Francisco at Denver, 8 p.m.

Monday, Nov. 18

New York Giants at Washington, 8 p.m.

Monday, Nov. 25

Seattle at San Francisco, 8 p.m.

Monday, Dec. 2

Chicago at Miami, 8 p.m.

Thursday, Dec. 5

Pittsburgh at San Diego, 7 p.m.

Monday, Dec. 9

Los Angeles Rams at San Francisco, 8 p.m.

Monday, Dec. 16

New England at Miami, 8 p.m.

Friday, Dec. 20

Denver at Seattle, 7 p.m.

Monday, Dec. 23

Los Angeles Raiders at Los Angeles Rams, 8 p.m.

1985 NFL PLAYOFF RULES

1. **First Round**—Wild cards play each other. Home clubs will be the clubs with the best won-lost percentage in the regular season. If tied in record, apply all applicable divisional tie-breakers.
2. **Other Rounds**—Sites for the AFC and NFC Divisional Playoffs and the AFC and NFC Championship Games are determined by the won-lost records of the divisional champions.

DIVISION TIES

If, at the end of the regular season, two or more clubs in the same division finish with the best won-lost-tied percentage, the following steps will be taken until a CHAMPION is determined:

Two Clubs

1. Head-to-head (best won-lost-tied percentage in games between the clubs).
2. Best won-lost-tied percentage in games played within the division.
3. Best won-lost-tied percentage in games played within the conference.
4. Best won-lost-tied percentage in common games, if applicable.
5. Best net points in division games.
6. Best net points in all games.
7. Strength of schedule.
8. Best net touchdowns in all games.
9. Coin toss.

Three or More Clubs

(Note: If two clubs remain tied after a third club is eliminated during any step, tie-breaker reverts to Step One of two-club format.)

1. Head-to-head (best won-lost-tied percentage in games among the clubs).
2. Best won-lost-tied percentage in games played within the division.
3. Best won-lost-tied percentage in games played within the conference.
4. Best won-lost-tied percentage in common games.
5. Best net points in division games.
6. Best net points in all games.
7. Strength of schedule.
8. Best net touchdowns in all games.
9. Coin toss.

WILD CARD TIES

If necessary to break ties to determine the two Wild Card clubs from each conference, the following steps will be taken:
1. If all the tied clubs are from the same division, apply division tiebreaker.
2. If the tied clubs are from different divisions, apply the following steps.

Two Clubs

1. Head-to-head, if applicable.
2. Best won-lost-tied percentage in games played within the conference.
3. Best won-lost-tied percentage in common games, minimum of four.
4. Best net points in conference games.
5. Best net points in all games.
6. Strength of schedule.
7. Best net touchdowns in all games.
8. Coin toss.

Three or More Clubs

(Note: If two clubs remain tied after third or other clubs eliminated, tie-breaker reverts to Step One of applicable two-club format.)
1. Head-to-head sweep (applicable only if one club has defeated each of the others or one club has lost to each of the others.)
2. Best won-lost-tied percentage in games played within the conference.
3. Best won-lost-tied percentage in common games, minimum of four.
4. Best net points in conference games.
5. Best net points in all games.
6. Strength of schedule.
7. Best net touchdowns in all games.
8. Coin toss.

Jim McMahon (center) and Willie Gault (right) are greeted by tackle Keith Von Horne after hooking up for a touchdown. (Chicago Tribune Photo)